To Denise,

Your Dad often
spoke of you.
You must be very
proud of his achievements

Best Wishes, Roz.

Reimagining Ireland

Volume 102

Edited by Dr Eamon Maher,
Technological University Dublin – Tallaght Campus

PETER LANG

Oxford • Bern • Berlin • Bruxelles • New York • Wien

Roz Goldie

A Dangerous Pursuit:
The Anti-sectarian Work of
Counteract

PETER LANG

Oxford • Bern • Berlin • Bruxelles • New York • Wien

Bibliographic information published by Die Deutsche Nationalbibliothek.
Die Deutsche Nationalbibliothek lists this publication in the Deutsche
Nationalbibliografie; detailed bibliographic data is available on the
Internet at http://dnb.d-nb.de.

A catalogue record for this book is available from the British Library.

Library of Congress Cataloging-in-Publication Data

Names: Goldie, Roz, author.
Title: A dangerous pursuit : the anti-sectarian work of Counteract / Roz
  Goldie.
Description: Oxford ; New York : Peter Lang, 2021. | Series: Reimagining
  Ireland, 1662-9094 ; vol. 102 | Includes bibliographical references and
  index.
Identifiers: LCCN 2020057168 (print) | LCCN 2020057169 (ebook) | ISBN
  9781800791879 (paperback) | ISBN 9781800791886 (ebook) | ISBN
  9781800791893 (epub) | ISBN 9781800791909 (mobi)
Subjects: LCSH: Counteract (Organization) | Labor unions--Political
  activity--Northern Ireland--History--20th century. | Violence in the
  workplace--Political aspects--Northern Ireland--History--20th century. |
  Peace-building--Northern Ireland. | Northern Ireland--Politics and
  government--1968-1998. | Northern Ireland--Politics and
  government--1998-
Classification: LCC HD6669.N67 G65 2021 (print) | LCC HD6669.N67 (ebook)
  | DDC 322/.20941609049--dc23
LC record available at https://lccn.loc.gov/2020057168
LC ebook record available at https://lccn.loc.gov/2020057169

ISSN 1662-9094
ISBN 978-1-80079-187-9 (print) • ISBN 978-1-80079-188-6 (ePDF)
ISBN 978-1-80079-189-3 (ePub) • ISBN 978-1-80079-190-9 (Mobi)
DOI 10.3726/b18004

Cover image: Mass Public Protest for Peace after first cease-fire collapses, Belfast 1995.
Courtesy Kevin Cooper.

© Peter Lang Group AG 2021

Published by Peter Lang Ltd, International Academic Publishers,
52 St Giles, Oxford, OX1 3LU, United Kingdom
oxford@peterlang.com, www.peterlang.com

Roz Goldie has asserted her right under the Copyright, Designs and Patents Act, 1988, to be
identified as Author of this Work.

This publication has been peer reviewed.

Contents

List of Figures

Acknowledgements

I am grateful to many people for help during the writing of this history. Indeed, the book itself is an acknowledgement of Counteract and a wide variety of people who worked for and supported the anti-sectarian unit. My thanks to those who gave me interviews in 2000–02 and who answered my phone calls and emails in 2020 and responded with information. However, I must first acknowledge the late Noreen Moore, secretary in Counteract. She gathered reports, minutes and information from the earliest days up to 2000 with constant patience and good cheer – no small task given Counteract was not strong on recording its work.

I began a final draft during the months of Covid-19 lockdown, when people could not meet and life was suspended in a virtual hub. Despite those difficulties, Kevin Cooper provided details about the few remaining people I needed to contact – some of whom had died or were too ill to contribute to this book. He waded through decades of photographs for this book, and shared his stories, experience and knowledge – all of which were invaluable. Imelda Cooper volunteered to proof-read drafts and encouraged me, as I tried to translate some rather turgid records into a readable text. Both she and Kevin spared no effort.

Billy Robinson's brother Gerard was a central person because, as nominal head of family after Billy's death, his approval was essential. He was open, trusting and generous in sharing photographs, records and many stories that would otherwise have been lost. It was important to get a well-rounded and verified picture of events. Jim Quinn's input was significant – as he had been the first 'leader' of Counteract. As with most people he had more to say than I had found on record and took the trouble to put this on (virtual) paper.

Pascal McCulla was a crucial source of information about the latter years. He came from the Northern Ireland Civil Service Department of Finance and Personnel with the expertise in organisational change to Counteract that Counteract needed to develop a framework for change. He was pivotal in developing the move from 'fire-fighting' to 'fire-proofing' that Counteract wanted. He read relevant drafts and provided detailed information – and amendments – on the Equity, Diversity and Interdependence Framework. He also shared photographs.

It would be invidious to single out particular individuals from over fifty interviews during the past two decades. However, information and quotations are credited, which acknowledges them. Thanks to those who also later confirmed facts and details by phone and email.

This book is part of my work as a visiting scholar to the George J. Mitchell Institute for Global Peace, Security and Justice at Queen's University Belfast and the Director, Hastings Donnan to whom I am obliged, but who obviously bears no responsibility for any deficiencies the script may have.

Abbreviations

ACPO	Association of Chief Police Officers
AEU	Amalgamated Engineering Union
AT&GWU	Amalgamated Transport & General Workers Union, now T&G (all references are made to T&G for uniformity).
BSI	British Standards Institute
BTC	Belfast Trades Council
BURC	Belfast Unemployed Resource Centre
CAJ	Campaign for the Administration of Justice
CBI	Confederation of British Industry
CCRU/CRU	Central Community Relations Unit
	(later) Community Relations Unit of OFDFM
CLMC	Combined Loyalist Military Command
CRC	Community Relations Council (for Northern Ireland)
CWU	Communication Workers Union
DARD	Department of Agriculture & Rural Development
DCAL	Department of Culture Arts & Leisure
DETI	Department of Enterprise, Trade & Investment
DFP	Department of Finance & Personnel
DHSS	Department of Health & Social Services (now DHSSPS)
DHSSPS	Department of Health & Social Services and Public Safety
DOE	Department of the Environment
DRD	Department for Regional Development
DSD	Department of Social Development

DUP	Democratic Unionist Party
EOC	Equal Opportunities Commission (NI)
ERDF	European Regional Development Fund
ESF	European Social Fund
EWU	Electrical Workers Union
FEC	Fair Employment Commission (NI)
FET	Fair Employment Tribunal (NI)
GMB	General, Municipal, Boilermakers Union
ICTU	Irish Congress of Trade Unions
LVF	Loyalist Volunteer Force
MLA	Member of the Local Assembly (at Stormont)
MSF	Manufacturing, Science and Finance Union
NIC ICTU	Northern Ireland Committee, Irish Congress of Trade Unions
NIHE	Northern Ireland Housing Executive
NIO	Northern Ireland Office
NIPSA	Northern Ireland Public Service Alliance
NUJ	National Union of Journalists
NUPE	Nation Union of Public Employees
NUS/USI	National Union of Students/Union of Students in Ireland
NUT	National Union of Teachers
OFMDFM	Office of First Minister and Deputy First Minister (now Executive Office)
PAFT	Policy Appraisal for Fair Treatment
PUP	Popular Unionist Party
RUC	Royal Ulster Constabulary
SDLP	Social Democratic and Labour Party
SIPTU	Services, Industrial, Professional Technical Union

STUC	Scottish Trades Union Council
T&G	Transport & General Workers Union
TUC	(British) Trades Union Council
UDA	Ulster Defence Association
UDP	Ulster Democratic Party
UFF	Ulster Freedom Fighters
UKUP	United Kingdom Unionist Party
UUP	Ulster Unionist Party
UVF	Ulster Volunteer Force

Introduction

The work of Counteract and its objectives has a long and largely untold history. Its roots lie in the public stance taken by the Trade Union Movement during the Northern Ireland conflict – when it directly challenged violence and sectarian intimidation in the workplace. As a longstanding member of the movement and the man who led Counteract for most of its time, this book begins with the thoughts of Billy Robinson:

> The Trade Union Movement has a very long history of fighting for workers' rights and during the Northern Ireland 'troubles' they did take a very strong stand against intimidation, sectarianism and violence. Major rallies and campaigns were organised to allow workers to publicly express their opposition to the violence. The reality is, however, that Trade Union members and officials do not come from some other planet but from the communities in conflict and as such carry most of the prejudices/fears. In consequence, it was challenging for the ICTU to maintain unity of the movement around the Equality Agenda.

> The name Irish Congress of Trade Unions in itself was perceived as a problem by a section of the movement. The protagonists expressed difficulty with the word 'Irish' in the title expressing the view that this implied acceptance of Dublin rule over the North. During the Loyalist inspired Ulster Workers Strike there was a call for the establishment of an Ulster Trade Union Congress. The attempt at splitting the movement along sectarian lines was encouraged by Unionist politicians.

> The workplace does not sit separate from society nor society separate from the workplace. What happens in society is reflected in the workplace and vice versa. This was a period when workers were under attack and murdered on their way to and from work and in some cases in the workplace itself. It may be reasonable to ask 'Who identified workers to the gunmen for assassination?' Is it possible that fellow workers or even the unmentionable 'Fellow Trade Unionist' conspired in those atrocities? Some would say 'tut, tut, no, no, never!' Others speak the truth. For some, supporting the Trade Unions is ok, as long as politics don't come into it.

> In this period of the 'troubles' the Trade Union movement had to walk a very fine line to maintain a semblance of unity and, despite the underlying sectarian nature of the membership, to their credit they were largely successful.

He cited an example of workplace sectarianism in the late 1970s – with an unusually personal touch:

> A cousin of mine was coming out of work one day when a fellow worker approached him and showed him a security photo of himself during his internment and said, 'Paddy, this photo is being shown around the workplace and I don't want to be part of this, I am just warning you.' Paddy never returned to work. He was lucky his fellow worker was brave enough to stand out from the rest, but not everyone has that courage. That particular workplace was very strongly unionized.
>
> One of the sensitive issues that was not really talked about at that time was the religious make-up of the Trade Union officials. For historical and cultural reasons, the majority were from the Catholic community. The interesting thing is that a Catholic would get elected as an official by a majority Protestant work force, as they would have seen the Catholic as being more bolshie. Even though you were a Catholic but a strong trade Unionist and seen as a bit of a commie that was acceptable so long as you were not one of those Republicans.
>
> The working-class Protestant culture was, in the main, I must say not all, but in general 'Don't challenge employers as to do so implies challenging the state and to challenge the state would suggest that you were disloyal.'
>
> One can understand why it would appear better not to openly discuss this problem. How can this issue be raised and managed in the middle of the serious conflict in society? Would the discussion allow others to capitalize on this to create greater division? So, the answer was 'just ignore it' – but it's not that simple. The issue is always in the back of your mind, especially when having to deal with conflict in the work place. Don't talk about the Elephant in the room.
>
> Long before I became involved in Counteract when I was working for the CWU as an assistant secretary for the external section of the union, I and others were aware that our committee had a greater number of representatives from the Catholic community. To address this, we had to take proactive action to encourage candidates from the Protestant community and support them. In dealing with this issue we firstly had to identify and agree that a problem existed then openly discuss an action plan to implement change. In addressing the problem openly fears diminished and representation from the Protestant community improved.
>
> Fear is the biggest de-motivator in dealing with conflict across the religious-political divide as inevitably we are defined by community and carry with us all the prejudices and the understanding of possible consequences in stepping out from your own side.
>
> At one point the Belfast Trades Council initiated a piece of research into attitudes of members to the Equality Agenda (diversity across the religious, political, race,

violence, intimidation and death was an everyday reality for many. The Trade Union Movement organised mass events and peace rallies – where thousands of people from across Northern Ireland registered their determination for an end to the conflict in campaigns supported by community relations, government bodies and other agencies.

The Northern Ireland Committee of the Irish Congress of Trade Unions (NIC ICTU) responded to widespread intimidation by setting up Counteract. They saw an urgent need for accurate information about the scale of sectarian intimidation and violence in the workplace, and finding procedures to deal with it appropriately. The original intention was to run a two-year campaign, with an Advisory Committee to comment and direct research, and a Management Committee representing the Peace, Work and Progress Campaign Group, trade unions, relevant voluntary and community organisations, and was also to involve appropriate academics.

The first Counteract leaflet on Housing and Intimidation gave advice to victims of intimidation and was distributed widely. Research was started. At the height of the murder and intimidation campaign against taxi drivers Counteract made representations to Government about improving safety. It also gave support to those drivers under constant threat of paramilitary hi-jacking and others intimidated out of their homes. Single-issue one-off campaigns would continue and remain an important aspect of the unit's work.

Leaving workplace prejudice, intimidation and discrimination unchallenged incurs huge economic costs. Bullying people in work because of religion, politics, gender or disability is against the law. It is not a matter of social or moral nicety. In 1990 it was yet to be recognised as both an economic and a political issue. Then there was little understanding of how to change long-established and deeply ingrained patterns of injustice. Until it became a crisis – for a manager, shop steward or businessperson – sectarian intimidation was not seen as having practical relevance to 'real work'.

This book is both a record of how such incidents were successfully dealt with and a tribute to the many people who made such progress possible. Counteract was a very small organisation that operated with trade unions and, later, government and business to make its indelible mark on how we work together, and played its part in changing what was once universally accepted as normal into an illegal, unacceptable relic of the past. In society, community and work we now know that we need relationships that appreciate fairness, differences and necessary alliances – that is, what happens when basic rights are enshrined in promoting equality and good relations – eradicating sectarian intimidation and discrimination.

Moving into this century we brought with us the feelings and fears of the last one – but learning to operate in a less threatening environment, with the help of the obligations in equality legislation, best practice and (for a significant number) the will to get past our sometimes-shameful histories. To put it in words that might have been the first motto of Counteract, *Everyone is to blame – It is in our bones.*

Notes

1. *Working with Emotional Intelligence* by Daniel Goleman, Bloomsbury Paperbacks, London, 1998 (and the original book by the same author, *Emotional Intelligence*) gives the reader an encyclopaedic thesis about the essential importance of EIQ in star performance in individuals, teams and the world's largest companies. EIQ is about using the 'soft' skills of dealing with people, reading situations and the politics at work. This is *'the capacity for recognizing [sic] our own feelings and those of others, for motivating ourselves, and for managing emotions well in ourselves and in our relationships'*.
2. Quoted from Bew, Paul and Gillespie, Gordon *Northern Ireland: A Chronology of the Troubles 1968–1999* (Dublin, Gill & Macmillan, 1999).

CHAPTER 1

Living in War – Working for Peace

The Trade Union movement was pivotal in working for peace by organising mass events, demonstrations and peace rallies – albeit at suggestions said to have come from government. Thousands of people throughout Northern Ireland voiced a burgeoning will for an end to violence at work and on the streets. These campaigns lasted throughout the 1970s until the early 1990s and were supported by community relations and the public, with the endorsement of certain government bodies.

Looking back over an eminent quarter century as the Northern Ireland Officer for the NIC ICTU and a lifetime in the trade union movement, Terry Carlin had many recollections about the development of Counteract in the 1990s. The history of trade unionism in Northern Irish politics was characterised by the deformed context of a sectarian society and the origins of Counteract lay in the movement's response to the violence, intimidation and discrimination that came from this – played out in the workplace. Counteract was the product of the movement's longstanding resistance to violence and intimidation of workers in Northern Ireland.

Since the 1960s a nucleus of the trade union movement had been concerned with social issues. In Terry Carlin's words, *A hundred thousand jobs would have done more than a hundred thousand guns – and forty thousand houses were needed!* Throughout the 1970s paramilitary intimidation and murders of working people were commonplace. Any security-associated work brought threats from the IRA, he recollected, including the telephone engineers in Portadown whose exchange lay within the perimeters of a security base.

In 1976 the *Better Life for All* campaign arose out of the focused anger of trade union activists who responded to *a vicious weekend in South Armagh.* What had been planned as a Saturday morning workshop in Transport

House for thirty people became a round table for nearly five hundred shop stewards and activists demanding action. That Tuesday the *Better Life for All* campaign was launched:

> Consistent with that theme, NIC ICTU resolved that threats to workers needed response. At a conference in the New Vic cinema in Belfast we determined to stand together, and drew up a set of principles that came to life under the banner 'There's no such thing as a legitimate target!' We promoted this with politicians, churches, and business leaders – what we now call 'civic society'.

Throughout the years pressure mounted:

> Calls came from people like community leaders and workers in the CWU. A union official from Newry rang because his men were being threatened – if they collected the bins from the police station the IRA threatened violence – if they didn't the UVF had warned 'collect or else!' That was what it was like.

This level of serious intimidation should have involved the unions, employers, housing, medical, social and other government agencies, but did not – so the feeling was if no-one else would act, the unions had to. *There's a circle to square, but that's what you're paid for!* Terry Carlin remembered being told. From this, and the work of other union activists in the 1980s, came the *Peace, Progress and Work* Campaign and from that, the anti-intimidation unit Counteract would emerge.

In the early 1970s the NIC ICTU *Better Life for All* campaign demonstrated Trade Union determination to act against sectarian slaughter in Northern Ireland. At this stage, the main players were John Freeman (Regional Secretary, T&G), Andy Barr (EWU) and Jimmy Graham (EWU). The most profound political effect on the Trade Union came from Betty Sinclair.[1] She enhanced political debate inside the movement and urged the unions to become more active and involved. Sean Morrissey was a member of the General Executive Council and Finance and General Purposes Committee of the T&G. He was also an active member of the Communist Party of Ireland (CPI) being involved in its Policy Committee. He instilled an understanding and acceptance of the politics of the anti-sectarian argument into senior officials of ICTU.

The *Better Life for All* campaign came about because all the unions and Trades Councils were involved which also encouraged the re-growth of Trades Councils in Belfast, Mid-Ulster, Fermanagh, Derry, Coleraine, Ballymena and North Down. Belfast was dominant with Joe Cooper, on Trades Council and President of the WEA, promoting a strong public profile. They organised a march where tens of thousands converged on London. They marched under the banner *The right to live free from violence, sectarianism, intimidation and discrimination*. In this they were mirroring Civil Rights movements of the 1960s, and establishing the benchmark for trade union activism and the eventual formation of Counteract.

These campaigns were very widely supported. Posters were printed in large numbers to publicise events. The Irish trade union movement inherently understood the complexities of sectarianism and Northern Ireland society which placed them in the vanguard for change. This was one of the most courageous decisions ever taken by NIC ICTU. They took it as a challenge, with a 'can do' attitude, and acted to subvert the otherwise negative views of sectarianism and what trade unions could do to address the issue.

Despite the dangers, the unions consistently condemned intimidation, sectarianism and violence. They condemned internment without trial. Internment was an ineffective but politically expedient response to civil unrest. It turned out to be counter-productive in stimulating deep resentments and motivating increased numbers to recruitment in paramilitary organisations, especially but not exclusively the Provisional IRA.

The trade unions were clear about the politics and violence of the time. The working class needed jobs, houses, social welfare and healthcare but they did not need sectarianism.

So, there were many attempts to address sectarianism before 1990. Terry Carlin recalled a meeting in the late 1970s with Bob Cooper of the FEA and the (then) Director of the CBI about publicly endorsing fair employment legislation. This had been a dramatic development for business in Northern Ireland at the time, and a step too far for many. As the CBI man said, 'I'm okay with it personally, but my backwoodsmen won't touch it with a barge pole!'

At that time, Terry Carlin had his own reservations on monitoring the religion of the workforce, as he had bitter experience of his religion being used against him in getting work. He talked of his being asked his religion when he went for a holiday job in Derry in the 1950s. When he asked why his employer wanted to know his religion, he was told *'It's in case you have an accident or get sick – we need to know who to call.*' He had retorted '*If I get sick or have an accident send for a doctor!*' That was common practice then and regarded as 'normal' in Northern Ireland. When mandatory religious monitoring of employees came in he resisted it:

> I believed, then, that you shouldn't ask people their religion. The unions had difficulties with this law, too. But unless you are up front about a problem, you'll never find a solution. So, we had to learn.

Peace work then was approved of in the trade union movement, but there was still a way to go in getting all round approval for the Fair Employment legislation.

Fair Employment legislation had brought many changes to the workplace in Northern Ireland in the 1970s and 1980s. On the streets and away from work people were openly sectarian and intimidation was violent. At work there was legal protection for individuals against discrimination in their recruitment, promotion and arrangements for pensions, retirement or redundancy. Fair Employment law made employers address fair selection and recruitment practices.

Yet, it was not until the 1989 regulations came into force that protection from intimidation and harassment at work became a legal right. This legislation established the Fair Employment Commission and the Fair Employment Tribunals. Their powers were strong enough to tackle unfair treatment, including sectarian behaviour in the workplace. Eventually these rights were to lead to discrimination being less blatant and open at work. Taking more 'polite' and subtle forms, sectarianism (like sexism a decade before) would become more sophisticated. There was a time when intimidation was violent and often fatal as with shipyard confetti. The term 'shipyard confetti' was the euphemism for the violent attacks in the Belfast shipyards in the early and middle years of the twentieth century when nuts, bolts and other metal objects were hurled from a great height down onto Catholics by Protestant workers, usually at times of cultural 'celebration' such as the 1st and 12th July. Far from 'shipyard confetti' intimidation would be expressed by graffiti in toilets, pointed jokes called banter or ostracising individuals. These could easily create a 'chill factor' and effectively intimidate people – but insidiously.

Although there was still widespread denial of its very existence in the early 1990s sectarianism at work was changing in order to get around the new laws. It was not disappearing but mutating to survive. This remained part of the complex tacit working culture of many organisations in Northern Ireland, although the business case for challenging prejudice and harassment in work was much more widely accepted than ten years previously.

In the 1980s sectarian intimidation and harassment were commonplace, but not dealt with, either as a workplace problem or as an economic issue. The Transport and General Workers Union (T&G) Equality Unit in Northern Ireland took up the issues and found funds to pilot test a new programme. T&G Education Officer Liam McBrinn was quick to use the opportunity and give anti-sectarian training, and worked with academic facilitators in delivering a new kind of course. Avilla Kilmurry, May Blood[2] and Liam McBrinn were central figures in the T&G's ground-breaking programme and in the development of Counteract (see Picture 2). Monica McWilliams[3] wrote the report on the T&G's programme.

Picture 2: May Blood and the Women's movement take part in mass protests

The original idea of a Trade Union–based unit opposing sectarianism came from Avilla Kilmurry (Women's Officer T&G, later Director of NIVT). The full impact of sectarianism in the workplace was only becoming apparent, and in the late 1980s there was nothing to support individuals experiencing intimidation and harassment in the workplace.

Avilla Kilmurry drafted a paper outlining the equality work of the Women's Committee and the possibility of establishing a confidential telephone help-line. She discussed this with Terry Carlin, Northern Ireland Officer of the NIC ICTU, and Quentin Oliver, then Director of NICVA. Funding from Comic Relief was identified and the foundations of an anti-sectarian unit were laid. The goal of a phone-line developed into a plan for proactive training and a point of contact for people fighting sectarianism in work. Trade Union activist Jim Quinn is credited with fashioning this objective.

May Blood still warmly commends the modest Avilla Kilmurry as the one person who 'could talk about ideas, and also put the vision into action'. She could always source funding, organise ideas and implement practical programmes.

The idea for what became Counteract came largely from anti-sectarian programmes the T&G ran in the 1980s. They had money for an internal two-year programme for their members including residential weekend courses. This was the T&G Education and Equality Office's response to the changing nature of sectarianism in the workplace.

The purpose of the internal T&G programme was to get Catholic and Protestant workers to look at themselves and their perceptions of the 'other side'. The sessions were to show that 'respectable' prejudice was no different from naked sectarianism, and that working-class issues were of particular importance.

T&G residential courses used their own two training videos and Liam McBrinn worked with Derek Wilson and Frank Wright to widen the members' experience. Frank Wright worked with Counteract as a tutor with Catholic and Protestant shop stewards in the transport industry. When he asked if the sessions were useful Frank was told they were extremely practical because they had given people their first opportunity to discuss sectarian issues – and this from men who had been working together for over fifteen years, and been shop stewards together for more than a decade. 'We never would've discussed these issues before.'

May Blood recalled that the perceptions that Protestants and Catholics had of each other were almost comically stereotyped, and that just talking about these openly was a good start in dismantling the myths that kept working-class people at each other's throats:

> Roman Catholics believed that all Protestants went to church with a hat on, every Sunday. Protestants believed that Catholics had priests in their homes every day who told them what to do.

In 1985 Belfast Trades Council had a preparatory motion adopted by NIC ICTU which led to resurrecting the *Better Life for All* campaign in the later 1980s. Liam McBrinn put the motion, and in the right to reply session was asked to enumerate the campaign's objectives. Temporarily stumped for precise wording, as he had not brought papers with him, he found Davy Wasson's helping hand reaching over with a card he had kept for over a decade, detailing all the campaign's objectives. From the acceptance of the motion came a working party of Belfast Trades Council and NIC ICTU representatives, who met in NIC ICTU's temporary premises.[4]

*   *   *   *   *

The working party wanted a forum giving advice on temporary housing, security, social services, benefits, etc., for people who had suffered violence and sectarian intimidation. The first organiser, Jim Quinn, recalls the original aims of Counteract were to

> Develop Anti-sectarian/Anti-Intimidation training in ICTU and individual unions affiliated to ICTU (As opposed to non-sectarian training).

> Develop policies and more importantly procedures for dealing with sectarianism and intimidation in the workplace for affiliated unions. NIPSA at the time had developed a policy of closing individual offices where threats were received until those threats were withdrawn. We were also trying to develop a system of contacts in workplaces who could be spoken to if workers were uncomfortable talking to the steward or managers about sectarian problems. We drafted a model procedure for dealing with sectarian harassment in the workplace which was later launched by either FEC or the LRA but without crediting Counteract as far as I recall.

> The third objective was around research and one of the early pieces of research we carried out concerned access to a scheme for workers who were intimidated from their homes. Up until then the scheme was quite restrictive and seemed to be aimed

primarily at members of the security forces who were intimidated from their homes. I think our intervention opened up that access to other victims.

Joe Bowers of MSF saw Counteract as coming from the 'left of the movement' with Jim Quinn generating its bona fides and raising questions. From its tentative beginnings Counteract would become a source of befriending, networking and advice – in league with key trade unions and NIC ICTU – and would access hundreds of representatives and thousands of members through its work.

Joe Bowers also remembered the challenging work at Shorts, where he would later introduce Counteract to the relevant people, and where he took on training sessions in its early days. Counteract would reveal what was happening, despite denials, and show how intimidation and harassment could be challenged:

> The people who worked with Counteract were not 'do-gooders'. They were effective because they had first-hand experience of harassment and intimidation and knew the scale of the problem. … they could expose the baggage and took a challenging approach to workers and managers. … It came out of the difficulties experienced in our own workplaces. It could demonstrate the size of the problem.

Joe Bowers saw the flags and emblems dispute in Shorts in July 1987 as prefacing the start of Counteract. At that time lorry loads of Union flags were on display in Shorts. On the ground it was commented 'It's like Mardi Gras – you know, colourful.' When these were removed, workers went on strike and MSF representatives had to speak out against the strikers. This led to the determination in Belfast Trades Council, and further afield, that something practical and relevant needed to be done. As things stood, the trade union movement was not well placed to resolve such divisive differences. The MSF, like T&G, was a very important union and their unequivocal support was to be a great asset to Counteract.

At this time trade unions pre-empted fair employment legislation and enforcement by talking of 'politically neutral environment' rather than 'harmonious workplace'. Their position on flags was that they should not be at work.

In 1989 Pearse McKenna of T&G and Belfast Trades Council moved the motion proposing an anti-intimidation unit at the annual NIC ICTU Conference. His speech was put together[5] at very short notice and, as is often the case, was all the better for lack of time to polish or adorn what he had to say. He made an impassioned and moving case for the entire Trade Union movement confronting sectarianism, wherever they encountered it, from the factory shop floor, to depots, offices and board rooms – arguing the Unions' duty was to provide education and training to combat the scourge of workplace sectarianism. He made no claim that they would defeat harassment and intimidation, but there was a certainty that these could be identified, isolated and addressed – so that such behaviour could at least be marginalised in the workplace. The goal was to reach a stage where people in work were clear that sectarianism was unacceptable, at every level and – with good management – would not be tolerated.

The proposal to establish an anti-intimidation unit was accepted unanimously and Counteract set up in 1990. The Movement recognised the urgent need for accurate information about the scale of intimidation in the workplace, and finding procedures to deal with it appropriately.[6]

So, the original intention was to run a two-year anti-sectarian campaign, with an Advisory Committee, and a Management Committee composed of representatives of the Peace, Work and Progress Campaign Group, specific trade unions and relevant voluntary and community organisations. NIC ICTU also wanted to involve academics with a proven track record in steering and evaluating research projects.

This Anti-Intimidation Contact Service would gain from the considerable experience of both Trade Unions and Trades Councils in dealing with the impact of sectarianism. Wide-ranging community contacts with Trades Councils across Northern Ireland also offered an established network.

As an action-research project, the unit planned to provide information on incidents of reported intimidation in the workplace and in the community over the preceding five years. They planned at least two seminars to examine research findings during that two years.

*   *   *   *   *

The Trade Union movement organised initial training for Counteract, as Jim Quinn vividly remembered:

> The first Counteract training session in November 1990 came about with the help of Frank Bunting (deceased) the then Education Officer of ICTU who introduced

us to Frank Wright. The training was held over the weekend in a hotel in Bangor and was attended by Trades Council Representatives. It was a total eye opener as we had never been exposed to Frank's styles of training before and his probing of the sectarian issue. We did quite a lot of work with Frank and his colleague Derek Wilson after that. Both were involved in the Centre for the Study of Conflict at the University of Ulster I think and also the Quakers.

The late Frank Wright and Derek Wilson began with searching and uncomfortable conversations that would be a defining feature of how Counteract talked about and tackled sectarianism in the workplace.

*   *   *   *   *

Whatever its precise work was to be, the embryonic Counteract needed to be housed. Brendan Mackin of Belfast Unemployed Resource Centre was closely allied to the core thinking of the unit and worked with them to find the space for the first small office.

As the first Chair of Counteract Avilla Kilmurry formed a core trade union group with Terry Carlin (NIC ICTU). Their aim was to secure ICTU support for the unit. And that support would have to be material because when asked to support the venture, the Rowntree Trust questioned why it was not getting enough money from Trade Unions.

Although the proposal at ICTU's 1989 Conference went through unopposed and had Trade Union backing, it was to take some time and much effort to secure substantial monies from some Unions. Even at this juncture it was evident that Counteract was to be sustained by charitable funding because the Unions regarded this work as over and above what they did in mainstream education. Some felt they could help their own members and did not need a more neutral venue for this.

Experience was to show that, in truth, they did need a shared Trades Union-wide initiative because sometimes people intimidated at work feared Union representatives because these people were involved, partial and sectarian.

Indeed, some trade unionists believed genuinely that they were elected, or not voted for, on openly sectarian lines. At times union officials felt they had to mend or make bridges in their normal union working relationships simply because of sectarian loyalties, cold-shouldering and exclusion of those from 'the other side'. Just as sectarianism has always been woven into the very fabric of this society – throughout the Islands of Britain and

Ireland, though most famously in Northern Ireland – prejudice and sectarian discrimination were perceived as being an everyday part of behaviour in the trade union movement:

> Limits to what Trade Unions could do. (Taken from an interview with Billy Robinson)
>
> People's fears of bias in the unions were common in the 1990s. For instance Counteract was phoned by an anonymous worker complaining about big union flags festooning his workshop. Had he raised the issue with management? No, '… because I take a certain route to work, and I don't want it to go out that I'd made a complaint. I'd be identified.' Had he raised it with the unions? No '… because the union man works in that room'.
>
> Asked, 'What's your union?' The response was 'I don't want to tell you because all you people talk.'
>
> So, what did he want Counteract to do? 'I was told you could deal with this.' All Counteract could do was to raise the matter with the FEC, which they did.
>
> A week or two later Counteract got a call from an irate union official, saying Counteract was '… causing major problems. The Director got a letter from the FEC quoting yourselves about this stupid flag. If it had been brought to our attention, we could have taken it down at night – we could have dealt with it.' To whom had the letter been addressed? Did the Director come to the unions? 'No, he went out and addressed the workforce.' A few weeks later a Counteract person had the case recited to him at a funeral on the Shankill Road. The issue had been raised in pubs and clubs and amongst paramilitaries. 'So, the fella was right in the first instance.'
>
> There are all those justifiable fears because trade unionists come from sectarian communities and, like it or not, community loyalties and concerns make an impact on decisions and judgements at work, and the working relationships that people have. Much as they'd like to be seen as trade unionists first and foremost, others don't see them that way.

Notes

1. Betty Sinclair was a member of the Communist Party of Ireland and after being interned in 1971 was most vociferous about the need for unions to challenge the politics of sectarianism.
2. Now Baroness Blood, she is the Shankill Road's only person to have taken a seat in the House of Lords where she has worked tirelessly on Northern Ireland issues. She was filmed at her honorary graduation in UU wryly noting 'I don't think I'll use the title. "Dr Blood" doesn't sound too good, does it?'

3. Monica McWilliams was then Professor of Social Studies (UU) but did not use her title during her time as Leader of the Women's Coalition party and MLA.
4. Their Antrim Road premises had been destroyed by three of the six IRA firebombs that greeted NIC ICTU's anti-violence stance.
5. Brian Campfield of Belfast Trades Council was unable to do so due to a family crisis and asked Pearse to step in for him.
6. 'The Northern Ireland Committee ICTU has consistently struggled against sectarianism and intimidation in Northern Ireland, as epitomised in its most recent 'Peace Work and Progress Campaign'. As an essential aspect of this Campaign, it is felt that there is a need to support on-going campaigning work against sectarianism and intimidation, with a concrete service which could avail of the extensive range of trade union contracts and networks throughout the community.

   The service proposed is essentially an Information and Support Unit which would be based in a broad trade union context, and whose remit would include the following:

   • to liaise with relevant trade unions, trade councils and community organisations concerned with the alleviation of the effects of intimidation;
   • to identify any strategies which might act to prevent sectarian intimidation and to develop a number of such strategies on an action-research basis;
   • to study the occurrence of intimidation through a number of pilot studies, and to draw out any apparent themes, patterns and policy implications;
   • to support the work of the Peace Work and Progress Campaign, and to identify priorities for the further development of trade union action against sectarianism and intimidation, which are closely inter-related problems in our society.

   The Anti-Intimidation Unit itself is envisaged as a two-year action research project to both provide a basis of the development of strategies and action against sectarianism, whilst at the same time, drawing together research findings on the impact of intimidation and the response of various agencies to it.'

   Quoted from NIC ICTU 1990 Congress Report.

CHAPTER 2

Meeting the Challenge

Although the new Fair Employment Commission had considerably greater legal power than its predecessor it was acknowledged that a pro-active challenge to sectarianism was needed to bolster the new legislation. Counteract would have that role.

The first Counteract Committee meeting was in September 1990,[1] having appointed its Development Officer, Jim Quinn and part-time Secretary Noreen Moore (who died before this book could be completed).

The name, 'Counteract', came from a competition for suggestions. The modest prize of a £10 book token was sent to the winner, one Brother McCullough, a printer in UNISON. 'Counteract' was felt to be the most expressive of their hands-on opposition to sectarian harassment and intimidation. The name was adopted along with the strap line 'An antiintimidation unit sponsored by ICTU' and Counteract had its public launch on 15 November 1990 in Belfast with significant media attention. Press coverage of the time reported

> *Unions go to war against intimidation*
> *Unions launch drive against sectarianism*
> *Anti-sectarian drive launched*
> *Group to Fight sectarianism*
> *Labour of Love*
> *Unions in 'clean up' pledge*
> *Jim gets job to fight fear in Belfast*
> *Anti-bigot task force launched.*[2]

The public and the media welcomed the work of the new unit.

As the first Development Worker Jim Quinn's unique background gave him a broad vision of community development plus solid Trade Union credentials. From work in the T&G in the late 1970s, through redundancy, community work, Welfare Rights work and Ruskin College in the 1980s, Jim Quinn had gathered a wealth of expertise and understanding before he came to Counteract.

In November Counteract held a weekend school for NIC ICTU. That training and education allowed people to talk openly, because it created enough safe space to outweigh if not completely remove people's fear. Delegates discussed sectarianism and intimidation, and identified five possible projects that could be undertaken by Trades Councils in local areas. They then met Trades Councils in Fermanagh, Dungannon, Newry, Belfast, Craigavon, Antrim, Ballymena, Derry and North Down, who appointed people to liaise with them on projects. Affiliated unions helped by encouraging participation in councils and providing material and financial support.

Brenda Callaghan, from NIPSA and Belfast Trades Council (BTC), was part of the active discussion about sectarianism on the ground:

> BTC was dealing with the consequences of sectarianism in day-to-day work and saw the need for some organisation to work with shop stewards because the unions were struggling to cope.

*   *   *   *   *

As Counteract opened their doors, they faced virulent sectarian rows about flags[3] and IRA threats to co-operatives supplying milk to the security forces. Unions opposing intimidation were reported as, 'Union leader condemns "bully-boys in balaclavas" '.

The early 1990s were a very active time with the staff and committee of Counteract heavily involved in making funding applications, participating in job panels and undertaking research.

The Trade Unions were crucial to Counteract in its early days. In March 1991 Jim Quinn had met nine unions and the remainder had been sent reminders. NUPE had agreed to give free printing of leaflets (in lieu of a financial donation) and develop guidelines on dealing with sectarianism and intimidation for their members. NUPE also organised a one-day Counteract seminar for their representatives, and delegated an officer responsible for liaising with Counteract. In sharp contrast, one union reported that as no problems existed at present, they saw no need for a meeting.

Counteract discussed with T&G and other affiliated unions how best they could help its work. A number of them and one council of trades unions pledged financial support for the unit. NIC ICTU authorised a £10,000 appeal to affiliated unions.[4]

*   *   *   *   *

New powers for mandating fair treatment paved the road to greater equality. Increased authority came with the new legislation, and arrival of the FEC and Fair Employment Tribunals. This created a sea change because fair employment was now clearly a matter of tackling prejudice and in-equality – including sectarian behaviour, harassment and discrimination at work. Sectarian harassment was declared illegal. The link between harass-ment and displays of flags and emblems was now recognised. The work that Counteract was starting was precisely in this area of workplace disputes.

The powers of the FEC were significantly more robust than those of other enforcers in the rest of the UK operating in the 1990s. No other body had the legal power to 'invade' – to go to a workplace complete an audit, report and make its findings public. At a time when Thatcherism had created a shift to right-wing politics and a culture of employers' rights, the FEC was creating a shift to employers' duties and a culture of equal opportunities and fair employment. The contrast was stark. Only after the FEC had merged into the Equality Commission a decade later, did their role and their powers stop being seen as highly contentious for employers in Northern Ireland.

Complying with monitoring requirements had become compulsory in 1990 for organisations employing over fifty people (later to be twenty-five and then eleven). However, it was not clear what the FEC or government could or would do if there was widespread resistance to this requirement. Publicly, there were loud protestations against providing the required stat-istics but ultimately compliance was forthcoming from employers. Most companies posted returns on time.

Many employers complained that their workers did not want to be identified by religion (or perceived religion). Also, unions were not entirely without cynicism about (if not occasionally resistance to) the exercise. The NUJ pamphlets of the time – on 'PRAM pushing' (Perceived Religious

Affiliation Monitoring) were indicative. A common quip at the time was, 'Ballylumford[5] was full of Shiite Muslims for a week!'

Monitoring the religious composition of the Northern Ireland workforce was necessary for confirming actual employment equality figures. If there was imbalance then that needed to be proven and addressed. It is a sad reflection on the broad trade union movement that the majority of members, at branch level and higher, had to be convinced at meeting after meeting that PRAM was a vital means to an end – the objective of fair employment. A decade later it was still a problem for people working in all areas of equality (whether in gender, ability, religion or ethnicity) that dis-aggregated statistics were not always kept by employers or government departments.[6]

There was a fear whipped up by political opportunists that Protestants would lose jobs and only Catholics would gain by monitoring. In hindsight the business case for monitoring was clear, but 'capitulation' (as compliance was widely regarded) took time. PRAM returns got figures to enable the FEC and government to estimate patterns in the entire workforce. It was not about targeting individual companies. Over the years the practice ceased to be a contentious issue. There was never any mass refusal to make returns, or any broad distortion of figures or personation.

*   *   *   *   *

The FEC and Counteract were working together but where the FEC had a defined framework and a clear remit to inform employers what the law required, Counteract was more involved with defining harassment and intimidation and confronting the underlying issues. Its role was to confront the 'fear, feelings and lack of trust' at the heart of sectarian actions and challenge these.

The FEC provided seminars and worked with both Counteract and the unions, but did not engage in 'hearts and minds' training. Dennis Godfrey from the FEC worked with Liam McBrinn, Avilla Kilmurry, and May Blood in the early training sessions for T&G, NIPSA and MSF. In these the FEC had input on courses for senior shop stewards, including information about the background, the legal requirements, case studies and the FEC Code of Practice. How managers and trade Unionists dealt with intimidation was not seen as the FEC's business so much as the role of Counteract and the Union Education Officers.

As the T&G Education Officer, Liam McBrinn was encouraged to operate in work places and in communities. As it was difficult for unions to deal with conflict in the community, unless it was a community-based organisation, T&G worked with Counteract, the WEA and FEC Education Officers – as partners developing their education packages, core modules on anti-sectarianism, and Equality of Opportunity training to include gender, sectarianism and young people.

This was a brave venture as criticism came from inside and outside the union movement. Some shop stewards challenged, arguing 'I am not an antisectarian worker, I am a shop steward.' Others said the developments were foolish and would not succeed. But the work went on and shop stewards were trained to deal with sectarian harassment. Advanced Shop Steward Workshops were organised, for the public and private sectors, men and women, who exchanged experiences, socialised and bonded. People felt passionately about the work and supported each other. This would become standard practice in Unions like the T&G.

The T&G was doubly determined to increase and enhance its anti-sectarian and anti-intimidation education. Nearly a decade on, their programme still included these courses. The T&G had the confidence and experience to do what Counteract called for because they worked in partnership. Liam McBrinn said he

> … couldn't overstate the contribution that people like May Blood, Avilla Kilmurray, Monica McWilliams, Sean and Hazel Morrissey have made in preparing the ground for what are now mainstream trade union activities. John Freeman (Regional Secretary, T&G) and Mick O'Reilly (current Regional Secretary) were champions of change. Their work gained widespread acceptance and support for the work of Counteract and all partners in anti-sectarian education and training.

At this stage they were only beginning.

Counteract was set up in the Belfast Unemployed Resource Centre (BURC). This was an auspicious place for them to be, as it was a city-centre venue and was independent. And BURC had an established network. It had accommodated the Campaign for the Administration of Justice (CAJ). In its early days, it hosted cross-community ventures with ex-prisoners and had established trust and credibility with both 'sides'. In the Thatcher years, and afterwards, BURC and Counteract could gain access to the business community and employers, despite their opposition to trade unions and ICTU. In BURC Counteract benefited from the political vision of left of centre radicalism.

1991 was a productive time. Counteract produced a leaflet on Housing and Intimidation giving advice to victims of intimidation. Jim Quinn recalls it was … *developed with the help of Joan Mc Crum who I think at the time was the director of Belfast Housing Aid and a member of the Counteract management committee who was always very positive and supportive.* This was distributed widely to individual unions, councils of trade unions, advice agencies, community groups and statutory bodies. Research was started. At the height of the murder and intimidation campaign against taxi drivers Counteract made representations to Government about improving safety; as did the T&G – as the records show.

The *Belfast Telegraph* reported, *Taxi men seek meeting with Needham on Terror attacks* (11 March 1991). The T&G union leader had pushed for a meeting after an emergency meeting in Transport House.

The *Irish News* reported: *Better fined than blown apart, taxi drivers told* (7 March 1991), noting that the T&G union leader had advised safety was more important than incurring fines; *Fearful taxi men threaten action* (11 March 1991) that paramilitaries on both sides were targeting taxi drivers; *Derry cabs in fear over hate letters* stating that the UVF was threatening drivers; and, *RUC 'booking' taxi drivers, says union*, demonstrating that the legal requirement for taxis to show their firm put them in danger of being killed (13 March 1991).

Similar stories ran in the *Newsletter* and *Irish Times* of that period. NIC ICTU made public statements condemning this ongoing merciless campaign of violence against workers in Northern Ireland. It also gave support to the drivers who had been subjected to armed high-jackings and unions got involved.

Counteraction, the unit's bulletin, was started. Education and training were introduced and developed.[7] The unit was represented at relevant conferences.[8]

In the North West Counteract was busy too. In May 1991 the T&G launched its three-year Equality Programme to address issues relating to sectarianism and discrimination.[9] A series of residential seminars brought Union members together to discuss the often-divisive issues of sectarianism, intimidation and discrimination. The first two of these seminars were in Lurgan and Strabane, training Union members as lay tutors to use the video and booklet materials in the Programme. Frank Wright of Queen's University Belfast agreed to facilitate the residential seminars.

There was a clear need to provide educational courses to explain in some detail the operation of then current Fair Employment legislation. T&G Regional Education Officer, Liam McBrinn, took up this issue and worked with the FEC to organise a five-day course. Courses ran throughout Northern Ireland where Jim Quinn facilitated discussion with shop stewards, on the more general issue of sectarianism. Counteract worked with a number of unions to develop anti-sectarian training in their organisations, and a programme of well-publicised seminars in 1991.[10]

*   *   *   *   *

Counteract had started research in February 1991 with a survey of Health Boards, Education Boards and District Councils. They got a response to from 17 (of 26) local councils and all Education & Health Boards finding only one council and not one board was even considering guidelines on procedures for dealing with sectarianism, harassment or intimidation in the workplace. This was a low baseline to start from.

Jim Quinn approached DHSS for statistics on people citing intimidation as a reason for leaving work but this yielded no results. Counteract wrote to the Industrial Relations Division for the number of intimidation cases dealt with by their tribunals. Months were spent on this, but to little avail because statistics were not kept. Ultimately Counteract could only try to influence and improve the existing Compensation Scheme.[11] A pilot study was be completed by Clem McCartney over the winter of 1991 and fuller research was undertaken in 1992.

*   *   *   *   *

Procedures for dealing with sectarianism and intimidation would be drafted as guidelines over the next year or so. These guidelines and the preliminary report were referred to the Equality Committee of NIC ICTU for further discussion. Paul Sweeney (then Director of NIVT), Pat McGinn and Jim Quinn worked on a detailed proposal for research into intimidation. Brendan Mackin suggested local companies that could be approached to fund it and worked with Jim Quinn approaching companies and charitable Trusts.

Fundraising used up a large amount of Counteract time.[12] At the outset the unit received funding from Telethon Trust (£20,000), Cadbury Trust (£10,000) and government's Central Community Relations Unit (£10,000 for the first year of two). To survive the unit had to obtain more.

At this stage Counteract was invited to sit on a joint advisory body made up of CRC, the NI Association of Citizens Advice Bureaux (NIACAB) and representatives of Independent Advice Centres. The joint working party looked at developments in best practice for advice for workers dealing with victims of intimidation whether in the workplace or community. In May that year the advisory group was broadened to include the Campaign for the Administration of Justice (CAJ).

May Blood recounted the T&G's work in Short Brothers (the Belfast based Aircraft Company) where Avilla Kilmurry and Liam McBrinn worked with Counteract and Dennis Godfrey (then at the FEC) training Senior Shop Stewards. Resistance was palpable from staff and management – who 'couldn't see what this had to do with work' – and hostility was apparent. Shorts' Personnel Director Rory Galway ensured that participants were given time off work to attend the course and smoothed over many ruffled feathers. In the early days, as still happens where an organisation's management practice is authoritarian, the training was ordered from above, with no explanation or follow through. Nevertheless, the training was completed. Sadly, there was not to be any further work.

Hostility to Counteract came from many sources, overtly and through resistance. Sometimes it was obvious, as when the accommodation was totally unsuitable or when supervisors or managers refused staff time off, stating this was 'for operational reasons'. At other times hostility was expressed as an implicit or explicit threat to trainers, made as they left the premises. Certainly, this work was not for the faint-hearted.

*   *   *   *   *

The politics and principles that defined Counteract came from the trade union movement and enlightened legislation. Sectarianism was (and in a less blatant way, still is) woven into the fabric of Northern Irish society. The overall pattern was clear. In general, Catholics felt they were discriminated against but that this was being denied – where Protestants disputed that discrimination existed. Everyone knew, but few would talk about it. If ever there was to be peace that would have to be recognised, and discussed openly, by workers and employers.

The role of trade unions and Counteract was sanctioned by a membership of over 200,000 people in NIC ICTU and 60,000 in the T&G. No political party could match that size of membership, nor claim to include people from the Orange Order, Hibernian, Free Masonic and St Columbanus. The Unions representing these individuals were not prepared to stay within the politics of condemnation but determined to use the politics of action and the Trade Union agenda.

July brought the annual, and by then traditional, heightened tensions as the marching season came to a peak. Orange Order marches and protests against these were the focus of 'community tensions', as rank sectarianism was euphemistically called. NIC ICTU spearheaded an anti-violence drive in both the North and the South of Ireland and they followed with a warning that manufacturing jobs were disappearing as a direct result of the violence – which the press covered.[13]

Counteract was profiled by the press then, too, as 'The bigot busters are on the job' and 'Shopfloor bigots "use jokes to bully"'.[14] The severity of violence perpetrated against workers was highlighted, and the subtleties of using 'banter' rather than open threats was given due attention. The anti-sectarian agenda was now becoming part of the wider public debate.

A huge row erupted at the Ford Autolite plant in Belfast that year, when management gave workers the option of working over the Twelfth of July holidays. The fact that this should be seen an issue at all spoke volumes.

* * * * *

All this work happened in an intensely violent time as records show. In summer 1991 Pearse McKenna was the only shop steward in Ormeau Bakery and was Catholic. He was mediating a dispute about flying union jack flags in the workplace after being approached by Catholic workers who'd complained about excessive and offensive displays of Union Jack flags. Pearse spoke to their shop steward.

A complaint was being formalised but the following day the flags had been removed. This caused deep resentment in some of the Protestant workforce and it was assumed that Pearse had removed the flags. In fact, the person who did take the flags down was a Protestant living in an area where, if the truth were told, he'd have been beaten up, put out of his home and possibly killed for his efforts. Pearse denied responsibility but was not believed. In an attempt to resolve matters he set about getting a neutral and trusted Union representative to mediate and 'clear' his name. Summer holidays and other things delayed matters and all appeared to be quietened down. However, in October he was 'taken to task' – and very lucky to survive the attack.

Two men on a motorbike approached him outside the Bakery as he left work.

'Is that him?' the pillion said.

The driver replied, 'Yes'.

Thinking they were about to ask about a chance of work – as people often did with shop stewards – he was not suspicious even when the passenger reached into his jacket pocket. Only when he spotted the gun did he realise the danger. He said

> If he'd just fired, he'd have hit me in the head at point blank range. I hadn't a chance. But he paused, put both hands on the gun, raised it over his head and took aim. I ran up the street. He missed my head.

Pearse heard two shots and felt a whack on the back. He rolled onto the ground and under a lorry. His friend and colleague, Derek Bryson, was in his car at that moment. He backed up to the motorbike threw and open the passenger door for Pearse.

The rider panicked. 'Forget about it, you've got him', he yelled and the motorbike sped off.

The two shots had got Pearse in the back. One into the left lower back and another through the right – penetrating the entire body. He wasn't sure he was shot, but the blood confirmed his fears. Thinking, 'I don't feel as bad as I should' he considered the damage. 'Are my legs working'? Only when he was in the ambulance, did the reality of his injuries come home to him.

Press reports included the front-page headline in the *Newsletter* 'Gunmen target bakery worker', and in the *Irish News*, 'Wife mystified by sectarian attack'. The Ulster Freedom Fighters claimed responsibility for the shooting.

Pearse McKenna, who later did voluntary work with Jim Quinn and Noreen Moore in Counteract, was never to be in paid work again. He was also a volunteer as part of the team working on the Museum of Citizenship project.[15]

After nearly a decade Pearse was still ardent about the importance of challenging sectarianism in the workplace. He was justifiably, bitterly disappointed in how his own former management responded to his situation:

> They just walked away from it. Not one person from management was disciplined let alone sacked. There were at least two other cases that I know about in there, and with mine that cost £60,000. No worker who had done £60,000 worth of damage to the business would have been let stay on.

It was also his opinion that Counteract should be careful in its relationship to corporate management, so that their involvement could not be used as an excuse in cases taken to Tribunal where – in reality – the company was not dealing with sectarian intimidation and harassment.

* * * * *

That October the IRA bombed Shorts aircraft company (again), threatened DHSS staff in Pomeroy and murdered Brian Haldane.[16] Counteract responded vigorously that 'There are no legitimate targets'.[17] Jim Quinn wrote to the press publicising the peace rally for 1st November.[18]

Counteract files on press releases reflect some of the innumerable contacts with press and media over the decade. They make chilling reading. Each page makes comment on the many violent incidents that are largely forgotten now. The 'big' events like the Shankill and Greysteel massacres may remain in our memory, and the attempted murders in Belfast, Ballymena, and throughout Northern Ireland that year.

However, the sheer volume of intimidation and the range of people in different occupations who were threatened shocked those who read of it. Shop stewards, social service staff, journalists, van and bus drivers whose vehicles were hi-jacked, hospital workers, technicians, shop assistants, engineers, DHSS and other civil servants, postmen, builders, lawyers, company managers and owners, postmen – the list goes on and on. The Unions re-peated their bid for peace, with Counteract, calling for marches and rallies.

Press and public comment became increasingly important. Incidents like the shooting of Pearse McKenna at the Ormeau Bakery were becoming 'normalised' in the media and public tolerance for intimidation and sect-arian murder had to be challenged. Only Counteract seemed to have to the capacity and the will to do this quickly – always without distinguishing between what 'side' inflicted violence on working people.

By then, in October 1991, Billy Robinson was surveying National Communication Union (NCU) members in Belfast about hi-jacking and was getting a good response. Jim Quinn wrote to the Chief Constable for statistics on hi-jacking of public and private vehicles. Counteract then contacted affiliated unions with members in the public services, that is, Busmen, Department of the Environment, Electricity, Telephone and Postal workers. Research on NCU workers continued in the Belfast branch that winter and members of the UCW were now showing an interest in the survey. Widening the survey on hi-jacking beyond the Belfast area, and developing a full research project from it, would require support and it was to take time.

Billy Robinson had considerable understanding of hi-jacking, including his personal experience – both he and his brother were hi-jacked on the same morning:

> The background to my raising the question of hi-jacking with BT was of my ex-perience of staff in the company being hi-jacked plus my own personal experience.
>
> The press and media would report 'Hi-jack vehicle with bomb on board exploded in city centre'. Neither they nor the public gave a thought to what took place prior to the vehicle's arrival, to the driver or how they were treated afterwards.
>
> A vehicle driver would arrive in the morning to do his day's work. Somewhere in the course of his day a gun is put to his head, his identity [badge/card] is taken, a bomb is placed on board his vehicle and he is informed he has to take it to a certain spot in the city – and if he does not do so he's told they have his ID and he will be got at, or his family hit. The driver then takes the vehicle to where he's instructed, but he's aware that this bomb might go off at any time.
>
> Consider the driver having a gun put to his head, he and his family threatened if he does not cooperate. That alone is very frightening, but then driving with the bomb and the danger of it exploding. After delivering the vehicle in most cases

he is treated as an accomplice by the police and taken to a police station for questioning. Depending on what time of the day the hi-jacking took place he may not be released until late at night, having to make his way home, maybe having lost his coat in the vehicle, no money – and then there were no mobile phones. So, it's a very frightening experience. The probability is that he would return to work the next day take another vehicle out.

The long-term effect was alcohol abuse, family abuse, depression. There was no provision of counselling. It was expected of you.

My own experience, the first time I was hi-jacked, was that I was waiting in a BT van on the Falls Road to meet a work colleague. He had asked me to bring his wages to him as he was off work sick. While waiting there I noticed a young man crossing the road in front of me, wearing a jacket with a hood pulled over his head. As it was a lovely morning, I thought it's not that cold so I immediately put the key in the ignition but did not see another person coming up on my side of the vehicle. He pushed a gun into my face and said, 'You're hi-jacked. Open up the other door.' Both got into the vehicle and instructed me to drive into some back street.

The problem for me was I was supposed to be working in the city center and under the rules of BT if you're not on your site of work then you could be disciplined or dismissed. I was very angry and started cursing and swearing. The person sitting beside me with a gun across his knee told me to stop using bad language. He must have gone to Holy Communion on a daily basis!

They put a bomb in my vehicle, took my BT pass (I never carried any personal ID), instructed me to drive it to the city center and I had 30 mins to get there before it would go off.

Driving the vehicle, I thought I don't want to be the cause of people being injured or killed. So, I thought, where can I take this? I put my full lights on, hazard warning lights, my hand on the horn and drove down the wrong side of the road. I reached some vacant ground and drove the van onto it. The police and army arrived. One of the police officers was a person I had worked with in the past. He asked me where I had been hi-jacked; I informed him of my situation with BT. He called the army officer in charge and informed him that no one was to know where I was hi-jacked not even BT. I asked, 'Is that ok?' He said, 'You can tell BT whatever you like.'

After the bomb was defused my vehicle was damaged by controlled explosions and was being towed to the depot. As it was towed away, it passed the shops where my mother was shopping – she saw the van and thought that it was my van even though there was nothing to identify it as mine. She did not know why, but maybe it was because my brother who worked for the Post Office had been hi-jacked earlier that morning.

Counteract then ran a campaign to at least get companies to provide counselling for staff after hijacking.

Since the issue had been raised, BT management agreed a number of measures to assist victims of hi-jacking. What was then a progressive step would be
the minimum expected of any employer today. Seemingly it took Counteract
and the trade unions to make the issue part of the corporate agenda.

*   *   *   *   *

Fair employment in Northern Ireland gained an international dimension
with the US intervention of the MacBride Principles.

The MacBride Principles shook the local business world when, in June,
the Mayor of New York David Dinkins signed a law banning contracts to
companies in Northern Ireland that did not comply with the principles.
(This also denied government contracts to employers who did not abide by
the rules of fair employment). In October a similar bill was endorsed by the
Governor of California. The FEC issued its first report, noting that according
to perceived religion of people, companies employing more than twenty-five
staff, 65% of those in work were Protestant and 35% were Catholic.

That same month, in the first case of its kind, the FEC had announced
that a south Belfast company had been disqualified from receiving government grants because it failed to return monitoring forms on the religious
make-up of its workforce.

In September John Taylor, a senior UUP member told the young
Unionist Conference that one in three Catholics is … *either a supporter of
murder or worse still a murderer.*[19] Overt sectarianism was still a hallmark
of politics in Northern Ireland politics.

In November the FEC publicised rules on religious or political symbols
at work that might be considered offensive, and caused uproar in certain
quarters by saying that pictures of the Pope or the Queen might be deemed
offensive. DUP MP Rev Willie McCrea described the ruling as 'treasonable'.

Peace talks began in March with a starting date of 30th April for peace
negotiations. The Loyalist cease-fire previously announced was then called
off. A fitful start in Strand One was called to an end by Secretary of State
Peter Brooke in early July, coinciding with the appointment of a Chair for
Strand Two. Talks in September proved to be no more than a sounding
board. Elections for the London Parliament were then in the offing.

A measure of the difficulty and danger of Counteract work can be seen
in the events of the time. In 1991 the conflict was still raging throughout

Northern Ireland and further afield. The IRA took to bombing England systematically,[20] starting with the bomb in the garden of 10 Downing Street during a Cabinet meeting chaired by John Major. Then the appeal trials and eventual release of the Birmingham Six happened, plus the appeal of the Maguire Seven leading to an upsurge of cases alleging miscarriage of justice.

The IRA onslaught on security forces in Northern Ireland continued and Loyalist paramilitaries responded with tit-for-tat sectarian killings and attacks. In prisons there was continued rioting for segregation between Loyalist and Republican prisoners, and the Crumlin Road jail was set on fire. The IRA bombed Shorts Brothers for a sixth time.

In the towns and villages of Northern Ireland more Catholic taxi drivers were singled out as the target of sectarian killings in the autumn. This year showed a marked increase in the number of killings by Loyalists, and a return to the IRA's bombing campaign. December brought the announcement from Peter Brooks that a freeze was to be put on public spending in several areas to meet the increased cost of IRA bomb damage.

The statistics for the years 1990 and 1991 told their story of unceasing mayhem. The figures[21] for 1990 are as gruesome as those for years before. Deaths arising from the Troubles: 76. Shootings: 557. Bombs planted: 286. Incendiaries: 33. Firearms found: 179. Explosives found: 1,969 kg (4,340 lb.). Persons charged with terrorist and serious public order offences: 383. Casualties arising from paramilitary attacks: 174. And, similarly, in 1991. Deaths arising from the Troubles: 94. Shootings: 499. Bombs planted: 368. Incendiaries: 237. Firearms found: 164. Explosives found: 4,167 kg (9,185 lb.). Persons charged with terrorist and serious public order offences: 404. Casualties arising from paramilitary attacks: 138.

Notes

1. The first Counteract Committee was Terry Carlin, Avilla Kilmurry, Brenda Callaghan, Joan McCrum (Belfast Housing Aid), Linda Walker (National Association of Teachers in Further & Higher Education), Billy Robinson (National Communications Union) and John Cassells (Services, Industrial, Professional Technical Union), who formed the working group.

2. *Newsletter, Irish News,* the *Irish Times, Belfast Telegraph, Daily Mail,* and *Birmingham Evening News* (15/16 November 1990), *T&G News* (December 1990), *Sunday News* (6 January 1991). The *Fermanagh Herald* covered the work in a profile of Jim Quinn and Counteract.

3. *Irish News*: 2 February 1991 'Row over Union Jack Policy' reported on the DUP railing against Ulsterbus for making staff take down Union Jacks in support of the Gulf War troops; and 30 January 1991.

4. As with most organisations of its type, finance is always a problem and fundraising has used up a considerable amount of Counteract time. At the outset Counteract received the following funding; Cadbury Trust: £10,000, Telethon Trust: £20,000, Central Community Relations Unit: £10,000 (first year of two).

5. Ballylumford was a key electricity power station, which was by the make-up and behaviour of its workforce, a byword for predominance of Protestants, and sectarianism, in the workforce. Also, Ballylumford had played a strategic role in the Ulster Workers' Strike in 1974 and was instrumental in bringing Northern Ireland to a standstill and collapsing the power-sharing Stormont government after the Sunningdale Agreement. Despite the privatisation of electricity 'Ballylumford' continued to signify Protestant workers' power for many.

6. The Training for Women Network has had substantial difficulties researching the gender breakdown in employment and training for just this reason.

7. Anti-sectarian work with young people had been dealt with mainly by the Youth Committee of Congress and its affiliated unions. Counteract did not seek to take a lead for fear of being seen as domineering and for the immediate future that relationship would be maintained.

8. As part of informing unions and others of its work and encouraging their participation Counteract attended a number of conferences. These included Irish Congress of Trades Unions Annual Conference (July 1991), NIC ICTU Annual Conference (April 1992), Fair Employment Commission Staff Conference (March 1992) and Centre for the Study of Conflict Conference (February 1992).

9. The T&G Programme was under the overall direction of the Union's Regional Equality Committee which met on a quarterly basis. Counteract featured in their 'Record' newspaper frequently throughout the years, detailing the work, ethos and objectives of the unit.

10. The first of these was on Saturday 25 May 1991, when a one-day Joint Seminar for Trades Council and Community Activists on Anti-sectarianism offered the opportunity for Trade Union and Community Activists to meet and talk about their experiences and the progress of anti-sectarian projects.

11. Counteract became aware of a scheme entitled 'The Scheme Of Compensation For Loss Of Employment Through Civil Unrest' by accident. It was designed to compensate workers forced to leave their jobs because of threats, intimidation or civil unrest. Cases were heard by a panel that had the power to award the equivalent of a

redundancy payment to victims. Payments were made from Government funds and so no claim was made against the employer. Figures provided by the scheme showed that some of the people disallowed claims under the scheme were excluded because they had not worked two years. Out of the 136 applications in the sample provided 34 were disallowed, and of these 14 (41.18%) failed because applicants had not been continuously employed for two years. Counteract Committee wrote to the relevant minister that autumn and questions asked in the House of Commons and the House of Lords on this issue. No changes were ever made. The only useful outcome was to publicise the scheme, flawed as it was.

12. On Paul Sweeney's advice Counteract prepared applications for core funding over a three-year period to Nuffield, Rowntree, Cadbury, Tudor and the Ireland Fund, arranging meetings with contact people before making formal submissions. Jim Quinn and Avilla Kilmurry liaised on this work and wrote to the smaller trusts for help. Income for these formative years also came from the Enkalon Trust, NIPSA, ATGW, GMB, NGA, FTATU, AEU, NUPE, NAPO, OPATS, Newtownabbey Trades Council, Course Fees, the Community Relations Council for Northern Ireland (CRC) Grants (Seminars) and the European Social Fund (ESF) Account.

13. *Belfast Telegraph*, 2 July 1991 reported ' "*Get off our Backs" unions tell bombers*' and called for a day of action with a massive rally to highlight the feeling amongst thousands of trade union members and their associates. *Belfast Telegraph*, *Newsletter* and *Irish Times* of 3rd July 1991.

14. *Irish News*, 4 July 1991.

15. The Museum of Citizenship project was inspired by the Museum of Tolerance in USA and planned as a museum for the twenty-first century placing prejudice, sectarianism and intolerance under the spotlight, where visitors learn to recognise and confront their most closely held beliefs. It was to predicates that Belfast could be 'European City of Tolerance'. A feasibility study was conducted and government pledged to help fund the project. This did not happen.

16. The *Irish News* of 20 October 1991 reported on the murder, the family's statement and the widespread condemnation from politicians. Brian Haldane ran one of the biggest timber companies in Northern Ireland and was targeted because he supplied the security forces.

17. *Morning Star*, 24 October 1991.

18. *Newsletter* 31 October 1991.

19. *Fortnight*, October 1991, quoted in Bew and Gillespie 1999.

20. Downing Street was bombed on 7th February. Eleven days later one person was killed and forty-three injured at Victoria Station in London. A series of incendiaries exploded in Blackpool and Manchester, causing considerable damage. In mid-December an incendiary device exploded in the National Gallery in London and explosive devices were found on railway tracks and trains.

21. Source: Bew and Gillespie, 1999.

CHAPTER 3

1991–92: Early Work

1992 began with two massive bombs exploding in Belfast and a five-pound bomb left in a briefcase near Downing Street. The IRA killed seven Protestant building workers who had worked at a military base as they drove home. A roadside bomb blew up their minibus at Teebane Crossroads near Cookstown. An eighth victim the driver died four days later. Just after news of this broke Peter Brooke sang 'My Darling Clementine' on the RTE television's *Late Late Show* and subsequently offered his resignation as Secretary of State for Northern Ireland. In February Albert Reynolds succeeded Charles Haughey as Taoiseach in the Republic. April saw a Conservative victory in the UK general election with a majority of twenty-one seats.

The FEC's 1992 report showed that although Catholics made up 35% of those in employment, 38% were available for work. The CBI and the NI Chamber of Commerce had opposed the publication of this information.

The *Belfast Telegraph* reported that two bombs in the centre of London attracted government compensation of a £800 million, as compared to £615 million paid since 1969 for damage resulting from the Troubles in Northern Ireland.

On the economic front, John De Lorean (the flamboyant US car manufacturer whose business collapsed) repaid £5 million to the Industrial Development Board and moves were made to reclaim a further £2 million of the £80 million that government had invested in the De Lorean project.

In mid-June, at the end of twelve hours of peace talks, and despite the deadlock in negotiations on Strand One (on the internal government of Northern Ireland) parties agreed a tentative move towards Strands Two and Three. Reports of speeches made by Sinn Féin at the annual Wolfe Tone commemoration suggested that '… the statement encourages the

belief in some quarters that Sinn Féin and the IRA might be moving towards calling off the campaign of violence'.[1]

A UUP delegation, headed by James Molyneaux, began three days
of Strand Two talks in Dublin in September. The same month a 2,000lb
IRA bomb destroyed the forensic laboratory in Belfast, injuring more than
twenty people and damaging more than a thousand homes causing damage
worth an estimated £6 million. In October the IRA hi-jacked a taxi driver,
making him drive a bomb to Downing Street where it exploded.

November 1992 saw the bombing of Canary Wharf, election victory
for the Republic's Labour party, and the introduction of 'goals and time-
tables' for promoting the number of Catholics in the higher reaches of the
Northern Ireland Civil Service.

In December the violence was escalated by both Republicans and
Loyalists, with bombs and incendiaries planted in Belfast, Lisburn, Dublin,
London and Manchester. In a controversial speech, Sir Patrick Mayhew
said that soldiers could be taken off the streets and Sinn Féin could be included in future talks if the IRA ended its campaign.

Grim statistics for that year show: Deaths arising from the Troubles: 85.
Shootings: 506. Bombs planted: 371. Incendiaries: 126. Firearms found: 194.
Explosives found: 2,167 kg (4,775 lb.). Persons charged with terrorist and
serious public order offences: 418. Casualties arising from paramilitary
attacks: 207.

In the midst of all this, a robust trade union campaign was started in
early 1992[2] with the first of a number of huge peace rallies. 'Trade Unions
Demand the Right to Live and the Right to Work' was the clear message
of a rally organised in Belfast on 4 February 1992. The general public,
community workers and clergy joined with ICTU and thousands of trade
unionists at Belfast City Hall in the biggest trade union rally seen here
since the outbreak of violence in the late sixties.

In an impressive display of trade union solidarity, Norman Willis
(British TUC), Peter Cassells (ICTU) and Campbell Christie (Scottish
TUC) along with other national trade union figures joined local union
leaders to reiterate the demand for the *Right to Live and Work* (See Picture 3).
As press archives show, the headlines got larger and the thousands attending
attracted photographers and increasing coverage by the media.

Picture 3:   Right to Life demonstration: Belfast 1992

Paying tribute to the movement in Northern Ireland, the TUC General Secretary, Norman Willis said 'You provide the strongest and most durable bridges across the political and religious divisions here.' (See Picture 4).

Campbell Christie, General Secretary of the Scottish TUC declared 'The STUC is solidly behind all the initiatives which will bring an end to this chilling scenario and we eagerly await the day when the slogan PEACE, WORK AND PROGESS is translated into actuality.'

Peter Cassells, General Secretary of the Irish Congress of Trade Unions, speaking as leader of 450,000 trades unionists and their families in the Republic of Ireland declared 'I am angry and sickened that the IRA claimed to carry out this massacre in the name of the people of the Republic of Ireland.''

Bernie McCrea, Chairperson of the NIC ICTU's Women's Committee said 'Women share the grief in our community in a very special way. How many times have widows had to pick up the shattered remnants of family life and try to rebuild it for themselves and the children left behind?'

Picture 4: Norman Willis (British TUC) speaks at the
Right to live and work demonstration 1992

Her words proved all too immediately prophetic, for within hours three
people were murdered in a Sinn Féin office by a disturbed policeman who later
committed suicide and the next day five people were murdered in a betting
shop in Belfast by the UFF. As a result, NIC ICTU was back on the streets
two nights later to join with the community of the Lower Ormeau in a silent
gathering, described in the media as 'impressive, solemn, and emotional'.
    Terry Carlin of NIC ICTU told the gathering

> There were two young girls in front of me, one about twelve years of age and the older
> one stood with her arms around her young sister. The younger girl's face was an image
> of grief I will never forget for the rest of my life. She obviously had been crying for
> three days and had no tears left. I'm not ashamed to admit that I did the crying for
> her on that Friday night.

As a follow-up to the demonstration, NICICTU had its *Peace, Work and
Progress Programme* and Counteract staged a series of six consultative

meetings with trade unionists and community groups throughout Northern Ireland to discuss how best the campaign could be brought forward and sustained. Ideas generated at these meetings formed part of a programme of work that would be endorsed by NIC ICTU.

The rallies throughout Northern Ireland were more poignant in the wake of the Teebane massacre.[3] Again, the message – reported in larger print by that stage – was 'There are no legitimate target's. Photographs of women and children carrying placards saying "Stop the killing and Smash the bigots" were printed beside headlines "Workers demand the right to life". There were reports that unions hinted at strikes for peace. Editorials repeated the message and the ethos of the moves for peace grew – on all sides.

These feelings had been intensified by the betting shop killings on the Ormeau Road in February. More rallies and demonstrations were planned and organised and heavily supported by the press and broadcast media. A sense of common purpose united all those people who were arranging or reporting on the movement from the people of Northern Ireland who now were beginning to register the increasing revulsion at the violence. The moral high-ground was now closed to paramilitaries of whatever brand.

Counteract ran the *Peace, Work and Progress Campaign* with the Trade Union Movement and organised events giving the Unions an increasingly prominent role in challenging sectarian violence. Long before the business community took an interest in challenging sectarianism and promoting economic inclusion, Jim Quinn of Counteract was working with the unions giving the clear message that sectarianism costs business, takes away jobs and robs workers most of all. In early spring 1992 Counteract sent more than six hundred letters to unions, union contacts, trades councils and community groups with information about regional meetings. More were to follow. At this stage, it was decided there would be no press publicity.

Hands Off My Mate was another anti-sectarian campaign, chaired by Joe Grillen a shop steward at Shorts Brothers. His work in this campaign led to him receiving the John Bosco Peace Award for 1992.

By March 1992 the education work of Counteract had been firmly established and the programme for spring/summer schools circulated. Jim Quinn teamed up with Frank Wright to deliver the first of many sessions. Frank brought a new way of training and adult teaching to the sessions.

His method was very different to the traditional lecture style of the union education programmes. His gentle nature and deep understanding gave inspiration to Counteract in its early days and the many union representatives with whom he came into contact. He facilitated discussion of difficult subjects that were normally 'off limits' and started what became characteristic of the Counteract method of talking about threatening topics in a safe environment – though without Frank's serenity.

Fresh ways of teaching and learning were successfully introduced into equality training – that foreshadowed the radical approach that Counteract would have to take to get its message across. Jim Quinn was now in the process of forming strong, mutually beneficial relationships between Counteract and the FEC, CRC and WEA, with a central and common agenda of training. Jim Quinn remembers. 'The individuals we worked with in the community at the start included Fergus Cumiskey – CRC, Colin Neilands – WEA and Edwin Graham – NICVA. There were also good relationships with Will Glendinning and Joe Hinds in CRC during my time.'

The media took a significant interest in the unit which now got widespread coverage in the local, national and international media. After the first year's work it was obvious that if contacts and supporters were to be kept informed of Counteract activities, a regular information bulletin was needed. And so, they produced *Counteraction* with a circulation of around 2000 for the first and 5000 for the second – anticipating the circulation would be increased. The second *Counteraction* was a collective effort by Committee members, each doing a specific report. One feature highlighted the serious problems faced by drivers in BT and the Post Office, experiencing hi-jacking.

*   *   *   *   *

Counteract recognised that hi-jacking was a key factor in the ongoing intimidation. Billy McCreight and Billy Robinson had been CWU colleagues and worked together before the days of Counteract. In 1992 and 1993 they felt the most pressing issue was the treatment of victims of widespread hi-jacking, where vehicles were used for carrying bombs and drivers often forced to deliver them. 'Hijacking was a major issue for bus drivers. … In particular the after effects of the trauma which were not always recognised sympathetically or treated' (Jim Quinn).

Case Study A

One van driver was taken from his vehicle, his driving licence, coat and money stolen, and told to sit in a public park *until four o'clock – and there's someone watching you. Don't move!* He sat without a coat and it started to rain. He did not dare move. He was subsequently treated as hostile by both the security forces and his employers.

Drivers were thus put in an impossible situation. Even if they could have named hi-jackers they knew their lives and those of their families were at stake. They were advised to say that they had been attacked by masked or hooded men to short circuit at least some of the escalating intimidation. They were also told by employers and security forces to avoid carrying driving licences, bills and other personal documents that might be used by hi-jackers to intimidate them further.

The effect of this trauma was not addressed and drivers went about their daily work in a state of extreme distress. Some of the more grotesquely humorous tales are still recounted. One man was taken from his vehicle to wait in a drinking club. Shaking with fear he was offered a drink. *A whiskey?* He didn't want one. *A pint? Harp? Bass? Okay – a pint. Bass.* After a while his kidnapper asked if he wanted another pint. He agreed. *Well, it's your round. You get this one – and get me twenty Benson & Hedges while you're up there.*

Coping with the effects of armed hi-jacking, kidnap and the arrest that followed drove some to depression, drink, marriage breakdown, medication and long-term mental illness. At that time employers saw no need to take this into account.

Case points

Other pressures were put on working men as a regular part of their job. After bombings companies were always keen to put up the 'Business as Usual' signs. This meant getting the phone lines working again immediately. Engineers were routinely sent into bombed buildings where no safety checks had been done. Shards of glass and metal were imbedded in walls, floors, handrails and furniture but the phone workers were told to get on with the job nevertheless. CWU were seen as 'a hindrance to fighting terrorism' when they questioned employers about the safety of their members. Employers understood the politics of the times but not the practicalities. Indeed, for many managers and employers the workers were being recalcitrant when they questioned these arrangements.

Hi-jacking affected both workers and local communities, and had a major impact on people delivering and receiving services, including bus drivers, taxi drivers, public utility workers etc. They had continuous experience of having their vehicles hi-jacked and being intimidated into driving bombs to various locations. The strain on victims was never investigated, nor was their treatment by employers, security forces and paramilitaries after a hi-jacking. Counteract focused on this issue and met officials of unions with members likely to be affected by this, as minutes record:

> Drivers having to drive with a bomb on board under threat either by gun or in some cases their families being held hostage, until they ferry the bomb to the paramilitaries' target. Adding to this trauma the driver may well be considered hostile by the security forces for their perceived co-operation with the terrorists and may face a lengthy period of questioning. The result of this may lead to depression, fear, alcohol abuse, marital breakdown and even loss of job. The unions within British Telecom and the Post Office were seeking practical support and assistance for their members suffering this trauma.

> We can now report a visit by Alan Johnston, General Secretary, UCW and his deputy Derek Hodgson who attended a meeting with P.O. managers, union representatives,

and postal workers in Belfast to discuss the problem. The result of the meeting was a more comprehensive guideline for managers than was previously in force. It is hoped that other companies will recognise the effects of hi-jacking on their staff and put in place some of the procedures outlined below.

Immediate Action

- *Notify the police and security immediately. Security will then notify all other interested parties.*
- *Speak to individuals to assess the incident and decide whether individual should*
  - *Continue working*
  - *Be taken to office*
  - *Be taken home*
  - *Be given medical treatment*
  - *Medical care must be arranged where necessary.*
  - *Family must be notified as soon as possible.*
  - *If an individual is with police, contact must be established, again family must be informed.*

Support Actions

- *Personnel service centre immediately contact Welfare/OHS/Counselling Services as appropriate.*
- *Inform senior managers on an ongoing basis of staff incurring sick absence.*

The Counteract annual report stated

At the height of the murder and intimidation campaign against taxi drivers Counteract made representations to the Government about improving safety. It also gave support to the drivers and unions involved. This type of support for single-issue one-off campaigns should continue and is an important aspect of our work.

Discussions between NIC ICTU and CBI on a joint declaration of
protection for workers in Northern Ireland were progressing – not yet
achieved but making headway. The very fact that it would be a joint declaration was encouraging. It was to mark the beginning of co-operation
by both sides of industry in a concerted effort to challenge, if not eradicate sectarianism, intimidation and discrimination in the workplace.

Originally, they had hoped for joint union/community anti-sectarian
projects in Belfast, North Down, Fermanagh and Derry. The first of many
obstacles to be overcome was the reluctance of local people to accept that
there was a sectarian problem. Even where there was acceptance, there was
a feeling that little could be done about it.

*   *   *   *   *

To get effective involvement with the community and voluntary sector
Counteract needed to work in collaborative ventures with CRC linking
into both community and statutory agencies. The first of these ventures
was an Advice Services Working Party whose remit was to develop best
practice for advice workers dealing with cases of intimidation and sectarian harassment. This would later become an information pack and
training programme for advice workers. The Counteract contribution
was its experience and its guidelines on dealing with intimidation cases.

In the voluntary sector, differences in the speed of trade union decision-
making and methods of working created impatience in community groups
who saw delays by unions (because of what they saw as democratic structures) as 'bureaucratic'. And then there were rivalries between community
groups in local areas.

On a more positive note, six regional meetings were held as part of
the *Peace, Work & Progress Programme*. These consulted local trade union
and community interests about the best way to advance the campaign, and
attracted representatives from forty-three community/voluntary groups.
Some joint union/community projects would develop as a result.

Another area of Counteract collaboration with CRC involved a series
of six anti-sectarian seminars in co-operation with NICVA, WEA, CRC
and Playboard (NI). These seminars were held in Ballymena, Omagh,
Newtownards, Derry, Belfast and Benburb and attracted some two hundred participants from community and statutory bodies. They generated

interest and work for Counteract in both the community and statutory sectors, and the evaluation showed that workshops on sectarianism in the workplace were the most popular and considered the most relevant. Meetings were arranged with the Community Relations Officers of Belfast and Derry City Trades Councils about ongoing training.

*   *   *   *   *

The killing of five Catholics in Sean Graham's betting shop in February created a flash point along disputed marching territories – one that would remain unresolved for decades. In light of increasing sectarian intimidation and murder by Loyalists, Secretary of State, Sir Patrick Mayhew banned the UDA from midnight on 10th August.

Working with Community Groups and activists in the early 1990s was challenging. For example, links were made with Community Groups such as Lower Ormeau, where Jim Quinn had been invited by the Management Committee to go as an observer. Planned demonstrations on the Lower Ormeau Road against Orange Order marches were not to go ahead until permission had been given from the most important people of the area – the families of the five people murdered at Sean Graham's Bookmakers on the Ormeau Road. Such meetings were not very constructive as much time was spent attacking the Orange Order, Security Forces or the Trade Union Movement. A lot of work would go into finding a constructive, viable and lasting role for Counteract engaging with the community. And this all happened against a backdrop of 'community activism' as local paramilitary engagement was euphemistically called, whatever the political hue of those involved.

*   *   *   *   *

Counteract was growing from small beginnings. Alongside CRC they started a preparatory alliance with the Industrial Society about training development. Work was developing with a number of employers in both the public and private sectors and Jim Quinn was confident that early in the New Year of 1993 they would have at least one pilot scheme on good practice in place.

It had been vital that employers were brought into Counteract work. Although progress had been slow it was encouraging to see some employers coming on board. To ensure this process continued and accelerated, plans were made to meet employers' representative organisations like the CBI, Institute of Personnel Management, Equality Managers Association and so on. Another breakthrough emerged from the fledgling unit with the start of joint union/management training courses. At this stage the potential collaboration was on trade union terms, so not yet perceived as an ideological conflict.

On another front, there were also possibilities for developing training in the Northern Ireland Housing Executive. Working with community/voluntary groups presented difficulties for individual groups. So, they operated via umbrella groups like NICVA, NIVT, WEA, Community Councils, CRC and so on. They'd approach organisations formally, explaining what Counteract offered and get involved in that way – a necessary method of engaging large community groups and statutory bodies like NIHE and Local Councils.

By summer 1992 the Counteract education programme had grown[4] and the autumn programme of seminars was being prepared. Counteract met Tom Moore about introducing anti-sectarian education into the general trade union curriculum, and followed up with a meeting between Counteract tutors, Frank Wright and Derek Wilson and ICTU lay tutors. Happily, at the same time, the FEC was in the early stages of developing a code of practice on harassment at work.

That June Terry Carlin told Counteract that NIC ICTU accepted their report on regional meetings and had endorsed the idea of using a declaration against sectarianism and violence as a means of bringing the *Peace, Work and Progress Campaign* forward. The leadership of ICTU, Belfast Trades Council (BTUC) and Scottish Trades Union Council (STUC) began the campaign of signatures. Away from Northern Ireland Counteract accepted an invitation to make a submission on its work to *Initiative 92* that summer and information went to the Scottish TUC to publicise Counteract among Scottish trade Unionists. – but this was not to progress.

*   *   *   *   *

Jim Quinn and NIC ICTU/ICTU launched a Workers Declaration against sectarianism in October, North and South, and invited signatures from the public, churches and so on. This was given considerable publicity in both broad-sheets and tabloids, locally, regionally and nationally. That month residents of the predominantly Unionist-Loyalist East Belfast housing estate Ballybeen were said to 'unite to reject Catholic's UFF killers'[5] making a clear statement of sympathy for the family of the murdered man and open opposition to this sectarianism. 'It's to let the family know we are not all cannibals' a resident was reported as saying.

The *Workers Declaration Campaign* was progressing well. There had been public signings across Northern Ireland.[6] Two meetings were held in Enniskillen, three in Lurgan, one in Belfast and one in Derry to promote the campaign. While press publicity for the declaration had been good, participation in local areas from trade union and community activists could have been better.

Although Jim Quinn informed the management committee that Ormeau Bakery had asked about training with management and unions in the Company – a full year after Pearse McKenna's near fatal shooting – even this gesture did not materialise. Counteract was never to be asked in. A year later things had not progressed. Although the FEC ordered Ormeau Bakery to train staff, as part of a settlement of a case in the FET, that training that never materialised. This was a condition of the Tribunal that was simply being ignored. So, despite their legal powers, there were limits to what the FET and FEC could make happen.

Autumn 1992 brought more progress, as the University of Ulster at Magee asked for training for first and second-year social work students – an excellent breakthrough for Counteract.

*   *   *   *   *

The results of pilot research into Intimidation Statistics[7] demonstrated the need for a more comprehensive study. Allied to Community Training & Research Services Ltd, based in BURC Counteract now prepared a major research proposal, which got CCRU funding. This was a survey of forty workplaces, in which both employers and trade unions were asked to complete a questionnaire and give an interview about incidences of intimidation and procedures for dealing with the issue. This formed the foundation of the first concerted effort to identify how sectarianism operated at work and how it could be dealt with.

Counteract reported excellent progress in the report *Two Years On*.
Work with individual trade unions represented the core of its work. Its
main objective – to develop work with as many unions as possible – was
being achieved. However, it was clear that more needed to be done:

> While Counteract's work with unions has been fairly successful, there is still a lot to
> be done if anti-sectarian/anti-intimidation work is to become a permanent feature
> of individual unions' activity.

Since its inception Counteract had met and received support from thirteen unions representing almost 150,000 members. An additional nine
made donations to its funds or took part in its schools. It had provided
eleven unions[8] with eighteen schools on anti-sectarian/anti-intimidation.

Jim Quinn was also piloting a three-module programme for trade
union lay tutors who gave talks to schools – to equip them with the necessary skills and materials to tell fifth and sixth formers about sectarianism
and intimidation at work.

Counteract was born out of and remained integral to the *Peace, Work
& Progress Programme*[9] and had a representative committee. Over its second
year the programme's activities increased and Counteract supported this
successful work. It had also played a leading role in organising the six regional meetings and expected to be active in promoting the declaration
against sectarian and violence shortly to be launched by NIC ICTU.

It now aimed to produce a series of posters outlining in simple terms
things such as a definition of harassment/intimidation, the unit's aims and
objectives, and the law on intimidation and harassment in the workplace. It
was also looking for more coverage in union and other journals in feature
articles. This came at a time when, coincidentally, the press was about to
experience sectarian intimidation first hand, and would thereafter have a
closer feeling for the work of Counteract.

October also saw the issue of sectarian intimidation hitting the headlines locally and nationally as the UVF threatened to close the Sunday
World, the largest selling Sunday paper in Ireland, by placing a bomb in
the door of its Belfast office in High Street. The newspaper's strong in-
vestigative political journalism angered paramilitaries and (alleged) drug

dealer-racketeers. They regarded this as 'provocative' and responded with force, threats and intimidation.

Press headlines read as

'Newspaper staff forced to jump bomb at office door'
'Show of Solidarity as Loyalist threats fail to shut down Sunday newspaper'[10]
'Newspaper Bomb Protest'[11];
'Belfast Journos defy UVF Bomb'[12];

The *Newsletter* quoted NUJ deputy general secretary, Jake Ecclestone saying, *the company must stand up for press freedom – it's vital. If one newspaper pulls out then it will only be a matter of time before another paper is forced to close down.*[13]

Five MPs and the general secretaries of nineteen trade unions were among the sixty signatories to a strongly worded statement calling publicly for the UVF to withdraw these threats.

The Sunday Times followed events closely with stories for three weeks in a row.

'UVF bombers declare war on top-selling newspaper'
'Bomb attack paper tones down coverage'
'Betrayal' talk at bomb-hit paper'[14]

The Sunday World responded with a denial of any 'toning down' of their reporting.[15] An already open-minded press was now seeing the relevance of Counteract work at first hand.

Andy Snoddy[16] from the Printing Union GPMU was part of the original discussion leading to Counteract. He and Kevin Cooper from the NUJ and the Counteract Management Committee were front men in a protest what would define future press and media response to intimidation (see Picture 5). The death threats to the Sunday World were not only to the journalist but also anyone who sold or who delivered the paper.

Initially Counteract had seen local Councils of Trades Unions as a way of developing joint anti-sectarian projects in local areas with community organisations. However, this did not happen for a number of reasons – the lack of participants and resources in local Trades Union Councils, a then general decline in Trades Council activity, and the fact that there were

Picture 5: Protest against sectarian intimidation outside the offices of Sunday World

few official links with local community groups or community relations officers. So, Jim Quinn now had to consider the best way to encourage involvement from local Trades Councils in Counteract work, as this was essential in spreading the work outside Belfast.

As the time approached for what was to have been the end of a two-year campaign Counteract was just gathering steam. Education, training and research had been put on a firm footing. The T&G with Counteract, supported by CRC, planned to develop and produce two training videos. The two themes were sex discrimination and sectarian violence and harassment at work. Counteract wanted to use videos like these, on fair employment and equality, as they considered following the ATGWU lead. However, the cost of professional production was then prohibitive.

The unit was involved in joint courses with the FEC and had an excellent relationship with them. Counteract had addressed their 1992 staff conference and exchanged information and ideas over the previous two years.

Reporting at the first Counteract AGM it was said 'Our links with FEC and CRC should be continued and strengthened especially through the development of joint training for unions and employers' and of CRC, that there was 'a good relationship with the council throughout [the unit's] existence. In terms of help, advice and publicity they have been more than helpful. We have also been involved and continue to be involved in a number of collaborative projects with the council. Hopefully this relationship will continue as they are important asset to our work.'

Over its first two years Counteract had also had discussions with individuals and groups from Canada, America, New Zealand, Australia, France and Belgium. There were lessons to be learnt from other countries, as for instance with the British and American approaches to racism, and widening links became policy.

It was vital that employers were brought into Counteract work. Although progress had been slow some employers were now coming on board. To ensure this continued and accelerated, plans were made to meet employers' representative organisations like CBI, IPM, Equality Managers Association and so on. Another breakthrough came with the development of joint union/management training courses. These changes were small

Picture 6: Noreen Moore, Counteract Secretary

but significant because Counteract was generated by the Trade Unions
and directed by a Management Committee of eight people representing
them.[17] The balance between Trade Union and Company management
perspectives was of some consequence, even at this early stage.

In the beginning Counteract was just one more campaign in a long
succession of Trade Union initiatives to address sectarianism in Northern
Ireland. It was conceived[18] as a help-line serving intimidated workers and
offering them advice. The funding was for an office with one development
worker and a part-time secretary, with a very modest budget. ICTU had
initiated anti-sectarian projects like *Hands off my mate* and *Peace, Work
and Progress* and this was envisaged as another short-lived campaign.

One very small room housed the two workers, with two chairs, an old
table and a makeshift desk made from an upturned door. What material
facilities they lacked were outweighed by the commitment of the drivers
of this new project and the first Co-ordinator, Jim Quinn. No-one believed Counteract would last more than a couple of years at the most when
Noreen Moore opened the door in 1990 (see Picture 6).

Notes

1. Source: Bew and Gillespie 1999.
2. Reference *Counteraction* Issue 2 April 1992. All local Northern Irish newspapers
    and trade union press carried features on the planned rallies, and the events them-
    selves, over a fortnight of constant reporting.
3. In January eight men died after the IRA bombed a minibus carrying workmen at
    Teebane Cross as they left work.
4. This included a one-day school in Dungannon, two schools for the T&G and dis-
    cussions with MSF, GMB, NUPE and NAPO.
5. *Irish News*, 28 September 1992.
6. Public signings of the declaration were arranged for Belfast (Thursday 8th October
    1992 in Cornmarket and City Centre), Enniskillen (Thursday 15 October &
    Saturday 17 October 1992 in the town centre and Bridge), Dungannon (Saturday
    10 October 1992 in the town centre & Curley's Supermarket).
7. Findings revealed incidents at work ranging from those leading to threatened or
    actual murder to sectarian name-calling and verbal abuse. Verbal abuse could not

be seen as trivial as it created fear within workplace. Sometimes union officials did not know about intimidation until the victim had left their employment. Episodes of intimidation seemed to have a tendency to escalate, especially when those in authority did not take incidents seriously. When incidents came to light it often appeared to be a matter of luck whether or not people with the appropriate will to take action were available.

8. The most successful of which were those for individual unions or two-day schools for workplace representatives. Schools aimed specifically at Youth and other categories of members did not get the same support. Workplace representatives' schools were modified so that half of the seminar involved awareness raising and prejudice reduction. The other half was a skills-based module designed to develop practical skills and build support mechanisms for representatives dealing with cases of intimidation or harassment in the workplace.

9. Specifically, it had given organisational and administrative help for the Belfast Trades Council demonstration (1 November 1991), NIC ICTU Cookstown/Magherafelt demonstration (21 January 1992), NIC ICTU Belfast demonstration (4 February 1992) and the Belfast Trades Council demonstration (21 February 1992).

10. *Irish News*, 17 October 1992 and 22 October 1992.

11. The *Irish Times*, 22 October 1992.

12. UK Press Gazette (front page), 26 October 1992.

13. *Newsletter* Ulster Edition, 22 October 1992.

14. *Sunday Times*, 18 and 15 October and 1 November 1992.

15. *Sunday World,* 8th November.

16. After being informed by Loyalist paramilitary that a catholic colleague had to leave work by lunchtime or face murder threat, Andy Snoddy took the man his coat and personal effects – and didn't return to work. As an official of the Printing Union GMPU Andy Snoddy had direct experience of sectarian harassment at work and faced the same difficulties.

17. Representatives included NIC ICTU (2 nominees), Belfast Trades Council (1 nominee), Affiliated Unions (3 nominees), Belfast Housing Aid (1 nominee), Belfast Centre for the Unemployed (1 nominee).

18. The original idea came from Avilla Kilmurry then working for the T&G. It was to change and grow organically as the political and economic climate changed and Counteract undertook more and more work.

CHAPTER 4

1993: Building Strong Foundations

1993 was the year of the Hume-Adams talks, political crises and changes throughout Britain and Ireland, as well as continued conflict in Northern Ireland. At a time when Counteract would have been ending as a campaign, it had only begun its work.

This was another year of violently and contradictory developments. There was change and progress with the talks between John Hume and Gerry Adams and the Downing Street Declaration. In January a Labour-Fianna Fail coalition government was formed in Dublin. At the same time, John Major wrote to John Hume rejecting the request for an independent inquiry into Bloody Sunday; adding, 'The government made clear in 1974 that those who were killed on Bloody Sunday should be regarded as innocent of any allegation that they were shot whilst handling firearms or explosives.'

A month later three of four bombs planted at a gas-works in Warrington exploded. In March another IRA bomb killed a three-year-old boy and injured fifty-six people in a shopping centre in Warrington. That day Terry Carlin and Jim Quinn were speaking to the MSF National School about Counteract. The UFF murdered four building workers in Castlerock and on the same day killed a Catholic teenager on the outskirts of Belfast. In April the IRA bombed a tanker at an oil terminal in Northumberland, and blew up the NatWest tower in London, killing one person, injuring over thirty and causing damage estimated at over £1,000 million. That month the UFF unsuccessfully tried to kill five Catholics in a Belfast bookmakers, murders only prevented because one of their rifles failed to fire.

Politics in London produced rumours of a deal between the beleaguered government and the UUP over voting on the EU 'Social Chapter'. While John Taylor of the UUP denied any such dealing, Rev. Martin Smyth UUP reported that he expected a House of Commons Select Committee on Northern Ireland to be set up in the near future.

The (Loyalist) Red Hand Commandos added folk-music nights in bars and hotels to their list of 'legitimate targets'. The UVF killed a Catholic van driver and a prison officer, and threatened to kill more prison officers unless conditions in prisons were reformed.

The autumn brought increasing Loyalist tensions about 'pan-Nationalists' due to the Hume-Adams talks. The Major government's delicate handling of these talks resulted, after much debate, in the Downing Street Declaration. That October saw twenty-seven conflict-related deaths, being the highest number in one month since 1976. Peace or the beginnings of it seemed nowhere apparent.

At the end of November, the co-ordinating body of the Loyalist para-militaries, the Combined Loyalist Military Command, made a press statement to the effect that they earnestly sought peace. 'In accordance with the overwhelming desire of the population.'[1] In early December two Catholic men were shot dead outside a taxi depot by the UFF, who later shot another Catholic at his Belfast home. The year 1993 was the first year since 1975 that Loyalist paramilitaries had killed more people than their Republican counterparts.

Controversial to the Unionist family, the Forum for Peace and Reconciliation was established in the Republic. The year ended with little stomach on the Republican side for the Downing Street Declaration, and the UVF declaring that they were not threatened by it. The UVF said they would not support another 'publicity stunt' by Ian Paisley protesting about the Declaration.

Figures for yet another year of the Troubles demonstrate: Deaths arising from the conflict: 84. Shootings: 476. Bombs planted: 289. Incendiaries: 61. Firearms found: 196. Explosives found: 3,944 kg (8,695 lb.). Persons charged with terrorist and serious public order offences: 372. Casualties arising from paramilitary attacks: 126.

*   *   *   *   *

In this turbulence Counteract pushed forward, its annual report stating

> As a result of research commissioned by the Community Relations Council a need for development in the area of community responses, community structures, information for advice workers, education for advice workers etc. has been recognised. To assist these developments, it was felt that an anti-intimidation support unit be

established and Counteract have been asked to head it up given our experience in this area of work over the last 3 years.

The Counteract Management Committee[2] continued to play a very important role in formulating policy and overseeing the unit's work.

Intensified sectarian intimidation of bus drivers led to a lightning strike of services in Belfast. The T&G worked with management to resolve the death-threatening situation of their staff.[3] Editorials and reporting were generally, and uncharacteristically, in sympathy with the strikers. Counteract continued to write to the press and make public statements opposing all sectarian incidents involving intimidation of workers. The message was loud and clear: non-sectarian was not enough, the move must be for all to get to anti-sectarianism.

School children led by four sixth formers in Belfast's Grosvenor High School held a large public rally on 31st March marching for peace. This was well attended, widely reported, warmly received and acknowledged (almost) universally as courageous.

* * * * *

Counteract had good working relations with CRC and was now involved with anti-intimidation groups from both the voluntary and statutory sector, and was collaborating very well in joint courses with the FEC.

CRC was involved with Counteract, first as a conduit for CCRU (government) funding and then directly as a core funder. Will Glendinning was CRC Work & Community Development Officer and had first-hand experience of Counteract, which he saw as, '... extending Community Relations beyond reconciliation into trade unions and the workplace'. CRC saw value in engaging Counteract in their working group, as CRC was working on its own anti-intimidation manual for the community sector *Action Against Intimidation: Information and Advice Manual*. So, CRC backed plans for a Counteract Community unit, and their efforts in updating the information pack in 1993.

Will Glendinning praised Counteract work:

> It had instant effect. It was as if there was an elephant in the room that everyone walked around but did not discuss. People could now deal with sectarian intimidation. ...

Their training was systematic, and supported by seminars. The subject was taboo but they challenged that.

CRC had documented the effect sectarianism had in the community, in housing estates, and there was a body of knowledge about graffiti, the 'chill factor', burnings, bullets through the post, petrol bomb attacks on homes and so on. It was known that in isolation people would not talk about this – so there was a need for community mechanisms to resolve tensions before they got out of hand. It took the co-operation of CRC, Counteract and many community-sector partners to develop those mechanisms. Therefore, CRC backed Counteract in their determination to tackle, '... the silence, safety and neutral [delivery of services]. Counteract are up front and there is no avoidance. What happens in work impacts on the community – and vice versa. It impacts on everything and cannot be ignored.'

During her maternity leave in 1993 Avilla Kilmurray developed materials to be used in Equality Seminars for the T&G Women's and Equality Committee Programme to address sectarianism, including Jim Quinn's input (for Counteract). Tony McCusker (CCRU) endorsed the T&G programme and funding for this, including the Counteract training element, was secured. Counteract would consolidate this work over the next two years. Avoiding the temptation to rush into new exciting things, they concentrated on building their expertise, organisation and influence.

Increasingly, statutory bodies, trade unions and employers were recognising that intimidation was damaging in every aspect of working life, from employees' morale to levels of profit.

Before the April Management Committee meeting started, Terry Carlin asked those present to stand in remembrance of Frank Wright. *Counteraction* also reported the sad news of Frank Wright's death:

> Since producing the last bulletin it is with great regret that we have to report the death of Frank Wright. Frank was involved with Counteract from November 1990 and facilitated our very first anti-sectarian school for Trades Council Representatives. He will be greatly missed but his work and that of his colleagues will continue as a lasting tribute to Frank.

Frank Wright's commitment to the work was such that his parents felt it appropriate to make a donation to Counteract from Frank's estate. Two years later Counteract dedicated its training video *The Inside Stories* to

Frank Wright, in recognition of his huge contribution in the formative stage in the evolution of its methods.

* * * * *

The major educational venture for Counteract in early 1993 was a cross-border school for forty MSF members from across Ireland – creating much greater understanding between Northern and Southern members about the problems faced by workplace representatives in Northern Ireland.

At this stage Counteract was intent on targeting the Health and Engineering sectors. That autumn Dennis Godfrey (then FEC Training Officer) worked on the weekend School in Mullingar for the MSF. In later years Trade Unions did their own training, sometimes using the Counteract video (produced in 1995). However, it was Counteract that began this work.

A promise of core funding for Counteract, and written confirmation from CRC, left an annual shortfall of £5,000-£7,000 per year – which would be sought from unions who had previously donated.

* * * * *

In summer 1993 the FEC's magazine *Fair Comment* featured Counteract in *Stop Watching … Get Active …* written by Jim Quinn:

> The biggest problem Counteract faces is convincing people that a problem exists in the first place. Unfortunately, it seems that people have become so case-hardened by the continuing violence that they only regard something as intimidation when violence, or the treat of it, are used to drive someone from the workplace or in some cases murder them. That is why Counteract has embarked on an education programme to create a greater awareness of how to recognise sectarian harassment and intimidation at every level. He went on to say, 'The unit has also recognised a change in the nature of intimidation and harassment. In the 1960s and 70s intimidation generally took the form of a section of workers being expelled from their workplace by their fellow workers during periods of political and sectarian tension. This type of intimidation it seems is now carried out by external elements while the internal intimidation is of a more subtle variety.'

Employers and managers had not responded to these changes and felt powerless to challenge sectarianism in work:

> As regards external intimidation or harassment Counteract again argues that while in many cases management and unions can help workers by improving their personal

security, relocating them etc., more can be done. One example is the civil service union
NIPSA, which has developed a procedure that allows the members immediately af-
fected to respond to intimidation and receive the support of the union when doing so.
A case in point was the attack by paramilitaries on a fraud investigator in Tyrone, when
DHSS staff closed offices all over Northern Ireland until the threat was withdrawn.

As the Annual Report records, Jim Quinn's commitment, dedication
and sterling work over these first three years laid strong foundations for
Counteract.

*   *   *   *   *

The summer saw the rise of serious tensions in Ford, the Fire Service and
Northern Ireland Electricity. The Fire Service in Maghera had openly
sectarian tensions.[4]

Billy Robinson recorded his experience:

> The fire brigade called Counteract in as they had a problem in their training school between
> participants on a training session. The background to the problem was that during a training
> session one of the participants made a remark that caused fear and apprehension in two
> other members. His comment was a reference to a 'Barrack Buster' – the two individuals
> that felt offended at this remark left the training session. A Barrack Buster is a name for a
> type of bomb used by the IRA to attack police stations. Unfortunately, the two individu-
> als concerned had previously been police officers who had served in Newry police station
> where a Barrack Buster had been used and a number of their colleagues had been killed.
>
> On having a conversion with the two individuals regarding their position and their
> feelings I then interviewed the alleged harasser. It turned out that when he made his
> reference to the barrack buster, he was referring to a 2 litre bottle of cider. In West
> Belfast, where he lived, if anyone, goes into an off license and asks for a barrack buster
> they are atomically set up a 2 litre bottle of cider. When I explained this to the two
> other people and asked if they would be willing to meet the other party, they agreed.
> When they met it was a little tense but the alleged harasser apologized for any hurt he
> may have caused, but was insistent that he was not aware of the other people's previous
> employment. The two other persons accepted his apology, but also stated that because he
> came from west Belfast it had coloured their view of him and his possible political view.
>
> Fears, feelings and the lack of trust?? This shows that words can affect feelings, can
> cause fear, and a lack of trust. It is like an onion: those three terms are the center core
> then all the layers are built on them.
>
> On discussion with the fire chief he informed me that it was a pity this incident had
> occurred on the last week of a 17-week course. I asked if there was any training on
> good relations and he said no. I asked him if it did not seem strange to him that on

a 17-week training programme there was no training on good relations, considering that these men depended on one another for their lives – this would be crucial in their training.

One of the problems that was prevalent in companies was the fact that although the director and the board would be committed to the principles of a harmonious workplace and even have instructions and routines to implement training etc. to achieve this – when this commitment clashed with other issues in relation to productivity etc. then you can guess which would take precedent.

For example, in one particular company we were engaged to deliver training. As I walked the shop floor and spoke with staff and first-line managers I asked them if there would be any problems if I were to seek a number of staff from the production line to attend a training session. They reacted and stated that they could not let anyone off the line as they had a target of 35k units per week and even one person missing would cause a major problem.

On returning to a meeting with the director and senior managers I posed the question of the level of sick absence per year in the plant. They responded, 17%. I then asked how much of this figure was due to stress emanating from flawed relations, and their figure was 5%. I then asked them to calculate the cost taking into consideration the loss of production, overtime, temporary recruitment, training of staff, and time allowed to pick up speed of the work. They came back with a figure of almost £200k. I asked 'was this good business?' I also asked the question regarding the release of staff from the production line. They responded that they would have to look at how they could manage that and would give me a call when they would find a way to facilitate. I never received a call. In most cases the judgment for companies is can we live with this loss or can we afford to engage in this training considering the cost, loss of production, training cost, risk of raising issues that may cause greater problems. Generally, their decision is, we will just live with the cost rather than deliver the training.

Ford's attempts to bring in an Equal Opportunities working group were resisted by two of the plant's three unions. Ford was acting on the advice of a US consultant body auditing companies for the MacBride Principles. The debate was about whether this was tokenism. One union decided to join irrespective, whereas the other two (T&G and AEEU) said they wanted action not committees. In the same edition of the *Irish News*, there was a report on the Northern Ireland Electricity (NIE) case in the FET. The following day the paper's feature title was succinct and informative, with '*NIE Catholic had* "no hope in hell of job promotion"'. This is significant because, at that time NIE was the state-owned monopoly electricity supplier.

Such public shaming and the powers of FET to fine and demand action from errant employers was now beginning to make a difference as the Fair Employment agenda took centre stage in the economy.

Work with heavy engineering company Mackie continued and the FEC was approached for funding towards this training as a pilot project.

*   *   *   *   *

Other 'everyday' work continued. Jim Quinn and Terry Carlin made a joint presentation to the MSF National School on Ireland in Whitehall (resulting in a donation) and more schools were planned with MSF. Presentations on Counteract work were well received at the NUJ conference, at a well-attended fringe meeting at the GPMU conference and the ICTU Youth Conference. Throughout 1993 other talks and information sessions were arranged with T&G Women's Committee, GMB, FDA, UCW, MSF Health Visitors and Unison, in events ranging from half-day to two-day courses. A number of unions wanted follow-on schools. Counteract developed links with unions and organisations across Europe to find out about their experience in dealing with racism and fascism.

Even though there was both financial and moral support from the Trade Union movement, there was not a universal acceptance of Counteract training – despite the fact that CRC's part-funding four residential schools for trade unions was potentially an opportunity. At this stage, some felt that they could help their own members and did not need a more neutral site for anti-intimidation work. That year progress was slow with Trades Councils – and they had other work on hand.[5]

*   *   *   *   *

Young people in Northern Ireland were regarded as a vital constituency by Counteract because they often started work with no knowledge about their peers from the other community. At sixteen, young men and women would enter the world of work or training without knowing what the cultural signals meant, other than in crude religious stereotypes. Frequently their perceptions were based on which newspaper was read (Did reading the *Irish News* signify Republicanism?) and what the conversations about sport were (few doubted that supporting Rangers signified Loyalist politics). There was a physical fear, common to young people, both Protestant and Catholic, about being with people from a strange and alien culture. Counteract was determined to confront this crucial issue, but how?

Billy McCreight and Billy Robinson found that access to schools was extremely difficult – with very few exceptions Counteract services were firmly rejected. Sectarian slogans on schoolbags were never challenged, as teachers and educationalists were too uncomfortable with what the anti-intimidation unit was proposing to discuss openly.

However, young people could be reached in community employment and training schemes. Billy McCreight (CWU) and Phillip Bloomer (NIPSA) prepared a presentation about how they came from the same working-class background but different religions, and still they had ended up in the same sort of work and got along without difficulty. Derek Wilson helped them to put this together as a training package.

Colin Glen Youth and Community Training Project was their possible entry into youth training. Counteract had met with the management and reached agreement about training. In the background, progress was being made with a CRC pilot training programme for community advice workers dealing with intimidation, held in Queen's University Belfast. Success was short-lived and ended in threats, as, on the very day they were scheduled to appear a phone call informed them *You bring any fenians here and they'll be shot. Take it seriously!* They did, remembering how many people had been shot for little or nothing, let alone for endorsing the forthright challenging approach of Counteract. Further work on that site was impossible.

Caution ruled on this occasion but, at the same time, the foundations of a programme for training youth were laid that in time would later become the proposed CYPHER programme.

* * * * *

Another important event was the 'Michael Rubenstein Seminar' (Fair Employment Complying with The Law) where Counteract presented *Policy and Practice on Dealing with Sectarianism in the Workplace.* This was particularly significant because the seventy-plus delegates were mainly employers or their representatives.

By then a number of employers were adopting the Counteract draft Equal Opportunity guidelines and training although usually only after being referred by the FEC. The FEC was reviewing the whole area of harassment at the time and asked for Counteract opinion.

Counteract was also developing relationships with public sector employers. They were involved with social workers in the University of Ulster at Magee Campus and community centre staff in the Belfast City Council. They discussed expanding the work in this area with the FEC using joint employer-trade union Equality Training in-house. The Labour Relations Agency training event brought them into contact with rural employers.

Never an outfit to rest on its successes Counteract identified other areas needing to be addressed, such as schools, T&EA centres, ACE workers and small employers. To defeat sectarianism and intimidation in the workplace there had to be equality education and training for young people at school, training or in job employment agencies. This remained an ambition that was not realised.

The pre-Halloween bombing on the Shankill Road galvanised trade Unionists. Solidarity was expected and shown.[6] Workers from across Belfast marched in respect and sympathy the following day.

Counteract, NIC ICTU NI Officer Terry Carlin, his staff, NIC ICTU and the whole trade union membership of Northern Ireland were praised for their efforts to restore peace and normality here – by the press and in various circles. In particular they were applauded for organising the Community Day for Unifying Peace.

On 18 November 1993 many thousands attended rallies throughout Northern Ireland to demonstrate their commitment to peace. People took the opportunity to express their revulsion at acts of mass murder such as the Shankill Road bombing and the shootings at Greysteel. As *Counteraction* stated at the time

> The question is, do we only react to multiple murder? If so, what is the number that requires us to express revulsion? The level of revulsion felt should be the same for single acts of murder as for multiple murder, but it is not. It is understandable that to react to every single incident would become a waste of time, yet it begs the question, should we build on the success of last year? If so, a total commitment would be required from all affiliated unions. A step has been taken at the NIC ICTU conference this year when the motion from the NCU was agreed. A motion from NCU

read 'In light of the unqualified success of the recent ICTU-led Community Day for Unifying Peace, Conference resolves that this scheme will be opted for all future ICTU May Day celebrations in Northern Ireland until there is an end to violence.'

The front page of the next day's *Newsletter* said it all. Above a half page photograph of the rally was the headline '157,457 say Stop the Killing', referring to the telephone peace poll. At the rally tens of thousands of workers, schoolchildren and other citizens observed a minute's silence. The drive to end sectarian killings had never been so strong. The message would, eventually, get through. However difficult the road to peace might be, and however long it took, the people of Northern Ireland were adamant that the killing must stop. Counteract support for the *Peace, Work and Progress Programme* continued and helped the various campaigns which NIC ICTU mounted under that banner.[7]

1993 saw another major expansion in this area with the 'Joint Declaration of Protection' signed both by the CBI and NIC ICTU and the *Let Us Work Together* poster campaign, the rallies and vigils leading up to the magnificent Community Day. The press reported this in detail:

> 'Bosses and Unions join protection plan'
> 'Action against intimidation'
> 'Pact against bias at work launched'[8]

On the same day, reports of Republicans putting a five-year-old boy off a bus, to wander lost, brought a stream of heartfelt outrage. Actions like this pepper the 'small' history of the conflict and epitomise the brutalising ways in which ordinary people had to live. Similar events continued unreported into 2000 and beyond, with all the predictable divisive effects on people young and old.

*   *   *   *   *

The Joint Declaration of Protection signed both by the CBI and NIC ICTU was an important landmark. As CRC's Will Glendinning saw it

> The joint ICTU/CBI declaration was significant. It was a huge move at the time. We come back five years later and see just how far that moved us along

the road. It was a matter of selling the benefits of anti-sectarian work and not the virtues. Counteract's work was organisational self-interest, and any risk in using them was well worth it.

Counteract produced and disseminated information as widely as possible, but needed to do more. In some unions the information only got to district or regional officers and did not reach the shop floor. Thousands of Counteract leaflets were circulated and 'Counteraction' had its widest circulation to date: one union alone ordered 3,000 copies. It had been too irregular, so an editorial committee was needed to make it both more interesting and more frequently produced.

Two key issues had sharpened a new focus on sectarian harassment and intimidation at work in the early 1990s: the murder of workers and the tribunal findings on sectarian harassment cases – the most noteworthy and one cited ever since was Neeson V Securicor. The case was widely reported and its judgement made a perfect example for Counteract purposes.

Neeson V Securicor. Case Ref: 153/91 FET and 2081/91 UD

Seventeen-year-old Liza Neeson started work in Securicor's Administration in October 1987 as the only Catholic employed in her department. She was dismissed in May 1991 because of the level of her absences due to sickness. Between October 1987 and by April 1988 she received three letters hand delivered by someone in the workforce to her desk, stating 'Fuck Catholics', 'We know where you live' and 'UVF Taigs Out'. The judgement states: *receipt of these letters was reported to Donegall Pass RUC station and the applicant made a statement to the police at Donegall Pass. Though the applicant subsequently withdrew that statement, the investigating police officer was satisfied that the applicant was withdrawing her statement because she was frightened.*

Securicor management did not investigate this and *none of the applicant's colleagues at work sought to comfort or reassure her during this period of her employment.* The company did not implement its policies and procedures. They did not practice fair employment, but discriminated in treating a Protestant co-worker in a more favourable way in similar circumstances. Management colluded with employees' harassing of Liza Neeson by accepting that deliberate threats were not significant and never challenging the supervisors concerned. In the Tribunal it was the word of Ms Neeson against that of an area consultant (who was a former RUC Detective Chief Superintendent), the security liaison officer (a former RUC Chief Superintendent), the parcels manager, office administrator, administrative officer and a traffic supervisor.

We say categorically that in our opinion, all of these witnesses were at times evasive, selective, incredible and downright untruthful in the testimony which they gave before us. The finding was in favour of Liza Neeson. Of £25,000 awarded, £10,000 was for injury to feelings and £10,000 for aggravated damages because: *it is our belief that the applicant was subjected to sectarian harassment over a considerable period when by age and community she must have felt isolated and vulnerable. The harassment was all the more serious because of her experiences in 1987/88 when not only did she receive vicious sectarian abuse in writing from colleagues she knew but she also knew (a) of management's indifference at best in the face of such outrageous conduct by its employees, and (b) that involvement of police made matters worse. [Her complaint incidentally was never logged at Donegall Pass RUC station and the statement which she made was destroyed when she withdrew her statement so that no record remained of her complaint at all when the Fair Employment Commission sought to investigate it. This was contrary to police procedures.]*

Although intimidation is much less blatant today this case demonstrates the culture of sectarianism and discrimination is institutional and not personal.

Notes from Neeson V Securicor Ltd.

Alleged harasser, Mr Taylor had … *a tattoo covering his forearm. It was in the shape of a dagger about six to eight inches long upon which were imposed the words remember 1690/Ulster/no surrender. In the words of his manager, this supervisor 'could be loud'* – *'you would know that he was about'.*

[The supervisor] … *told the Tribunal, under oath, that he did not know that the year 1690 and the Battle of the Boyne were matters of significance to the Orange Order because he was not a member of that Order. He did not think his tattoo could be described as sectarian. He saw no sectarian implication in the words no surrender. Even as a police officer [reserve] he did not believe that July was a sensitive time of the year. He never heard the term fenian at Orangefield school.*

Ms Young was a colleague of the applicant who was aware that the applicant had received threatening letters. She did not express sympathy with the applicant because the applicant never approached her. She never looked at Mr Taylor's [the supervisor] tattoo because she did not like tattoos and she did not know what was written on the tattoo. She did not know if it contained a union jack or a red hand. [Ms Young lived with Mr Taylor for a year.] She has never heard the words taig or fenian spoken at home or in Kelvin school which she attended in the 1970s. She had heard those words used only on television – but had no idea when she heard such words on television. She had never been in company where such words were used. She only understood what the words meant when she heard it explained in the Tribunal at the hearing. She had lived in the Donegall Road area but had never seen the words taig or fenian written on gable walls. The applicant alleged that Ms Young was one of the persons who regularly addressed her as taig or fenian.

He stated that he did not know the significance of Celtic and Rangers football teams. He only knew that they were Scottish football teams.

The time when employers and managers could simply deny sectarianism and intimidation was coming to an end, and the power of the FET was gaining more recognition, if not respect. Cases like Neeson V Securicor were to become relatively rare, and employers took fair employment issues increasingly seriously.

*   *   *   *   *

Clem McCartney, Avilla Kilmurry and others produced a substantial report on Counteract's first piece of major research[9] which was a study of policy and practice on sectarian harassment in the workplace.[10] It found three broad strategies were used to deal with sectarian behaviour. These were avoidance, troubleshooting (or confrontation) and building a positive work environment. Of these only a proactive approach tackled the culture of intimidation at work, and that existed only in the companies with the best management practice:

> Though some notorious incidents make headlines in the papers (often relating to flags and emblems) much workplace intimidation is more subtle and covert. Such insidious intimidation based on innuendo is particularly difficult to deal with because it is hard to pin down and often it is difficult to identify those responsible. This report gave a valuable insight into relations on the shop floor and in the office. Most of those interviewed spoke openly about practices in their workplace, problems that had arisen and how they dealt with them. They not only talked about cases of flagrant threats, but also about the operation of more subtle ways in which the minority are frozen out and made to feel unwelcome – the 'chill factor'.

At that time many employers and trade Unionists preferred to avoid sectarianism, not for lack of support for fair employment practices, but in the hope that sectarianism would simply wither away without their involvement. Worries that highlighting the issue would exacerbate the situation were common. Both 'sides' in a sectarian incident might be union members, and union officials did not want to be in a position where they had to support some members against others. There were stories of union officials and supervisors being threatened and their property damaged because they had supported management and acted to deal with sectarian incidents. Foremen and shop stewards were vulnerable if the workforce turned against them because they came from the same community and they normally relaxed and socialised together:

> It could be difficult for management to find out who is responsible and they look weak if they cannot control what happens in the workplace. They may have to make decisions which might include suspending the perpetrators of the intimidation. Not surprisingly if this could be avoided and the problem swept under the carpet then

both management and union were happy to concentrate on what they saw as their role: running the company or protecting their members.

It is easier to take this stance when incidents of intimidation were less blatant. Some of those interviewed were not aware of the potential intimidation in their workplace, or discounted its significance if they did know. One manager did not know that there were sectarian slogans in the toilets. Some union officials could not see anything wrong with sectarian jokes even though some workers might be worried and offended by them.

However, it was clear that both management and union were prepared to act when there was clear evidence of intimidation, and act decisively. If in normal circumstances the motto was 'sweep it under the carpet' when that deteriorated the motto became 'nip things in the bud'. The situation was more clear-cut and the management could assert their authority. The union also took the line that those responsible for intimidation acted outside the union rules and ethos and the intimidated worker needed union protection. Management was no longer worried that the situation will blow up into a public confrontation because it would already be out in the open and they no longer felt they needed to act cautiously.

Once management acted to stop intimidatory behaviour, they kept a close eye on things to ensure that there is no reoccurrence. In fact, they thought that close monitoring was necessary on many occasions, otherwise their authority might be undermined. This form of trouble shooting seemed effective in changing attitudes towards flags and emblems. Initially they were removed unwillingly on orders from management creating rumbling resentment. In many firms there had apparently been a change of attitude and for the majority of the workplace the display of bunting and flags is no longer an issue. (Billy Robinson)

However, while this reactive approach was sometimes effective, it did not deal with the underlying causes of a specific incident. That needed a broader approach, as seen in firms that were building positive work environments. Clearly, management and unions in these companies were co-operating to improve the work environment.

In contrast, although most people interviewed said they supported the idea of close co-operation between unions and management, in reality there was often a reluctance to exchange information when problems actually arose in companies using avoidance or trouble shooting strategies. Management believed that union involvement would complicate matters and the union preferred to deal with things internally to avoid anyone facing normal disciplinary procedures. Only when it came to taking positive steps did both union and management recognise that they needed each other's help and support.

Proactive companies provided training, sometimes in-house. And, sometimes organisations like Counteract were invited to lead a short course. These companies developed a fair employment policy and signed a joint management-union declaration on protection of workers. More importantly they discussed the implication of these documents with management and workers. In too many companies the fair employment policy was found to be simply a paper exercise with little participation or understanding of what it meant.

In this report and in subsequent research by Counteract, it is evident that companies already practising a progressive approach to management found that anti-sectarian work was simply applying good management practice.

Research played a pivotal role in further developments for Counteract. CRC research findings demonstrated the need for development in community responses to sectarian intimidation, community structures, information for advice workers, and education and training for advice workers, and had involved Counteract at its core.

* * * * *

Internally, there were changes for Counteract. A special Management Committee meeting was called at the end of November. Jim Quinn was going to another post and Counteract needed to recruit a new person as soon as possible. Billy Robinson would become the next worker, under the new job title of Organiser. Billy McCreight replaced Billy Robinson on the Management Committee as the CWU nominee. The formative years were complete. Jim Quinn left Counteract an established unit recognised for its effective education and work for peace. The scale of his contribution merits public recognition.

Notes

1. Source: Bew and Gillespie
2. At their AGM on 2nd February Avilla Kilmurry was elected to the Chair again, with Brenda Callaghan as Vice-Chair and Terry Carlin as Secretary/ Treasurer. Other members of committee included John Cassells, Brendan Mackin, Billy Robinson and Lynda Walker.

3. 'Buses back on roads after lightning strike', report *Belfast Telegraph*, 10 February 1993.

4. 'Fire men move to relieve tensions' reported in the *Belfast Telegraph* of 4 August 1993.

5. Jim Quinn had previously made contacts with individual community groups through larger umbrella organisations like NICVA, WEA, CRC with positive results in Dungannon, Enniskillen, Belfast and Bangor. Counteract was now recognised for its expertise in dealing with sectarianism, discrimination and intimidation in the workplace and its education programme. That coincided with a marked increase in Counteract involvement with Community Relations Officers (CROs) in Dungannon and Enniskillen. The education programme extended beyond the Belfast area because of collaboration with the WEA. Plans were made to develop in Derry and the North West as well. Work was developed with the NI Sports Council through the CRC. Assistance was provided to NICVA, Save the Children Fund and with workers in the Belfast City Council through the Belfast Trades Council's CRO. Plans for work with a number of private employers were also well advanced.

6. The *Irish Times* Monday/Tuesday 25/26 October 1993, plus coverage in local and Northern Irish papers and broadcast media throughout the islands.

7. Terry Carlin was justly proud when the joint CBI-ICTU declaration was launched and well received. That autumn he went to 'Peace, Work and Progress Campaign' demonstrations in Dee Street, on the Shankill Road and at Belfast City Hall. Against a background of escalating violence, he told Counteract that NIC was to hold a special meeting.

8. *Belfast Telegraph*, 28 September 1993, *Irish News*, 21 September 1993.

9. This study was undertaken by the Community Training & Research Service in BURC. Its findings were based on interviews with management and trade unions in a cross-section of 40 companies. Of the many people involved, the Annual report made a note of thank to 'The Advisory Panel, CTRS (especially Mairead Abraham & Nigel Collins), Clem McCartney who carried out the analysis and authored the full report, Avila Kilmurry, Chair of Counteract who prepared the text of the summary report, the 40 employers who participated, the union and other employer representatives. Thanks also to the Central Community Relations Unit and the Enkalon Foundation for funding the survey. And last but not least Jim Quinn for his driving force in making sure it was brought to a conclusion.'

10. The study included interviews with representatives of management in forty firms across the whole of Northern Ireland and in each sector of commercial activity, apart from services. These firms were both locally owned and large multi-nationals. They varied in size from the largest to almost the smallest in the province. The religious composition of the work force ranged from those which are well balanced to those where there is a preponderance of Catholics or Protestants. Where there was union representation a shop steward was also interviewed.

CHAPTER 5

1994: Developing Work in a Changing World

1994 saw the first and short-lived IRA cease-fire. In January Northern Ireland's first woman Minister of State in the NIO arrived, when Baroness Denton replaced the Earl of Arran. The Irish government announced they would not renew their broadcasting ban on Sinn Féin. At the beginning of March, the IRA mortar-bombed Heathrow airport and shut it down for two hours. At the end of March, they declared a three-day cease-fire to demonstrate their sincerity towards the peace process.

The particularly repulsive murder of Margaret Wright in the Donegall Road 'Bat Bet' band hall in Belfast (solely because she was mistakenly thought to be Catholic) resulted in the later murder of the two UVF members who had killed her – by Loyalist paramilitaries. There was public revulsion at the murder, its method and the fact that other women had been involved.[1]

In May two Catholic workmen were shot dead by the UVF in Tigers Bay area of North Belfast, and two more Catholic men were wounded in Armagh by Loyalists.

At a Belfast press conference, responding to preliminary peace talks, Ian Paisley called UUP Leader James Molyneaux 'Judas Iscariot'. In June The Dail Minister of Foreign Affairs, Dick Spring (Labour) said that Sinn Féin were key to the political discussions on a permanent cessation of violence. That month the UVF killed six men and wounded five others watching football on television at a bar in Loughinisland. The government announced a week later that forty prisoners would be transferred from prisons in England to Northern Ireland.

August brought the Hume-Adams statement on a just and lasting peace, and Gerry Adams' public statement that he believed the conditions existed for moving the peace process forward. On 31 August 1994 the IRA announced its cease-fire. Unionists remained sceptical. The CLMC asked UUP and DUP leaders to meet John Major to find out 'what deals were done'. The *Belfast Telegraph* polled public opinion on the cease-fire finding with 56% believing it was the result of a secret deal and only 30% believing it would be permanent. Albert Reynolds met publicly with John Hume and Gerry Adams, provoking Andrew Hunter, Chair of the Conservative's Northern Ireland Committee on Northern Ireland to describe this as a 'disastrous miscalculation'. When Ian Paisley and the DUP delegation refused to take John Major's word that no secret deal had been done, they were thrown out of the Prime Minister's Office.

In September the UVF injured two people with the explosion of a small bomb on the Belfast-Dublin train – it seemed that just going to the Republic of Ireland was apparently deemed a crime – and the US lifted a ban on a visa for Gerry Adams.

Loyalist leaders were given permission to enter the Maze prison in October to discuss a Loyalist cease-fire with 'their' prisoners. A cease-fire was called – announced by the CLMC – three days later. Premiers in both London and Dublin welcomed this. Ten days later Malcolm Moss replaced NIO minister Tim Smith who resigned amidst a furore about political lobbyists paying MPs. The next day Labour replaced Kevin McNamara with Mo Mowlam as party spokesperson on Northern Ireland. Within the week leading Loyalists were in the USA to make their case to the National Committee on American Foreign Policy.

November saw the murder of a postman in a raid on a Newry Post Office. There was a mass public protest about the Newry murder and the Irish government suspended the release of nine Republican prisoners the following day. The IRA made a statement that they had not given permission for this raid, nor for the use of any arms. In the heat of another controversy, about the appointment of Harry Whelehan, Albert Reynolds resigned to be replaced by Bertie Ahern as the leader of Fianna Fail.

The USA was high profile in Northern Ireland that December when President Clinton appointed former Senate majority leader George Mitchell to be special economic adviser on Ireland. The economics of the changing political landscape were already being played out, as John Major and US Commerce Secretary Ron Brown spoke at a two-day investment conference attended by three hundred delegates in Belfast. The following day John Major announced a £73 million investment package for Northern Ireland. Within hours there was a newly elected Fine Gael Taoiseach, John Bruton, who was a strong critic of the IRA, and known to be pro-Unionist. Dick Spring remained in government as deputy Prime Minister and spokesman on Foreign Affairs. That day Loyalist political representatives from the UDP and PUP held explanatory talks with British government officials at Stormont. Christmas parole was granted to ninety-seven paramilitary prisoners in Northern Ireland and thirty in the Republic.

Deaths arising from the conflict in 1994 were 62. Shootings: 348. Bombs planted: 222. Incendiaries: 115. Firearms found: 178. Explosives found: 1,285 kg (2,835 lb.). Persons charged with terrorist and serious public order offences: 349. Casualties arising from paramilitary attacks: 192.

*   *   *   *   *

Counteract was working at home[2] and further afield in challenging the thinking and policy of people in work, trade unions, economy and politics. They went to a European Conference *Peace Making and Conflict Resolution*. Co-ordinator Billy Robinson was now meeting trade union representatives throughout Northern Ireland, and the two-person Counteract staff could report progress on a number of fronts. As their Annual Report went public the key message was to employers, saying 'Don't take the "let sleeping dogs lie" approach. Research shows there are business reasons for tackling sectarianism in work.'[3]

That spring Derry Trades Council worked with Counteract organising a Seminar *The Key Role of the Unions in the Fight Against Sectarianism*. This was to include Derry Trades Council and local groups. Eamonn McCann's introduction to the report set the tone of the work accomplished. He stated

> All of the solutions on offer in the current 'peace process' have this in common: they set out not to overcome sectarianism but to manage it, not to bring people together but to police them apart, envisaging as an ideal that the Protestants and Catholics of the North should live at one with one another, rather than that we should live as one together. It should surely be the role of the trade union movement …. to rekindle and sustain a transcending vision of unity.

The seminar's workshops and discussions were not uncritical of the trade unions. Class analysis of institutionalised sectarianism concluded that sectarianism was inimical to working-class people. Equally the historical 'ownership' of human rights issues, such as Bloody Sunday, by Republicans was challenged. The fact that there was a substantial over-representation of Catholics and community groups was openly discussed and seen as an issue to be addressed. Community development in the North West was inextricably linked to challenging sectarianism. The agenda was set for an open recognition of diversity, conflicting constitutional aspirations and cultural identities, and the established denial of division would be declared unacceptable.

The seminar report cited numerous ways of finding common ground between the interests of Protestant and Catholic working-class people and supporting local community initiatives. The role of community development in de-escalating political and sectarian tensions in the community was seen as crucial.

Counteract was now in demand in unions[4] and at their conferences[5] and they approached the NCU Treasurer for funding support for their increasing work. Now they also had plans for training NIE staff and MOD police recruits.

Spring brought press debate (in the *Irish Times*) about how sectarianism was as much the preserve of the middle class as that of the working class. In 'Ulster's hate that dare not speak its name' Counteract was reported as flagging up the issue of prejudice about prejudice.' *Most striking about these mainly middle-class people was their culture of denial'* in both Protestant and Roman Catholic communities. And, alongside the denial of sectarianism and prejudice, 'fear palpably crackled beneath the polite restraint of both communities.' The hallmark of Counteract training and 'fire-fighting' had always been the refusal to politely deny or avoid the tough issues. The media would now take notice of the culture of denial, and look behind it.

By the summer Billy McCreight could tell the Management Committee that as a result of a Counteract fringe meeting at the NCU Conference in Blackpool some branches had asked about affiliating to Counteract. Counteract also contributed to a CRC Management Course, three NICVA courses on Equality, two WEA Schools, a one-day school with Belfast City Council Community Centre Workers and gave a presentation to the Local Government Staff Commission.

Counteract's relationship with the Trade Union movement included work with the unions in GB as well as NIC ICTU. Since most of the big unions were British-based, their policies were made in London and these marked the position for trade union members. In the early years Counteract had an important job to do in raising the standard of debate and challenging a simplistic received wisdom that 'Brits Out' was appropriate for trade Unionists in Northern Ireland. Trade Union members and representatives from a Unionist background were opposed to what they saw as Nationalist ideology and a 'green' agenda – green being a synonym for Republicanism rather than environmental issues.

Billy McCreight and Billy Robinson were with Terry Carlin when he took the NIC ICTU message to London. Fringe meetings at conferences in the mid-1990s were the seedbed of a more informed debate. If Trade Unionists in Northern Ireland were going to challenge sectarianism, they needed to change the knee-jerk slogans of the GB trade union movement.

At the London conference Counteract brought in the Society of Black Lawyers to address the issue of immigration. Sponsored by unions from the North and South of Ireland and from London, these discussions widened the debate. They were setting the agenda for developing a Counteract strategy of analysing prejudice and intimidation in a broader context. On the basis of the strong foundations laid by Jim Quinn Counteract credentials were established and others in the movement now wanted to work more closely with them.

*   *   *   *   *

A working Conference on sectarian harassment was organised in Hillsborough during April 1994 with input from the key players of the time. Keith Brown Director of Advice and Information (FEC) gave a presentation on *Guidance for Employers*. Fiona Cassidy of Jones & Cassidy Solicitors gave an update on recent cases, good practice and procedures. Harry McConnell Equal Opportunities and Corporate Services Manager of NIE spoke on *Practical difficulties in implementing a sectarian harassment policy*. Counteract provided the trade union perspective on dealing with sectarian harassment. These workshops were effective in opening up meaningful discussion and providing a significant exchange of information.

Then Equality Manager for NIE,[6] Harry McConnell, was tasked to support initiatives on anti-sectarianism in the company. NIE was perceived as being a predominantly Protestant workforce with a history of political strikes which was not good for a business that was on the verge of privatisation and in contact with US companies who looked to the MacBride principles as their benchmark. NIE were serious in this endeavour, putting anti-sectarianism on a similar footing to Health & Safety at work. Counteract was able to help NIE implement new policies in the early 1990s because it had credibility as a Trade Union–based outfit. Management-driven initiatives alone would not have succeeded in challenging sectarianism in NIE and certainly would not have taken hold at shop floor level. Counteract was non-management and therefore more acceptable.

Harry McConnell remembered that considerable work was needed to convey clearly what constituted harassment, and to emphasise that displays of flags and emblems, jokes, 'banter' and sectarian tunes were unlawful behaviour in work. He and Billy Robinson worked on these sensitive issues by beginning where they were reasonably sure of getting general agreement.

For instance, they would paint a picture of inequality and discrimination against, say, a disabled person. That would be universally recognised as unfair. Then the theme was taken to include race and sex and still there would be a reasonable consensus about this being discriminatory. When a basic level of agreement was established sectarianism could be introduced. It was about getting workers (and management) to recognise that everyone had rights. Harry McConnell recollected 'Knowledge didn't come naturally … but the passion and creativity of Counteract made for excellent training. Best training adds value to each session and has real life examples. Counteract did that.'

At the same time there were frequent difficulties, as for example, when two Belfast supervisors at a training session (one Protestant and one Catholic) refused to do basic exercises. They did not trust that their input would be kept confidential and simply would not co-operate. Fear, ubiquitous in anti-sectarian training, always posed difficulties. Like other large service industries in Northern Ireland NIE had 'orange', 'green' and 'grey' teams, in which the divisions of society were frequently mirrored – whether as workplace issues or individuals opting out of promotions etc.

The FEC was a statutory body advising on the legal requirements on employers. Their contribution was to push for fair participation in the long term. Counteract was voluntary and therefore less constrained. It operated well on the shop floor, rather akin to a Health & Safety Risk Management capacity, in the short term and so provided solutions for employers.

Harry McConnell's view was that companies would only address an issue or make changes where there was a threat to business. Sectarianism was clearly identified as a threat to NIE business. That was why they created Equality Management, monitoring and training. That was why they were happy for their staff to appear in the media in association with Counteract. It was a pragmatic approach, taken for much the same reasons as Shorts, and giving anti-sectarianism work a high profile and some clout. The MacBride Principles were taking effect.

*   *   *   *   *

Picture 7: Kevin McNamara at Counteract Conference

Counteract was gaining an increasingly public and political profile through conferences.

*   *   *   *   *

The impact of US commercial leverage was changing the landscape. The possibility of losing business for infringing either legislation or the MacBride Principles was what drove organisations like NIE, rather than moral arguments. Shorts employed a highly paid Equality Manager just like NIE and they were there to deliver solutions to the problems that left their companies vulnerable. The implications of failure to turn these problems around were too important to be left to chance or middle ranking managers and the strength of the MacBride Principles was a potential threat to their core business.

One of the MacBride Principles was busing minority workers to their place of work. This was a contentious issue because the very act of putting any minority into a bus that was scheduled daily would identify them and potentially leave them open to attack. Many were understandably reluctant to accept this principle or practice in the early to mid-1990s.

The New York-based Investor Responsibility Research Centre (IRRC) provided information for big New York pension funds investing in companies in Northern Ireland (then accounting for between 14% and 15% of all jobs). Their analysts visited and talked to people like Harry McConnell and Billy Robinson, looking for evidence of the development of good practice. Counteract was therefore integral to the potential economic development of Northern Ireland in its work with large employers, although this has never been acknowledged. IRRC visited Northern Ireland regularly and kept in contact with Counteract after that time.

As time went by, employers worked with Counteract developing solutions to crises and training options. Holistic training that included discrimination in general, rather than sectarianism alone, was viable where there was serious commitment from senior management to make change happen. That meant that the resources and power to drive change were made available.

Large employers brought Counteract in because they recognised the business case for tackling sectarianism in the workplace, whether that was internal to the company or external (e.g. hi-jackings, threats and attacks on workers). Others less committed to long-term change called for Counteract help when they had lost, or were about to lose, a Fair Employment Tribunal case. The Counteract opinion was 'These were organisations with the wrong mindset – it was a purely reactive response.'

What distinguished Counteract was its visible presence as a voice of the Trade Unions working with management. Its strength was in bringing managers and union representatives together, and in working cultures where the workforce believed that this would be a matter of negotiations, brokering and dealing. (Though it must be said this was a combination forged by the statutory powers of the FEC and FET.) In this Counteract echoed the voice of the workforce and made substantial progress in introducing a more neutral working environment. As someone in senior corporate management at the time, Harry McConnell, in NIE, was well placed to see the advantage of Counteract in other ways.

At that time the unit was based in the BURC, home to many similarly radical projects and initiatives. In having to go to Counteract, and thereby come into contact with radical organisations and people, Corporate Managers like those in NIE learned a considerable amount. Incidental to their 'official' role, they were also widening the horizons of potential 'drivers' and administrators who had a sometimes-limited vision.

In the CRC Conference Report[7] *Accommodating Change* NIE's stated goal to 'have a workforce representative of the community we serve' prompted the question *What moved NIE to take on such a commitment?*[8] Harry McConnell responded as their Equality & Corporate Affairs person:

> There are three or four business reasons why equality of opportunity and maintaining good relations with the community are very important. … People should get somewhere on merit rather than background. There is also the commercial self-interest argument for operating an equality policy … [without equality] … you are not drawing on the widest pool of possible employees and you are losing out on good people. … There is real merit in diversity. … In a group this stimulates better team spirit and a better product. … If you have a workforce representative of the community it serves, it is likely that special needs in the community will be better understood in the workforce. If you have a workforce representative of people with disabilities, you will be more aware of the special needs of customers with disabilities. If you have a workforce representative of women, there will be a greater awareness of the special childcare obligations society tends to impose on women. That is maybe less obvious than the Protestant/Catholic thing.

And what were the material benefits of such a policy direction?

> The bottom line is if there is a community significantly under-represented in your workforce, that community may decide not to buy from you.[9] Other bottom-line factors are, of course, the MacBride Principles, which means American investment.

If you are recognised as an employer who is not providing fair treatment for the two sides, that may affect your ability to get financial investment for the future.

As regards NIE dealing with '*the main issues of cultural diversity in the workplace*' changes had occurred:

Well, from 1988, like a lot of employers, we started taking the issue of offensive flags and emblems very seriously. Like a lot of big factory-based employers in Northern Ireland, we had a number of sites where bunting was flown at the relevant times of year. We introduced a new policy and made it very clear that any breaches of the policy would involve discipline and people could ultimately be sacked. That was a very difficult phase – we had managers receiving bullets in the post, we had to relocate managers, we had a lot of threats made to the firm. But we took down all the bunting.

It was quite a culture change and it was achieved by working closely with the unions and having senior managers deal with the problems. It wasn't left to the equality person to take the flags down. The compromise was to have the Union flag flying all the year round at headquarters which is the same arrangement as at Shorts.

At this stage NIE had trained staff throughout the company, providing forty harassment advisers and fifty managers able to investigate complaints. Complaints of sectarianism in NIE were taken to senior management. NIE's position was clear:

Anyone can have any political views they want and I would say that anyone with bigoted, sectarian views has those views protected under the Fair Employment Act. But as employers, we must show that they do not bring these views into the workplace. As an employer, I protect your right not to have extreme views taken into account in any employment decision made in relation to you. What I do not protect is a perceived right you may have to make comments on those views you have which may be offensive to other people in the workplace.

What are the prerequisites for changes such as those you outline at NIE? To secure change you have to have total senior management commitment. The top man or woman has to be behind the policy totally. They have to make it clear they will 'pull the plug' or sack people if they don't toe the line. You also have to have a major communications exercise and the only meaningful way of doing that is to get the support of the trade unions. Trade unions and management must work together to ensure that as much is done as is reasonably possible to ensure a new neutral working environment. There also needs to be training of key people … [and] a focus on awareness raising.

Protestants are not particularly aware that poppies might be offensive if worn outside the normal period and Catholics are not aware that speaking the Irish language may be offensive in the presence of Protestants. There is such segregation in society that there is a low level of awareness of what constitutes offence. The law is very clear on this for employers. The offence is based on the impact on the individual. A Catholic might have tolerated a King Billy poster or a Protestant a tricolour, but they don't have to; and they have a very strong case if they want to make it.

At the same conference Pat Dougan Chief Executive, Mackie International Group Plc, was asked *'Do you have any sense that society is dumping its ills on business to sort out?'* He replied

> They [FEC] have a clear brief. I had a problem with one of their requirements to put on ads that 'we welcome applications from the Catholic community.' They threatened me with legislation. We do receive applications from a broad spectrum. There is a problem convincing the Catholic community that there are opportunities in Mackie; but I don't see writing 'We welcome ...' at the bottom is of use, because even the Catholic community will see that as obligatory.

Evidently, at this stage in the development of the commercial equality agenda, the business perspective was not yet fully endorsing the need for a perceived neutral workplace or working practices.

Another speaker, Paul Browne (then) Equal Opportunities Unit QUB, is quoted answering the question:

> Does the University have a policy of encouraging greater understanding between the communities in its environment, as well as of discouraging tension? He said Toleration you mean. Each member of staff has to do a one-day equal opportunities workshop
>
> ....

To this, it must be firmly said that toleration is not part of equality, but a way of managing inequality. As a black delegate at a US seminar remarked 'I don't want you white guys to tolerate me and my kind. I want my rightful place as your equal!' There was still a way to go, even with the apparently most enlightened senior managers.

In the same CRC conference report John McVicar of NIACTO (the umbrella organisation for over thirty community training groups) reflected on the value of workshops they had run with Counteract facilitating:

The first event was primarily to give the managers within the organisation an idea of some of the issues around. The second was to involve some of the trainers, those who actually have influence over the young people. There was a two-pronged attack. Yes, we extend the sessions into each of the organisations; yes, we begin to think about 'peer education'. As far as young people are concerned, anyone over 20 is old. The best vehicle to put a message across is their peers. These are the two points that came out of the two workshops we have run. It is a case of putting the case back into the T&EA's court and with the CRC. But it was the conference which triggered us into doing something, and for us it is back to the drawing board to see where it all fits in.

The difficulty is that throughout Northern Ireland there has been a shift towards vocational training and away from personal and social development. The training organisations I deal with would recruit from the 'low achievers', the 'drop-outs', what education would regard as the 'no-hopers'. A lot of them come with a lot of personal baggage problems of numeracy and literacy and as well as that many of them don't know what a Catholic is, or a Protestant.

So how was NIACTO training young people?

Much of it is down to common sense. But it is not a priority, I feel, given the vocational emphasis. To be blunt, most organisations depend for survival on young people getting qualifications as quickly as they possibly can. Those are the hoops the government puts up and people have to jump through them. So, unless it is within the context of that type of training, people tend to ignore it. Also, there are neither the financial nor human resources to make it a priority.

John McVicar's opinion was that the emphasis on vocational training excluded vital components, such as

… personal and social development, literacy, numeracy, teenage pregnancies, drug abuse, solvent abuse, sectarianism. It is a bit like saying, 'We are a training organisation but we want you to come in and hang all the real problems you have with solvent abuse and reading on the coat hook. Bring the training part of you in and pick up those other things on the way out.' It doesn't work!' … The primary objective for any training organisation is the £ sign over the head of every young person who enters the door. How much are they worth to the organisation, both in terms of generated funding and in terms of output-related funding. The organisation and the young person get a bonus for qualification. There are no pounds and pence for social issues, so you've got to drop it if you want to survive. … All too often government departments are looking for quick-fix solutions to long-term problems, and that's like the area of sectarianism and community relations.

Case Study: Used by FEC in April 1994 conference workshop

Background

Nothread Ltd is a multinational tyre company based in the North West of Northern Ireland. They employ 150 workers, 90% of whom are Catholics and 10% of whom are Protestants.

Throughout the Troubles there have been very few problems in the workforce, and management and unions have a very good relationship. The Tyre Workers Union organises all the workers in the company and has a full-time convenor and five shop stewards.

Scenario

On Friday morning John the union convenor is approached by a Protestant worker called Jack who is employed in the finishing department. Jack is in a very distressed state and explains to John that all the Catholic workers in the Company have been saying to him 'I hear you're leaving on Friday.' Jack was not planning to leave but feels that the Catholic workers are trying to force him out of the company. He has been employed for fifteen years in Nothread.

Discussion Points

- What should the union do for Jack?
- Should the union involve the management in the case?
- What lessons are to be learnt from this case by both unions and management?

Clues

- Policy, Procedure and named persons;
- Facts, evidence and rumour;
- Assumptions, perceptions and previous experience.

At this time Counteract was still developing relationships with public sector employers. They were involved with social workers in the University of Ulster at Magee Campus and community centre staff in the Belfast City Council. They discussed expanding work in this area with the FEC using joint employer-trade union Equality Training in-house.

*　　*　　*　　*　　*

The working relationship of Counteract and the FEC, as providers of advice, training and education work, can be tracked through both organisations' annual reports. Clearly both saw the importance of the Trade Unions in challenging discrimination and sectarianism, and began with 'maintaining contact' from the earliest days. The FEC developed a 'Code of Practice' which, although not legally binding, had been given significant legal status under the legislation. This was distributed widely in the early 1990s.

Counteract acknowledged the FEC contribution:

> Commission staff contributed to equality training schools for shop stewards and branch officers organised by ATGWU and NIPSA. … and … made available to a number of employers a draft policy and procedure for dealing with sectarian harassment. In the incoming year this model policy and procedure will be widely distributed and additional advisory materials will be prepared for both employers and employees.

Case Law: Employer's Liability

An employer is vicariously responsible for acts or omissions of an employee during the course of their employment (Section 35 of the 1976 Act and Article 42 of the 1976 Order). The liability arises whether or not the act/s were done with the employer's knowledge or approval. An employer has a defence if he/she can prove *He took such steps as were reasonably practicable to prevent the employee from doing that act or from doing in the course of his employment acts of the same description.*

Reference McGibbon v Murphy T/A Carol's Restaurant Case No 63/90 FET.

The significant increase in both public and private sector employers[10] taking a positive approach to addressing sectarianism at work was reflected in the level of requests for training seminars both to management and staff. The FEC and Counteract gave joint seminars to a number of employers, getting positive feedback; the companies involved said they found it created a more harmonious workplace. It was not clear whether this was the result of declining levels of violence or simply a greater confidence on the part of management and a willingness to address the subject. However, the important fact was that sectarian attitudes and behaviour were increasingly being acknowledged if not always effectively tackled.[11]

Teresa Moley, formerly FEC Complaints Officer, later with the Equality Commission, recalled working with Counteract at that time with Billy Robinson and Paul Oakes in Conferences and training input for both the MOD and Ulsterbus:

> It was extremely useful. Hard issues were on the agenda. Counteract went beyond the standard FEC training. Counteract's work took risks, developed its methodology, made a video for training and took more risks – that made for better learning.

She also appreciated the moral support of having Billy Robinson around when facing sometimes very hostile people. 'The training took people out of their comfort zone. When debate got heated, they would get out of their seats.'

Teresa Moley courageously chose to work alongside Counteract in physically intimidating circumstances. Like them and other FEC staff, she would be on the receiving end of anger, hostility and outbursts of prejudice because she was seen not as representing a statutory body, but as the perpetrator of new, challenging legal requirements.

From a safe distance the threats and stresses of this work can be underestimated. Certainly, this is the stuff of burn-out. Evaluations of these sessions and workshops were extremely positive, despite the heavy work involved in accessing hidden prejudices and exposing strong emotions.

During the 1990s the FEC-Counteract relationship was constructive. However, they had different approaches and a sometimes-impatient Billy Robinson tended to expect too much from the FEC. There was always a healthy debate and occasionally there was argument on vital issues. Their operational remits overlapped and their training materials had common elements. As importantly, their alliance was stormy on a couple of occasions.

One instance was over a disputed passage in the Counteract report *Sectarian Intimidation and Harassment at Work*. It read as follows

> There is a feeling that the FEC has little understanding of how the workplace func-
> tions and therefore they are not able to make relevant suggestions about handling
> real problems. Even more worrying is the opinion that the FEC is unwilling to
> take responsibility and give advice for fear that it might be challenged in a fair
> employment case, and it is not even willing to enter into discussion of cases. The
> perception of the Commission is that, when a company wants advice or guidance
> on a particular case they will 'follow the law' and 'will know if you are wrong or
> right when you go to a tribunal'. It was felt by some that the Commission had not
> consulted with business on how to address the issue.

A special meeting of the Management Committee had been called in March to discuss the FEC's reaction to this report, where 'the Committee then reviewed the correspondence and an open and frank discussion took place.' The FEC requested a change to the report to clarify the roles of both the FEC and Counteract in advising complainants and respondents. The Committee agreed to insert change:

> Counteract acknowledges that the Commission's Advisory Unit does give advice to
> employers on a wide range of fair employment issues. If, however, an individual case
> of alleged discrimination is notified to the Tribunal Office, the FEC or the LRA, the
> Commission is required in law to decide whether or not it will assist the complainant.
> In these circumstances it is therefore debarred from advising the respondent employer.

This was the first in a number of controversies that were to arise between Counteract and the FEC.

While the Counteract report may have accurately reflected the opin-ions given in a survey, it was not taken kindly by the FEC whose statutory duties were defined and limited by law. In retrospect, the incident appeared to lay heavier on the minds in Counteract than it did with the FEC.

Work with both union[12] and non-union[13] groups continued and was developed. Johnathon Stephenson[14] (NIPSA) agreed that summer to pub-lish the next edition of *Counteraction*. Although it was hoped that the bul-letin would be published at least four times a year, the overload of work for all concerned restricted its frequency. Upping the profile of the unit was also on the agenda now as NIE and Queen's University Belfast featured Counteract in their in-house magazines.

After press coverage of the 'Jobs Bias hearing for Queen's University' earlier in the year, the university agreed to sign a policy pledge preventing employment bias. Against its very public record of having FET cases taken against it, QUB was more open than some other large public employers. They did not pay off complainants who had a good case, using public monies that then somehow disappeared in the accounting system. Counteract welcomed the move as 'the first step in establishing an equality policy'.[15]

* * * * *

Linking the trade unions and FEC into the voluntary-community sector was not easily done. Brenda Callaghan recalled that the trade union movement lacked real involvement with the sector, where Counteract was to make a huge impact. NIC ICTU was, in those years, concerned about 'what constituted a bona fide community group':

> Counteract was born out of the trade unions but I'm not sure the parents followed the baby. Counteract had principled support from ICTU and practical help from Terry Carlin. It developed way ahead of mainstream thinking. It had a straightforward working-class political agenda and was able to tread where the mainstream movement feared to go, and explore the darker and more sensitive issues.

Billy McCreight, who was to be the incoming Chair, believed that one lesson learned along the way was that Counteract could and would tackle what was too 'dangerous' and therefore had been avoided by others. Individual Trade Unions had difficulty facing intimidation and had no desire to address issues surrounding it. Both local union representatives and activists could be targeted in reprisals. The response was, understandably, to protect union people from attacks by avoidance. Throughout the 1990s Counteract work was to demonstrate that there was an effective alternative to ignoring sectarian intimidation at work. Today few would question the importance of challenging prejudice and harassment, however troublesome that may be.

* * * * *

Counteract was one of sixteen Northern Ireland organisations dealing with conflict and community relations that were represented at a 1994 European Conference *Peace Making and Conflict Resolution*. Three hundred delegates gathered in the Basque region in one hundred and twenty workshops, where people shared experiences. Topics covered ranged from responding to racism, human rights and minorities, Gypsies, gender identity and conflict, religion, culture and conflict.

Questioned about whether European Trade Unions were taking issues of xenophobia, racism and fascism seriously, it was apparent that this was not seen as part of their role. Counteract workshops were very well attended. There was almost awe that the trade union movement in Ireland had taken such a progressive step in addressing sectarianism by setting up the unit. The European experience was that although unions had an overall policy in prejudice, they did not generally try to address conflict, racism or xenophobia in the workplace. However, they did agree that the movement in Europe should consider establishing a similar unit to Counteract to promote workplace awareness and prejudice reduction.[16] This gave Counteract and ICTU even greater impetus to develop the work and spread it beyond Irish Unions.

Away from the intensity of Conference Billy Robinson met a number of representatives from the Basque region to discuss issues like work committees, how they coped with them, whether they were productive or if they inhibited the union's ability to represent their members. The Basque response differed from other European unions. Political division in the region meant members joined a union on the basis of their politics, not on an industrial basis and so election onto all committees was important. Basque unions had to actively campaign to get their members elected to these committees and so ensure their political views were heard.

*　*　*　*　*

Minutes of the November 1994 Committee meeting record what is the start of a process of gradual change, as Counteract was facing potentially conflicting aspects of its development. Given the origins of the unit Counteract had a potential problem if their fee-earning developed. To ensure that services generating a modest income from fee-paying organisations would not conflict with its articles of association, a new account was to be opened under the name 'Counteract Services'. As the anti-intimidation unit had outgrown its original remit, and core funding had to be supplemented, the Committee realised that some of the Counteract work had to generate income. Donations from various unions were coming in, in response to the 1993 Appeal, but this would never cover all the costs.

Training in NIE and MOD police recruits was proving successful and would produce more work as did training managers at Queen's University Belfast, and staff at Post Office Parcelforce. NSPCC wanted training and, as they were a charity CRC funded this.[17] The Northern Ireland Association of Community-based Training Organisations was looking for Counteract services too. BT was still undecided.

Costing and pricing its training brought the Counteract Management Committee up against the commercial realities of running a service organisation which had to break even. Also, at this stage, there was such a volume of training work that Counteract obviously needed another employee.

Billy Robinson had the idea of producing a Counteract training video and the Committee agreed that he should look into that. Counteract believed strongly that companies should address sectarianism and harassment in the workplace, not just as an equality issue but also as a question of Total Quality Management.[18] With TQM there was a recognised cost to failure and addressing failure. So, there were hidden costs for companies failing to address negatives like sectarian attitudes and behaviour because they impact on relationships between company-customer, management-staff, staff, departments etc.

To substantiate this view Billy Robinson suggested Queen's University academics could research it, adding, as he'd do characteristically, that CRC had said it would finance such research. Within weeks Billy Robinson, Oliver Johnston, Gilpin Black Consultants and CRC's Will Glendinning were developing a research project with CBI, LEDU and IDB to investigate the negative cost to industry in failure to address sectarian attitudes in work.

The outcome of this was to be the production of leaflets, a checklist and advice for employers – all of which made an important supplement to existing resources for employers and managers.

Notes

1. The memory of this killing remained in the public consciousness so that the Sunday World reported on 8 October 2000 that one of the men at the heart of the 'brutal murder saga' was in a mental hospital. One of those convicted left Northern Ireland with his family as soon as he was released from prison.

2. The 1994 AGM elected officers as per: Avilla Kilmurry (Chairperson), Brenda Callaghan (Vice-Chairperson) Terry Carlin (Secretary) and Brendan Mackin (Treasurer).

3. *Belfast Telegraph, Newsletter* and *Irish News*, 8–9 March 1994.

4. As regards work with the unions, CRC funded four residential schools for unions after NCU, GPMU and UCW declared interest. The Post Office asked for and funded a joint Management-Union course. Billy Robinson had been asked to talk to the Confederation in AEU House and take part in a T&G school in Belfast & Portadown.

5. Billy Robinson went to a joint conference of NUC-UCW and met the Education and Equality Officers, took part in a women-only seminar organised by NCU, and was invited to speak at a fringe meeting in Blackpool.

6. Harry McConnell went on to become an Equality Commissioner for Northern Ireland.

7. The Conference Report was published in February 1996.

8. Quoted from '*Experience of Change*', pp. 5–9.

9. A note of caution should be sounded here. Consumer power (whether to buy or not) assumes choice. Unlike supermarkets and travel agents, NIE then had a monopoly on electricity in Northern Ireland. In the same way, public services – like health, education and social services – are 'monopolies' and people cannot shift their custom (or need) to another service provider.

10. Newry and Mourne District Council, Omagh District Council, Derry City Council, Golden Vale UK, Premier Power, Moypark and Unipork. MOD recruits began introductory sessions at this stage.

11. Counteract was negotiating for training and renewed work with Newry & Mourne District Council, Derry District Council, Lisburn District Council, Probation Officers – Maghaberry, Golden Vale UK, Premier Power, Moypark, Unipork & QUB.

12. At this time, Unison was about to incorporate Counteract training programme into their own Education Schools and wanted it to train shop stewards and management in the Ambulance Service. NCU, UCW, NIPSA and GPMU planned four residential schools.

13. The Equal Opportunities Commission had requested Counteract training on anti-sectarianism for their staff. Billy Robinson was discussing the possibility of addressing fifth and sixth-year pupils in schools with Tom Moore of NUT, ICTU and Declan Cairney.

14. Johnathon Stevenson was Chairman of the Social Democratic and Labour Party (SDLP) and had been involved in trade union work, and radical journalism (such as the Northern Irish monthly journal, *Fortnight*) for many years.

15. Sunday Life, 14 August 1994.

16. Edited from *Counteraction* Issue 1.

17. Counteract produced a leaflet informing organisations about this.

18. This was featured first in 'Impact News' (NIPSA's paper) October/November 1994.

CHAPTER 6

1995–96: Peace Breaks Out for a While

After the London government lifted its ban on ministers having contact with Sinn Féin, and the Loyalist UDP and PUP parties, the Dublin government would formally meet Sinn Féin. There were signs of progress. In February the Dail lifted the Republic's state of emergency declared in 1940 and renewed in 1976. 'Framework' documents were published on government for Northern Ireland and North-South relations.

These events brought the inevitable, predictable debates – the hotly disputed issue of linking arms de-commissioning (by the IRA) and political negotiation (including Sinn Féin). Never slow to anticipate the turn of events, Sinn Féin had begun their 'parity of esteem' campaign earlier that winter, arguing that as elected representatives they should not have to negotiate their political status – or that of their voters. Gerry Adams bitterly opposed the exclusion of Sinn Féin. In March James Molyneaux was re-elected UUP leader, throwing off a challenge from Lee Reynolds.

And in April the RUC re-routing of a contentious Apprentice Boys march on the Lower Ormeau Road in Belfast presaged another year of disputes about Loyalist marches in Nationalist areas. The unremitting bigotry, cynicism and political-sectarian symbolism on all sides was evident in reports of the meaning of the acronym 'TUAS'. Did Republicans mean 'total unarmed struggle' or 'tactical use of armed struggle'? Whether or not the devil was in the detail, this was a typical example of the importance of innuendo, hidden meanings and ambiguity – played out by all interests, and sometimes for no greater gain than malicious pleasure as causing fear and offence.

The NIO and Ministers met Sinn Féin, while the Dublin government held talks with the small Loyalist parties the UDP and PUP. Secretary of State Sir Patrick Mayhew and Gerry Adams met privately after a Washington conference on investment in Northern Ireland. John Major saw off opposition to his leadership, thereby allegedly stabilising the peace process. Belfast got its first ever Nationalist Deputy Lord Mayor, Alban Maginness.

July ushered in a series of escalating confrontations between Loyalist marchers, counter-protesters and the RUC. That was the birth of the phenomenon known as Drumcree, as Orangemen and their supporters converged on a small church on Drumcree Hill on the outskirts of Portadown to drive their march back through the predominantly Nationalist Garvaghy Road. When the march was 'forced through' Anglo-Irish relations were strained at the highest level. Sectarian attacks on Protestant and Catholic homes and Orange Halls formed the backdrop to official complaints from Dublin to the Maryfield Secretariat about the bias of the RUC. Orangemen started to picket Catholic churches during mass – stating their position 'if we can't worship, then we will stop them from their worship' (Bew And Gillespie, 1999).

Sectarian attacks on businesses were followed by widespread boycotting of Protestant businesses with immediate and bitterly felt economic consequences. Burning of Catholics schools followed. In August the Apprentice Boys followed the lead and supported the Orange Order in their demands to march wherever they wished to go. Clashes broke out and people were injured in protest and counter-protest throughout the summer.

At the end of August James Molyneaux resigned making way for David Trimble as UUP leader. Trimble made his position clear. There must be de-commissioning of IRA arms before an Assembly including Sinn Féin could be set up.

As the university year began the Queen and President Mary Robinson shared their first public engagement in London celebrating the 150th anniversaries of Queen's University Belfast, University College Cork and University College Galway.

Next month saw two important developments. An Orange rally was organised by the 'Spirit of Drumcree' group who argued for radical change within the Order, the resignation of the Grand Master and the severing of links with the UUP. Senator George Mitchell took the chair at the Mitchell Commission, alongside former Prime Minister of Finland Harry

Holkeri, and Canadian Chief of Staff and former US ambassador General John de Chastelain.

The international influence on Northern Ireland continued as the year ended with the European Court ruling that the Prevention of Terrorism Act contravened the European Union's law, under the Treaty of Rome.

Deaths arising from the conflict in 1995: 9. Shootings: 50. Bombs planted: 2. Incendiaries: 10. Firearms found: 1718 Explosives found: 5 kg (11 lb.). Persons charged with terrorist and serious public order offences: 440. Casualties arising from paramilitary attacks: 220.

*   *   *   *   *

At the start of 1995 Counteract had heard informally that funding for the new Community Unit would be coming from CRC. Later, CRC confirmed funding for the poster campaign *Live without Labels*.

Brenda Callaghan[1] asked the Committee to record formal thanks to Jim Quinn and the current staff of Counteract for securing this funding.[2] Counteract welcomed the NIC ICTU initiative *Investing in Peace: an Interim Programme for Reconstruction* fully endorsing their statement. 'Ending violence is only part of the process of creating a new peaceful and stabilised society in Northern Ireland in which economic prosperity, full employment and equality of opportunity could become the norm.'

Nevertheless, in the 1995 Counteract Annual Report Billy Robinson wrote

> I have difficulty with the continuous use of the word peace, intimating that we ever had peace. Neither I nor my parents have ever known peace – we have known a number of ceasefires but never peace. The English dictionary defines peace as 1) 'a state existing during the absence of war' 2) 'a state of harmony between people and groups'. If the latter is not present the former will break down for fear and mistrust are the main elements that have to be addressed in a peaceful society.

However, the longer that the level of violence continued to fall in Northern Ireland the more optimistic people were that this would create a climate to allow a peace settlement to be agreed. Counteract called on political leaders to develop the trade union negotiating skills in finding a middle course.

On more traditional ground Counteract provided a stall and spoke at a number of conferences that year, including NUJ (London and Dublin), CWU (Bournemouth) ICTU Biennial (Newcastle) and the Anti-Racist Alliance (London). It played a full part in the debate on 'what happens after the cease- fires?' in fringe meetings and formal discussions with the trade union movement in Ireland and Britain.

*   *   *   *   *

Condemnation of sectarian harassment at work was increasing and challenging it was becoming recognised as a business issue – because failure cost time, productivity and profits. Counteract now argued that: 'It should be part of the criteria laid down by the British Standards Institute (BSI) equality standards for those companies wishing to attain recognition that they create a neutral and harmonious working environment.'

Peace and the construction of a conflict-free society in Northern Ireland would bring industry, unions and workers along the same path – making companies more effective, thus helping to create a competitive region in the European and World markets. Challenging harassment (of any kind) in the workplace was clearly a common goal.

Counteract went on providing seminars, workshops and speakers at various trade union events.[3] In October 1995 Counteract organised a very successful weekend school for GPMU/CWU women's committee members on sectarian harassment in the workplace. This was the first ever women-only seminar organised by Counteract and it proved to be a very enlightening event, both for the delegates and for Counteract itself. It highlighted the fact that addressing sectarianism had been looked at from the male perspective and that one of the problems women had was if the harasser is male then women have a dual problem in terms of sectarian/ sexual harassment.[4] The event exposed other issues that had not been fully examined, so Counteract decided that, where possible, it would in future conduct women-only seminars to develop a better understanding of the problem from a feminist perspective – no small ambition as Counteract had, like the Unions, a solidly male culture.

Records for the year report a slight increase in the number of unions taking up the services of Counteract. However, there was still a large number that did not. Dialogue began with the Northern Ireland Council for Ethnic

Minorities (NICEM) to develop anti-racist aspects of anti-prejudice training programmes. This would develop substantially in the coming years.

* * * * *

At a conference in Madrid on racism at work, Terry Carlin and Billy Robinson joined representatives from the European Commission, European Trade Unions Confederation, the Union of Industrial & Employers Confederation of Europe and representatives from the German, Swedish and Spanish Governments. The main area of debate was integration of emigrants into the host community and workplace and providing support and training. Another question was whether or not there should be a European directive on xenophobia and racism in the workplace. This would be integral to establishing a practicable equality agenda.

At European level, however, there did not appear to be a serious attempt to address the question of prejudice in indigenous populations or the need to provide awareness training in workplaces. In this respect the Northern Ireland trade union movement was still far ahead of anything in Europe. These issues remained a powerful challenge in Ireland, the UK and Europe. Yet Counteract continued its commitment to addressing these head-on.

Community-based organisations, and public and private sector employers wanted Counteract services that year.[5] Employers' positive approach was reflected in the level of requests for training both management and staff – with the FEC and Counteract in joint seminars.

After this, organisations reported increased numbers of complaints about harassment but this was predictable; a better-trained management could deal with complaints in a more professional manner – which seemed to make for better staff-management relations and a more efficient and productive workforce. Counteract continued to make the business case.

* * * * *

The credibility and importance of Counteract's ground-breaking work was given a high profile at the 1995 AGM with the presence of President of the Republic of Ireland, Mary Robinson.

* * * * *

Billy Robinson recounted his now predictably challenging experience during training at Queen's University Belfast. This session was to include issues that would be core to the unit's work – and its challenges – for the next few years:

> When we were delivering training to QUB staff we tried, for the first time, to introduce the question of wearing the poppy at work. There were 25 people present plus the Equality Manager. At the start of the session on the wearing of emblems the Equality Manager immediately left the room – and at this point I was approached by a participant who said that I was going to do more harm than good and stated that he was considering leaving the room. From his bearing and his clothing, I guessed that he was of a military background. I asked him to bear with me for a while and if he thought I was doing anything wrong he could leave the session and I would understand. At that he said he would stay but if he thought that, in the course of the session, I was causing a problem, he would leave.
>
> The presentation I made was really on the fact that the poppy was used and claimed by one group, denied by another yet should be embraced by all. I recalled that when I was a child, I witnessed a priest at a mass lambasting an individual for wearing the poppy at mass, denouncing it as 'a load of nonsense'. I also told the group that touring the North of Ireland I'd witnessed monuments and statues to the fallen of the two wars, yet there was no monument or memorial to the only person, in Northern Ireland to receive the highest award, the Victoria Cross, from the king at the time. Why? Because he was a Catholic from the Falls Road in Belfast, – 'a load of nonsense'.
>
> In Ballymena, on Remembrance Sunday, the local [Catholic]cleric and some politicians absented themselves from the platform because a representative of the Parachute Regiment was present, despite the fact that he was a Catholic Priest and Chaplin to the Regiment – 'a load of nonsense'. When someone wears the poppy from the end of September to December, they are not remembering the dead but using it to make a statement – contrary to what the poppy stands, for which is to remember all the fallen irrespective of religion.
>
> At the end of the session the person who'd said he had concerns spoke up in the group and stated that he supported this view and that the abuse of the poppy in the manner described did not honour his fallen comrades.
>
> The Equality Manager later informed me that he had panicked when I started to introduce the issue as it was a very sensitive matter that he had never occasioned in discussion before. He informed me that when he left the room he had returned to his office and stood watching from his window to see if the participants were going

to leave the room. He was surprised when no one left. His fear was that I would cause problems in the University by raising the subject matter but expressed relief and joy that the issue had been broached and could now be discussed openly.

*   *   *   *   *

The cast

Presenter
Adrian Dunbar

Emma Moylan

Ian Beattie

Jacqueline Magowan

Patricha Irvine

Richard Orr

William Walker

Michael Foyle

Peter Balance

Brónagh . . . . *Emma Moylan*

Billy . . . . *Ian Beattie*

Jeannie . . . . *Jacqueline Magowan*

Mrs Patterson . . . . . *Patricha Irvine*

Jimmy . . . . *Richard Orr*

Personnel Officer . . *Stella McCusker*

Sammy . . . . *Peter Balance*

Tommy . . . . *Michael Foyle*

Sammy Barns . . . . . *William Walker*

Joe . . . . *Derek Halligan*

Valerie . . . . *Moya O'Hara*

Sammy's Son . . . . . *Michael Diamond*

Picture 8: The Counteract video, *The Inside Stories*

The Counteract video, *Sectarian harassment in the workplace: The Inside Stories*, was filmed during October 1995 (see Picture 8). Sponsored by industry, government agencies, unions, charitable trusts and the EC, it had a budget of around £80,000.

Billy Robinson explained how important it was to make *The Inside Stories*:

> The idea of making a training video on sectarian harassment in the workplace first came to me after I'd watched other trainers delivering awareness training. They did not address the hard issues and for two reasons – the fear of raising contentious issues and the lack of proper training material. As most of the materials and especially videos were from outside NI there was nothing produced here that related to our specific problems.
>
> I thought if I made a training video which portrayed the real language and behaviour of the community then that would take some of the fears away – because it'd be the video not the trainer saying the words. Most training videos were face to camera interviews and speakers reciting the information. Counteract's product exposes sectarianism in the two dramas and it was produced totally by NI people in NI.
>
> In the video there's a scene where Irish language is used as a way of making a fellow worker feel isolated. I was challenged in the local press, claiming I was portraying the Irish language as being anti-Protestant. My response was that the Irish language was not of itself sectarian, as a large number of the founders of the Gaelic league were Protestant – but it's often used to exclude Protestants in the workplace and society.

Production got underway after only two months in scripting and development. The timetable was remarkable enough but making the film was a story in itself.

The whole project came together in three months but before it started the producer gave Billy Robinson some uncharacteristic advice. Richard Abbott had a great respect for what Counteract did, and plenty of experience making corporate videos that would sit gathering dust on the shelves of senior managers. He advised Billy Robinson 'Keep your money in your pocket' but once he understood the content and the purpose of the video and work-book that went with it he rapidly reversed his decision. 'It's really intriguing as a subject and a production.'

Directed by Ian McElhinney and starring Adrian Dunbar, the making of the video was an extraordinary operation. It just happened that Ian McElhinney and Adrian Dunbar were in Northern Ireland, and a lucky accident that David Barker was home from Hollywood for the space of a few weeks. Everyone involved in the production was from Northern Ireland and understood the issues. They supported Counteract thinking and ethos. They all felt the video was important and put their hearts into it.

Renowned cameraman David Barker is said to have commented that he had never worked on a shoot that had gone so smoothly. Others in the crew remarked that 'there was no bitching and ego-trips' and that this was a project where everything had meaning and got the commitment of the team. Individuals worked for minimum rates, less or nothing at all, just to finish the production. The fact that the whole project was backed by government and large corporate sponsors, who went on to use it in their own organisations, was already a significant endorsement.

Sponsorship was generous[6] but not sufficient and CCRU made up the shortfall in a relatively expensive but very cost-effective new development. There would be a widespread use of *The Inside Stories* by both Counteract and a range of employing organisations across Northern Ireland in the coming years.

Counteract opted to make the video on film, which cost considerably more but was the best quality for production. Like everyone who worked on the production Adrian Dunbar was wholly committed and extremely enthusiastic. Years afterwards, Billy Robinson remembered the project with warmth and respect for all those involved, and wanted recognition of their contribution:

> The quality of the film was a result of the commitment of the people. They had a feeling for it. And that went through Counteract to people outside who supported us, opened doors, and helped in different ways. The quality of the film was the people who were making it. This wasn't their area but they all did their bit. The fella who filmed it (David Barker) said 'I've worked on numerous projects with people bitching but everybody is doing their bit here. It's going so smoothly.' Typical was Dunbar, who just said 'I support you, Billy.' He was brilliant, very professional – an idiot like me telling him what to say. But they said, 'No, you're the man. You know' 'Everybody on it was great and I really enjoyed it.

The respect and trust between the production team, actors and Counteract was mutual and strong. Richard Abbott and Ian McElhinney were professionals and more than capable of making films, but they wanted Counteract advice on the finer subtleties, to give them the right steer. 'On this subject I haven't a clue – you're going to have to sit in on every word in filming and editing – language, tone, body language and the smallest facial expression. It's your area of work.' This scrutiny was seen as vital in the attempt to get the authentic experience on camera. Sylvia Sands came from the BBC to script the film with Billy. He was, at the same time, reassuring the production company that finance was *no problem – sound as a bell.* The reality went like this:

> Trevor helped me by giving me bills to pay as the filming went along. That was fine until the night Noreen and I were standing in the street and they were filming around the back of the Unemployed Centre and Trevor came up to me and gave me the next bill for over twenty thousand pounds. I said, 'No problem, I'll sort it out tomorrow' and put it in my pocket. Noreen said to me, 'Billy, what are you going to do? We only have two thousand pounds in the bank.' I said I'd sort it out in the morning so I had to get up next day and start phoning around to squeeze the money out. And the CCRU made the final contribution. When it was finished the CCRU pulled me out of a hole. And the reason they supported us was, I think, because there were so many different factors involved and so many sponsors. So, they saw that employers and the statutory sector were backing it and went with us.

The video was dedicated to Frank Wright who had generously shared his educational expertise in the early days:

> Dedication: Frank Wright 1948–1993), Lecturer in Politics at Q.U.B. and first Professor of Peace Studies in Ireland dedicated many years work to building rela-tionships between all the people of Northern Ireland. Through Counteract and the Understanding Conflict Project (UU) he facilitated the first meetings between trade Unionists on sectarianism which later led to this video.

The Inside Stories video was launched in November 1995 at the Belfast Europa Hotel, with Jane Morrice, Head of the European Commission Office in Northern Ireland officiating. In her address she welcomed this innovative project by Counteract and praised the co-operation between trade unions, employers, community relations agencies and universities in sponsoring this video, adding, 'Hopefully this will be the beginning of future co-operation in addressing sectarianism – an area where we all have a common purpose.'

Having been involved so closely at every stage of the production Billy Robinson couldn't watch its premiere in the Europa Hotel and stood outside chain smoking:

> We looked through the door and saw the last of the credits coming up, so we sat at the back. When the film finished there was total silence, and I thought 'Oh ****'. But then everybody got up and applauded it. It was like we found afterwards. We'd always leave people for a minute to have time to take a breath because there was so much in it and it's so powerful that you need time to come back afterwards. It was good. There were over two hundred people there and after spending the money and doing it I didn't know if it was good or if it was relevant and would connect with people. But it worked.

According to Billy Robinson, Ian McElhinney wanted to enter *The Insides Stories* for a film award. He had been so enthused by the work on sectarianism that they discussed making a film about racism in European countries. In the end nothing came of these plans, but these like many episodes in the history of Counteract were good ideas but not, at that stage, viable.

Counteract staff who later used the package recalled its impact:

> People talked to Counteract about the video, and said it disturbed them. They said one of things that upset them was that they knew it. They recognised things, things they hadn't challenged. All of a sudden it was there – in their face and they knew. People felt guilty. It affected people who saw it, and especially Protestants – the bottling plant manager who asked for the video to take it to show his family saying 'It's a powerful message and needs to be heard outside of here.' One youth worker on the course had 'let it ride' but went back to work and brought it into his work – creating a new ethos and environment. (Paul Burke)

The video and training package came from the vision, tenacity and infectious commitment of Counteract. Brenda Callaghan, Chair at the time, said 'Billy Robinson brought a broader vision of the work. Counteract might not have survived without that. One example is the decision to produce the video, *The Inside Stories*.'

She remembered the night before its launch when he'd said 'I don't have the money for it.' As Chair she took a reasoned view – given her knowledge of him – replying, 'Launch it and see about that afterwards.'

Counteract did not have a business board and made mistakes. In the absence of a copyright on the video, consultants (from large and small companies) used it with neither payment nor acknowledgement. To remedy this in part it is now freely available on YouTube (https://www.youtube.com). As in other respects the Management Committee learned what they needed to know as they went along – from statutory requirements as an employer to the decision to work with employers as well as workers and trade unions. 'Counteract developed because there was a deep belief that it could contribute to society. It caters for a gap in the 'market' as there are no other Northern Ireland based resource materials on this issue.'[7]

While the debate in Counteract was about keeping to the value base of trade unionism, this was an era of marketing with an impetus towards self-financing of projects. Counteract was slow to exploit its unique product:

> The [video] pack is currently priced at £100 for voluntary organisations and unions and £350 for employers. The price for employers is too low. The market price for other video resource packs in Human Resource Development is at least twice this price. There is a danger that a personnel manager in looking at the price and not knowing about it might assume its cheap price was an indication of poor quality.

The Inside Stories comprised two dramas depicting sectarianism at work with the commentary by local actor Adrian Dunbar highlighting the main issues involved. The first story involved a young Catholic woman, Bronagh, in her first job experiencing obvious threats and hostilities from her Protestant co-workers.[8] The second was about a Protestant man, Sammy Barns facing a more subtle form of harassment from his predominantly Catholic work-mates of fifteen years. The few words *hear you're leavin' Friday* confused, then worried and ultimately intimidated Sammy to the edge of despair.

There was generous sponsorship[9] and total commitment from Advertising Partners, the company who produced the video and workbook package, and Adrian Dunbar who gave his time and enthusiasm freely. Counteract went on to show the video at the ICTU and other conferences, integrated it into training and presentations, and sold it to unions and private, public and voluntary sector organisations. Note should be made, however, that the use of *The Inside Stories* by employers, managers and industry was frequently for in-house training. Employers were keen, even years later, to say they did not need Counteract – that is, to be seen NOT to have a problem of discrimination or intimidation in their workforce.

Sadly, indicative of the times was the press report 'Anti-bias video man rebuts Gaelic critics'[10] Briefly, the issue was 'The maker of a campaigning anti-sectarian video has dismissed claims that it depicts the Irish language as anti-Protestant.' The Irish language lobby were a trifle disingenuous in very publicly responding 'that's good news for all of us who see Irish as being above politics and religion'.

At the same time, FEC and FET were very quick to acknowledge the value of these new training materials and used them consistently. And there were some employers who did admit to having an internal need to address these issues but who used the video as part of a package worked out with Counteract.

* * * * *

A Community Unit was set up in 1995, with a remit based on the research findings of an anti-intimidation working group under the auspices of the CRC – to include Counteract, NIACAB, Belfast Law Centre and CAJ. It was proposed that the aims of the unit be

- Collating information from agencies giving advice and support to the victims of intimidation and harassment;
- Updating the advice workers information pack;
- Developing models of anti-intimidation practice which can be used by local communities to reduce the isolation of victims;
- Assisting local groups to develop such initiatives; and,
- Assisting the development of overall strategies and programmes of prevention where possible, in conjunction with the relevant agencies.

A now expanding Counteract had to spend time on staffing matters. First Jim Quinn and Noreen Moore, then Billy Robinson and Noreen had been the sum total of Counteract staff. Additional capacity was needed to cover the increasing amount of work, and Counteract needed people who had maturity and experience in trade union work. So, a new post of Trainer/Development Worker was advertised and by 1st July Jim McCabe was in place, although only for some months, as he went on to other independent work.

Counteract welcomed its next recruit, Joe Law, as Trainer/Development Officer into its new community unit. He came from the T&G and had been a member of their Equality Committee and Executive member of Belfast and District Trades Council. As a former Orangeman, he brought another dimension of experience and credibility. Counteract work was progressing beyond crisis management into a more strategic approach to challenging intimidation in the workplace. 'You got to be pleased you don't have to do the same thing. Counteract played a part in reducing intimidation'[11] (Joe Law).

Counteract Community unit was launched by Mr Michael Ancram MP, (see Picture 9), Minister with responsibility for Community Relations, who said

> Counteract's new unit has an important role to play in promoting community reconciliation, fostering a new climate of thinking and creating a better future for everyone. The Trade Unions have adopted a courageous and responsible lead against all forms of sectarianism in the workplace and have helped to insulate the workplace from the worst aspects of community division.

Picture 9: Billy Robinson, Terry Carlin and Michael Ancram

The first objective of the Community Unit was to update the *Action Against Intimidation Information & Advice* manual. Joe Law and Noreen Moore completed the update and had discussions with CROs, District Councils and housing groups about developing training on the use of the manual.[12] This was Counteract's pathway to engage at community level, years before it was government policy to embed community development in mainstream statutory services.

NICEM, who had contributed to the manual, now asked for a Counteract nomination onto their newly established Advisory Panel. This was Paul Oakes who joined people from the various industries that had also been nominated. This was also significant in that the ICTU Conference passed a motion extending Counteract work to include addressing racism in the workplace, in light of its equality agenda and the introduction of the Race Relations Act in Northern Ireland. The trade union movement was keen to be seen to be proactive rather than reactive.

Although racist violence happened in Northern Ireland it did not get the same publicity as sectarian attacks. Also, it was now apparent that children of ethnic minority families did not necessarily want to work in the traditional areas of work like the family business and looked for jobs in industry and trade, where they had never been represented. So, racism at work had to be addressed and Counteract began talks with NICEM to develop anti-racist aspects in training programmes.

With less of a public profile, NIPSA, and especially Jonathon Stephenson, pulled their weight in the production of *Counteraction*.

*   *   *   *   *

The continued commitment of core funding from CRC went well towards keeping Counteract afloat. To be viable they also had to ask the unions for support, and launched another three-year appeal, which met with a positive response from many[13] ICTU affiliated unions.

At this stage, the Management Committee represented both unions and voluntary organisations.[14] It was decided that the Committee should be seeking nominations from organisations that would, in future times, also reflect the breadth of its service users. This entailed going outside the realms of the trade union movement and was a substantial development. Counteract needed to widen its contacts, and have itself more realistically represented rather than as being bluntly 'cloth cap' and perceived as anti-management. That consideration remained an issue, though a smaller one, for many of the larger companies and senior public service figures.

Incoming Chair, Brenda Callaghan, agreed that

> The committee needed to expand because they were people from the same background and value base. Formal issues got attention but strategic development was lacking. We needed to expand the management committee's membership and representation. Gaps in our knowledge became more obvious and the weakness of informality showed. We needed a shared vision but also practical skills and people to act as a sounding board and perhaps challenge the committee with a more cautious approach.

It was with deep regret that, after five year's dedicated work, Avilla Killurray's resignation had been accepted. She had chaired the committee since the inception of Counteract and worked tirelessly to support it.[15] Her successor, Brenda Callaghan, believed that Counteract was growing because it took an intelligent approach and the ingenuity and courage to forge new paths:

> The organisation developed with a lot of vision and luck and because of its ability to identify needs, take risks and not fear the outcomes. It was a bold step in relation to workplace issues, violence and intimidation, because workers perpetrate sectarian acts. They are members of Sinn Féin and the Orange Order. Before Counteract, unions would bury the personal, emotional and economic issues. Billy Robinson started to see sectarianism in business terms – but from a trade union perspective. If sectarianism cost money then money saved by dealing with it should recompense the people who suffered, not just go back into a big company pot.

> Counteract had established credibility with the unions long before employers came on board. Counteract came in speaking shop floor language, not board room language. That was its strength because it was talking to ordinary white collar or shop floor people. The message relates to their experience due to the intense belief of the trainers.

*   *   *   *   *

Expanding Counteract education into the community sector and growing its services coincided with more strategic thinking. A network of committed friends, experts and fellow-travellers around Counteract fed into that thinking. Changing how people behave in work or the community would be more likely if organisations changed how they operated – there had to be more than 'fire-fighting'. Containing intimidation alone was important but on its own it was a second preference. Ideally intimidation would not happen and to achieve this, organisations would have to alter their ethos.

This was a huge challenge because changing the working culture and the ethos of an organisation always creates difficulties. It requires 'drivers' of change and commitment at the highest level of management and needs direction. Addressing change of this order would become a central part of Counteract thinking and development in the coming years. Yet, however much Counteract wanted to see organisational change there was neither the expertise nor the necessary leverage to deliver this – that kind of change would have to come from within the organisation.

Meanwhile Counteract asked T&EA to fund a youth training project. This was planned as the pilot youth training project CYPHER. At this stage Billy Robinson met Annie Moore, Director of the Open College Network about accreditation and writing up of the project. Everyone was keen to see the project take off but this elaborate initiative would take time to plan and think through – as well as getting the people to deliver it.

As ever Counteract was on the lookout for opportunities – for funds, support, training contracts and anything else that might help them. A meeting had been arranged with Doug Riley, Chief Executive, BT (NI) about future training. As far as BT was concerned Billy Robinson had his own 'history' as a former employee and union representative (CWU) – and he would be known to have understood the problems since he had been hi-jacked at gun point in the past. He expected that there would be a certain suspicion of him, and the assumption that he would bring in moral arguments and left-wing politics to make his case. He did not.

His message was sectarianism, intimidation and discrimination must be addressed because there is a business case to be made. Although BT did not take their services for long, and had their own training, Doug Riley invited Counteract to help out in the call centre in Portadown and train managers. In later years BT would have a person on the Counteract Committee (albeit representing CBI).

*　　*　　*　　*　　*

Counteract had argued strongly that workplace sectarianism and harassment was not simply an equality issue. The problem was to be addressed as a business issue, like Health & Safety. They now made the case that it was a question of TQM – Total Quality Management – which most employers understood as having costs attached to failure. Just like addressing any negative factor, employers should confront sectarianism in work because it was detrimental to business relationships, like relations between company and customer, management and staff, between and within departments, etc.

A measure of the success in getting this message across was the full-page feature on the back cover of Business Telegraph (see Picture 10).[16] The regular 'Company Profile' piece was 'Counteract poses the question, should TQM address Sectarianism?' and included a list of negative elements affecting efficiency and profitability of organisations:

- *Sectarian attitudes, fear and stress in the workplace can lead to absenteeism, particularly at certain times of year;*
- *Sectarian attitudes can cause lack of co-operation between staff;*
- *The stress and anxiety produced by sectarianism leads to employees taking time off due to illness;*
- *For employers the cost of investment in training and development is lost when employees leave and must be duplicated with new employees;*
- *Loss of confidence by staff in the company, lack of commitment to the organisation and low morale has a negative effect and can lead to failure to seek promotion within the company;*
- *When a company is brought to a tribunal, litigation and possible adverse publicity can damage its reputation, which in turn can lead to customer loss.*

… it therefore makes sound business sense to promote and maintain a neutral working environment. Addressing these failures should fall within the concept of TQM. TQM addresses the question of 'human relations management' … if an organisation wishes to achieve quality recognition then it must address the question of prejudice within the workplace. … Trade unions and employers have a common purpose; working together to create a harmonious environment, rejuvenation of the company and the creation of job opportunities.

Picture 10: Billy's fight for fairer play in the workplace

The business community was as sophisticated as the general public, having learned through the years that old ways of doing things, and habits of tolerating unacceptable behaviour, was costing Northern Ireland a lot more than simply a bad image.

Billy Robinson pushed that message in the press throughout the year.

*   *   *   *   *

Nominating Billy Robinson to the CRC Committee was an indication of the unit's contribution, as was the invitation to sit on NIVT's Vulnerable Groups Advisory Grants Committee. Counteract was being recognised as tackling the injustice of sectarianism at work and so enhancing community relations work in Northern Ireland – and doing this without equivocation about the importance of equality.

After years of 'talks about talks', cease-fires and the beginning of negotiations, peace appeared to be within reach. And the solution to conflict was to be political. Life in Northern Ireland changed dramatically for most citizens in 1995, if only temporarily. Living beyond the clutches of war had become a reality for some and an aspiration for the majority. It was not the end of violence, but the beginning of a fragile set of peace negotiations that lasted until 1998. Like many other associated phenomena, sectarianism 'had not gone away' and Counteract services would still be needed.

Notes

1. At the same time Johnathon Smyth (NATFHE) and Janet Hunter (Housing Rights Service) were formally welcomed onto the Committee of Counteract.
2. The CCRU (later the Community Relations Unit of OFDFM) agreed three years' funding for the new unit. CRC gave a grant and the balance was financed by IFI.
3. Over 1995–96 they worked with T&G, NIPSA, CWU, CWU – Women's Committee, GPMU – Women's Committee, MSF, NUJ and SIPTU.
4. This was never been fully explored and remained a challenge for the future progress of Counteract and its partners.
5. These included Women Together and Shankill Women's Network. Newry and Mourne District Council, Omagh District Council, Derry City Council, Golden

Vale UK, Premier Power, Moypark and Unipork. Prisoners (Maghaberry), Probation Officers (Maghaberry), CRC, QUB and the Centre for the Study of Conflict at UU also used them. Training prisoners for their release and re-entry into the workplace, and becoming involved with women's groups was a new area of work for Counteract.

6. NIE gave support in the form of £5,000 sponsorship plus the use of their premises for filming and their own editing facilities (worth another couple of thousand pounds). Ford asked what they would get for sponsoring the video. The reply was they would be named on a package about tackling sectarianism in the workplace; eliciting the response '*that's good enough for us*'. Queen's University was another sponsor and like many others they had experience of being brought before the FET. When the subject was raised at the University of Ulster, and mention was made of Queen's University's giving support, they came on board. Funding for the project also came from CRC, CCRU, EC, FEC, NIVT, T&EA, NIC ICTU, Shorts, Citybus, Northern Ireland Bankers' Association and the Equality Forum Northern Ireland.

7. Quoted from the CENI Evaluation Report 1997, this is accurate, except for the T&G education equality programmes.

8. This drama was based on the facts of the FET case taken and won by Lisa Neeson.

9. The Annual report states, 'The total cost of production of the video was £86,000 and we would like to take this opportunity to thank those organisations who contributed both financially and in kind in meeting the above cost.' The sponsors of the video were CCRU, NIC ICTU, EC, FEC, NIE, QUB, UU, T&EA, NIVT, Ford Motor Company, NI Banders' Association, Equality Forum NI, Citybus, Shorts Bombardier, Harland & Wolff, Telecommunity.

10. *Andersonstown News*, 4 November 1995.

11. Quoted from an interview with Billy McCreight, former Chair of Counteract Management Committee.

12. Three years' funding for the unit was obtained from CCRU and IFI.

13. USDAY, CPSU, IPU, NUJ, INTO, PSEU, ATGWU, AUT, MAS, UNISON, CWU, NATFHE, AEEU, ASTI, INUVGATA, NIPSA, UCATT, GPMU, IMPACT, NIBCAWU.

14. Of a committee of eight there was one nominee from NIC ICTU, four nominees from affiliated unions, one nominee from Belfast Trades Council, two nominees from voluntary organisations working in the areas of housing and the unemployed. That year Maria Graham (NIC ICTU) joined the Management Committee.

15. Avilla Kilmurry went on to work just as assiduously as Director of NIVT, founder member of the NI Women's Coalition Party, quietly making a substantial contribution to the creation of a working peace process – politically and at community level.

16. *Belfast Telegraph* Business Telegraph, 30 January 1996, p. 24.

CHAPTER 7

1996–97: Strategic Development to Change Organisations

From its initial role of crisis management and 'fire-fighting' Counteract was increasingly involved in preventive or 'fire-proofing' measures – and this was becoming more widely recognised as essential in both workplace and community settings. The unmistakable reality of sectarian hatred and violence was no longer being denied by employers and managers, particularly after the experience of Drumcree 1996 – when swathes of the business and public sector were forced to close days early for the annual 12th July holidays. Few could deny that this directly impacted on relationships at work.

In 1996 a number of significant developments changed public perceptions and the progress of the peace process. At the start of the year the Chief Constable of the RUC Sir Hugh Annesley said the IRA was responsible for the spate of killings claimed by 'Direct Action Against Drugs' that winter. The Mitchell Report was published, stating that there was an obligation on the part of all those holding illegal weapons to de-commission. However, paramilitary organisations would not de-commission before there were all-party talks. The report called for confidence-building measures and the setting up of an elected body with an appropriate mandate.

In public and in private, meetings between the governments and parties continued. On February 9th while UUP MP Ken Maginnis and Sinn Féin's Mitchell McLaughlin were debating on live BBC TV, the IRA bombed Canary Wharf and the cease-fire was broken. Bitter recriminations came from all round. In the short term, the reaction of Loyalists was very restrained, and peace of a sort held – albeit in great tension. Security in Northern Ireland was stepped up immediately and the Irish government pressurised Sinn Féin to produce a permanent cease-fire.

In a year that could have marked the beginning of substantive peace negotiations, events began badly with the Canary Wharf bomb. Protests and rallies took place across Northern Ireland where calls were made for a return of peace, calls to *Give us back our peace* were recited from platforms. Four thousand people attended a peace rally at Belfast City Hall organised within days by ICTU and Counteract, and widely supported by government bodies. A peace group collected more than half a million signatures calling for the cease-fire to be reinstated.

Splinter Loyalist groups threatened more sectarian murder in March but the CLMC asserted firmly that the Loyalist cease-fire would stay in place. The INLA declared its 'tactical' cease-fire was at an end. In London, government introduced the Prevention of Terrorism (Additional Powers) Bill and increased police powers of search. Despite Labour abstaining, the Bill became law immediately.

Throughout April and May tensions were very high but with Sinn Féin accepting the Mitchell principles, elections to all-party negotiations went ahead. New parties were in the minority but drew sufficient electoral support to be included. Thus, the UDP, PUP, UKUP and the Women's Coalition all had their say in the peace negotiations over the coming year. Inclusiveness and interdependence became the language of mainstream politics in Northern Ireland, however disagreeable that was to some of the participants and those, like the DUP who boycotted the talks.

John Bruton kept up the pressure on Sinn Féin to declare an 'unconditional and irrevocable cease-fire' as Unionists complained about the chairmanship of George Mitchell. Negotiations, however, were beginning for real.

July brought what would become an annual mass protest at Drumcree. The murder of a Catholic taxi driver by the UVF set the tone for a bloody and tumultuous summer. All Unionist party leaders negotiating on Drumcree took a hard line that the march should be allowed through despite local Nationalist opinion. Loyalists blockaded roads and towns, closing businesses and transport systems. This widespread protest was seen as an echo of the 1974 Ulster Workers Strike – which had brought down the power-sharing government after the Sunningdale Agreement. So, a thousand extra troops were brought into Northern Ireland, and the

Orange Order march was allowed through – to the outrage of John Bruton's government and Nationalists. The fact that TV news showed the leaders of both the DUP and UUP dancing down the Garvaghy Road holding hands only increased the bitterness felt by Nationalists and Republicans.

Rioting in Nationalist areas spread throughout Northern Ireland, lasting for some days. The SDLP withdrew from the Northern Ireland Forum, the IRA blew up a hotel in Fermanagh and Sir Patrick Mayhew announced that Dr Peter North would lead the new Parades and Marches Review.

Amidst the tensions, recriminations and 'bunkering down', splits in Loyalism became apparent. The CLMC ordered extremists in their ranks to leave Northern Ireland, though the Rev Willie McCrea was still happy to appear on a platform with the well-known paramilitary leader, Billy Wright. At the end of August Ronnie Flanagan was named as the next Chief Constable of the RUC signalling the potential for a new era in policing. After this the DUP began to publicly demonise fringe Loyalist parties.

Autumn brought a more measured party-political response as Labour spokesperson on Northern Ireland, Mo Mowlam met Loyalist prisoners in the Maze prison, as did David Trimble some days later. Orange Order and Loyalist reaction to events was clear and uncompromising, as picketing of Catholic churches continued on a sustained basis. In November 1996 the Poppy became an issue when a BBC news presenter was publicly censured for not wearing a poppy on screen reading the news.

As the year came to a close Sir Patrick Mayhew announced a £120 million investment package for Northern Ireland, underwriting the economic as well as the political importance of peace negotiations. Shortly before Christmas the IRA wounded a policeman guarding the child of Nigel Dodds MP (DUP) inside the Royal Belfast Hospital for Sick Children. Two days later a prominent Republican was wounded by a Loyalist booby-trap under his car.

Statistics for 1996 show: Deaths: 15. Shootings: 125. Bombs planted: 25. Incendiaries: 4. Firearms found: 98. Explosives found: 1,677 kg (3,700 lb.). Persons charged with terrorist and serious public order offences: 595. Casualties arising from paramilitary attacks: 326.

*   *   *   *   *

The combined efforts, thinking, collaboration and progress made by Counteract, with its partners, trade unions, funders and sponsors had started a sea change in the workplace agenda. Primarily the anti-intimidation unit was there to focus on the workplace, and originally only through the trade union movement. Progress and public demand were about to alter this restricted remit.

The business case for fighting prejudice and sectarian intimidation at work was established and now community and voluntary groups wanted to know how to deal with these problems on the ground. Counteract had evolved from crisis management into helping workers, managers and the voluntary sector develop proactive methods. These preventive measures were now welcomed as both necessary and fundamental to managing working and community relationships – and integral to what Europe called Peace and Reconciliation.

Clear connections between intimidation, violence and sectarian conflict on the streets and workplace relationships were now more accepted, which was key to developing Counteract and its work.

The restoration of the IRA and Loyalist cease-fires generated a popular but short-lived opinion that 'peace' would bring an end to sectarian attacks, on workers and in the community. Counteract argued strongly against this view, prefacing their Annual report with the assertion that Sectarianism dictates the quality of all our lives:

> Too much of a generalization? Consider these questions.
>
> Where do you work? What area do you live in? What sports do you play and which clubs do you support? Where do your children go to school? Do you have any friends or colleagues whose religion you don't know? Where do you buy your groceries? What do Harryville, Dunloy, Drumcree, and Garvaghy Road mean to you?
>
> If you have not found sectarian reasons in any of your answers you don't live in the real world. Sectarianism has dictated our lives from the moment we were born, if not before. It has made our parents socially accepted or isolated. It has determined who our first friends would be, commanded our allegiances in play and sport, and decreed our 'colour' from the very first.
>
> Sectarianism dictates – it orders us and puts an order on our lives. It orders where we can and can't go for a quiet night out. It puts an order on how and with whom we can live in peace. It has ordered which schools we would attend, and which routes we might safely take to work. It has put an order onto our adult life, and what we

could expect. It is still ordering us about – and our children and grandchildren. It effects the quality of life for everyone in Northern Ireland.

Widespread intimidation throughout 1996 led to a dramatic increase in the demand for Counteract services. Deplorable though the causes were, it brought about a certain if reluctant admission that ultimately sectarian intimidation had to be challenged across the board. Stark realities could not be denied, especially in the wake of the violence around the Drumcree protests of 1996. Counteract had a clear message – there are ways to address intimidation and sectarianism, but they must be adopted properly.

*   *   *   *   *

Counteract continued its work with unions giving seminars, workshops and speakers at various events,[1] and interesting questions came from these. Could Trade Unions discuss the conflict of ideas in the workplace and community? The answer was a resounding YES, because trade Unionists were trained to discuss ideas, to negotiate and compromise. When the same question was asked about the possibility of discussing conflict arising from feelings in the workplace and/or community there was a resounding NO. This demonstrated the need to include training on how to deal with feelings – because most conflicts arose out of feelings because intimidation and harassment were about how people were feeling. They felt marginalised, they felt intimidated, they felt harassed, isolated, afraid, humiliated and so on. Counteract would soon be reaching the stage where the bywords for tackling prejudice and inequality were 'fear, feelings and lack of trust'.

In April 1996 Billy Robinson and Brendan Mackin met George McKay of the Gorbels Unemployed Centre and Bill Spiers from the Scottish TUC to discuss how an organisation like Counteract could be set up in Glasgow. Sadly, there was a consensus that there was 'no problem'. This was despite the fact that when discussion on racism had turned towards sectarianism, it was readily admitted that sectarianism was rife. For instance, NCA was an organisation where its acronym was known in the vernacular as standing for 'No Catholics Apply'. It seems that there was just not enough interest in taking things forward. Initiatives started tackling sectarianism in football in Scotland some years later. UK-wide there was recognition of the sectarian significance of supporting Liverpool, Man United as well as Rangers and Celtic and that sectarianism and racism in sport needed serious attention. There was no progress as was clear when, five years later, the Irish premier Bertie Ahern postponed a trip to Glasgow for 'security reasons'[2] because of sectarianism surrounding the Celtic-Rangers football match.

The ICTU and the International Labour Organisation facilitated a conference, *Societies in Civil Conflict: The Role of Trade Unions* to include representatives from Bosnia, Mozambique, Palestine and Northern Ireland. It considered the role of trade unionists and their possible contribution in resolving civil conflicts in their societies. The diversity of participants added considerably to positive reciprocal learning. Despite exchanges being slowed down by the need for interpretation, language barriers did not present insurmountable problems. If NIC ICTU had ever needed vindication for creating a proactive anti-intimidation unit it had a resounding endorsement there, as Northern Ireland was clearly greatly in advance of other unions in Europe and further afield.

*   *   *   *   *

More employers, both public and private, asked Counteract to train staff. There was a shift from training management and senior staff only, to employers placing greater importance on training blue-collar workers. Companies already had policies and procedures in place and they made their workers aware of this by producing company handbooks and so on. However, a common concern was whether or not employees read the material provided. If so, did they understand what harassment/intimidation really meant? Some basic practical work was still needed even by more enlightened employers.

Allied Bakeries and Glen Electrics in Newry used Counteract for training seminars to shop floor workers. Counteract provided training seminars to Ulsterbus-Citybus-NI Railways alongside the FEC. The NI Ambulance Service, NIE and Golden Vale, Coleraine bought training. Counteract was asked to make a presentation to 500 pupils in St Louise's Secondary School. The Department of Agriculture asked for detailed costing on providing training seminars to 850 staff and a meeting was arranged at the request of BT about buying a supply of training videos for their use in team briefs.

At this time Counteract had started training seminars for trainers in the RUC. Policing had been a political issue throughout Northern Ireland's history. The RUC had traditionally been seen as, and recruited from, a predominantly Protestant-Unionist section of the population. There had also been much publicity and some serious criticisms surrounding the summary of the Stevens Report in May 1990, which declared that there was not institutional sectarianism and that collusion with Loyalist paramilitaries had been limited (subsequently more incriminating findings were reached and made public). The RUC had been found wanting by the Fair Employment Tribunal in the Neeson V Securicor Case (1993). The relationship between the RUC and Counteract is therefore of both historical and political importance.

Billy Robinson was invited to give a session in three RUC Trainers' courses. Inspector Cindy Mackie was at those sessions and continued to be a key contact with Counteract. She had completed the Future Ways course at UU where she experienced at first hand the Counteract approach to sectarianism and harassment and was impressed with the courage and conviction of the presentation, and the candour of Counteract. Where others have made anti-harassment into a profit-making business Counteract remained committed to its values and displayed great integrity. It was apparent that Billy Robinson was talking from experience on the street, and he gripped his audience.

Ronnie Flanagan's leadership as Chief Constable, signalled a new era for policing and training, not least in equality and diversity. Counteract was to be brought in, like others with expertise,[3] as co-facilitator as the RUC Training put together an equal opportunities programme for all its officers, both for new recruits and those with service reaching from two to thirty years. This was effective because there was a 'champion for change' at the top and the will to drive through change from the highest level.

Counteract made a submission to a Working Party, *The Underrepresentation of Women, Roman Catholics and Minority Groups within the RUC*. As ever, their position challenged the received wisdom that Catholics did not join the police simply because they were intimidated by Republicans in their own community. Counteract cited the sectarian treatment of Catholics in the RUC as a major part of the problem.

In practical terms the Counteract video was the most effective tool for RUC trainers and was used in training 6000 police men and women over a seven-week period. The video was part of training at grass roots, in RUC stations throughout Northern Ireland. It formed part of the first module of the 'Policing with the Community' programme, and was to be embedded in the ongoing RUC development and promotion process.

Counteract materials were used to inform officers about prejudice and harassment and provide an awareness of perceptions that need to be re-formed or better informed. Priests and ministers from churches were used to answer officers' questions about religious beliefs, practices and to help dispel myths about 'the other side'.

The object in this training was to address equality and diversity – as both internal to the RUC and in relation to policing and the community. The value of the video was its relevance to everyday policing and perceptions – 'there is nothing else like it here' – and its stories could be studied in the framework of formal training modules.[4] From the video, examples were used to bring to life the sophisticated models and theories at the core of this training.

Equality, community and race relations training was central to attempts at transforming the culture of the RUC in the late 1990s. It was provided for Assistant Chief Constables and throughout the ranks, and intentionally to change perceptions that influence the policing of 'normal' incidents.

Specific anti-sectarian training became a mainstay in RUC training and was woven into the fabric of programmes, as policy was made operational and integrated into formal training and assessment, and monitoring. Police training had to be progressed on five counts – knowledge, understanding, skills, behaviour and attitude. Each of these was a vital part to equality and anti-harassment training. Not only was training assessed and directed by the national Police Training Council, but also there were strategic directions from HM Inspectorate of Constabularies and ACPO which had to be adhered to. In meeting these standards and new targets the RUC saw the need to bring in external trainers – for many years – and engaged Counteract as a training provider and consultant organisation (among others, it has to be said).

Later, when all examinations for RUC promotion were assessed by National Police Council personnel, the Counteract video was still given to assessors[5] from Harrogate, in England, to familiarise them with sectarianism and harassment in Northern Ireland. Counteract materials and services were used in police work in communities as well. It was not just the information that Counteract provided but the experience of their methods of educating people. Lessons learned from the early days working with Derek Wilson and Frank Wright and Trade Unions had given Counteract an edge – without blunting its somewhat confrontational approach.

The relationship with the RUC was mutually beneficial. Both Counteract and the police gained. The RUC found Counteract welcoming at a time when many organisations would not openly work with them. And Counteract gained credibility in its work with the police. Superintendent Cindy Mackie regarded them as courageous for the work in those more difficult days.

Even in retrospect Billy Robinson underplayed the courage needed in this work:

> One difficult issue for the management committee was a request to provide training for the RUC in the period before the cease-fire and the Good Friday agreement. Counteract was asked to provide sectarian awareness training to their trainers at police headquarters.

> At that time a request like this was politically sensitive. It would have been wrong for me to make a decision on my own without the committee having an input into the final decision, so I brought the request to the committee for their decision. The initial decision was to say no, for obvious political considerations. I outlined the danger of such a decision in that Counteract was an anti-sectarian organization, established by the ICTU to address sectarianism in the workplace. I asked the question 'is there sectarianism within the RUC?' And if so, 'is it a work place?' The answer was a resounding 'yes'. Concern was expressed around my personal security. I said I was prepared to take the risk as to do otherwise may be construed as sectarian, thus signaling the end of Counteract. The committee agreed and we started working with the RUC.

> The problem of introducing the question of diversity and ant-sectarianism into the RUC was the culture of the organization. At that time only approximately 8% members were from the Roman Catholic community. Since the establishment of the RUC it had been seen by the Catholic community as a paramilitary organization, established to support and maintain a Protestant government and suppress the Catholic community. The Protestant community, on the other hand, saw the police as their main defense against a takeover by the Republic of Ireland and the Roman Catholic

Church. The organization was also very strongly structured militarily. Clearly the history of the State and the political divisions within had a major influence on the attitude of both sections in the community. Therefore, one can understand the culture that would be held within the organization.

One of the main problems in providing training was that people were instructed to attend – it wasn't a matter of choice.

Initially we were involved with the police training division and new recruits. Our observations were, that in a majority of cases the subject was approached by participants to some degree with tongue in cheek. We had an opportunity to have a conversation with the chief constable Ronnie Flanagan when we were invited to a Christmas reception in Police Head Quarters. On that occasion Mr Flanagan thanked us for working with the RUC in these difficult times. I stated we were pleased to provide any assistance we could to progress change within the RUC, but I pointed out that we can train all the young men and women you can give us on diversity and anti- sectarianism, but when they are dispersed to various police stations, inevitably the existing police officers will say 'Forget whatever you heard. We will tell you what is the real world here.' In other words, you have to change the culture and the only way to do that is to retire some officers, put others on non- operational duties, and make it quite clear that to gain promotion they have to show clearly they embrace the whole question of equality to each community.

On reflection looking back over that period a number of questions come to mind. In 1996 Counteract was invited to provide training sessions firstly to RUC trainers then to new recruits. At this time Ronnie Flanagan had become the Chief Constable. His leadership ushered in a new era for police training particularly in the area of equality, diversity, community and race relations. It became central to transforming the culture of the RUC in the late 1990s. This was before the Patton Commission when reform of the RUC was a major political debate, with questions around the acceptability of the RUC in Republican areas, the need to change the name and recruitment arrangements – all these made for protracted and difficult discussions.

To support what must have been preparations for these changes there had to be some ground work in preparing for a massive change in the mind set of people. The question I have been asked since then is, 'Did I think that the sole reason for Counteract being invited to train the RUC was because of our great training skills or was there another motive?'

A decade later he put his thoughts into words:

Counteract engaged with the police and security forces when others were being shot for that. So why were we not shot? Did the IRA not know we were going into Police Headquarters? People who were simply delivering milk to police stations were being shot. I am quite sure they were aware of our activities. The point is nothing happens by accident there is a lot of preparation required to create a change in people's attitude. The question hangs: was there an agreement between the Government and Sinn Féin to work towards creating the conditions or doing some proper work prior to the Patton Commission? Because of its Trade Union background was Counteract acceptable to both the RUC and Sinn Féin?

It is inconceivable that the IRA did not know where Counteract was working and there is no question that Billy Robinson risked his life taking on that job. What events and agreements operated in the shadows of peace negotiations cannot be evidenced in this book – but it is clear that only Counteract could have delivered the hard-hitting anti-sectarian message, and Billy Robinson knew the risks.

*   *   *   *   *

It was apparent that, while developing organisational or company policies, procedures and providing training was important, it was not enough to create a neutral working environment, let alone a harmonious workplace. At the policy and procedure stage real change was only beginning. Fear would continue to force people to conform to the old sectarian divisions and behaviour. Employers needed to provide support and visible commitment to eradicate this fear and ultimately to embed an anti-sectarian ethos within their organisation.

Counteract was clear. Creating an anti-sectarian ethos was as important as good Health and Safety practice in work, and must be taken seriously. Business would not prosper simply because a mission statement was written up. A company might even have all the right ingredients but these were only building blocks for the structures, relationships and processes that enable the creation of an anti-sectarian ethos:

- Anti-sectarian Policy and Procedure
- Joint declaration of protection signed by the company/unions
- Implementation of all procedures
- Management Commitment – at the highest level
- Permanent agenda item at Board meetings
- Item of agenda on team briefs/quality circles
- Equality Committees
- Training for all existing staff, follow through training and evaluation

- Anti-sectarian training within induction training for new employees
- Two-way communications between staff/management
- Continual review and monitoring of policies and procedures

Like creating a Health and Safety ethos, it would demand commitment and continuous attention:

> You wouldn't create a Health and Safety Policy and then let it sit gathering dust on a shelf. You would know better than to risk industrial injury, court cases costing time, money and bad PR for your company, wouldn't you? So, neither can you take a 'quick fix' approach to anti-sectarian work.[6]

*   *   *   *   *

At this juncture Counteract had two people employed in the Community Unit.[7] Joe Law was Trainer/Development Officer and Paul Oakes was Administrator/Collator. They developed as more and more organisations asked for their help. The Community Unit played a central part in a Community Inquiry Panel in North Belfast, which had been set up to look at the incidents over the summer period of 1996 – with widespread rioting and violence emanating from the Drumcree protests. The panel took written and oral evidence from a range of sources including community groups, individuals, statutory and other bodies, elected representatives. Meeting and discussing these issues, the problems that were common to many community organisations emerged.

Principally, there was a basic deficiency since some groups had no policies and procedures to deal with sectarianism. For those that did have policies and procedures, these had not been reviewed since they had been written. When it came to Fair Employment legislation, many community groups believed that this did not affect their group – even though some employed up to thirty people.

In response, the Counteract Community Unit organised a conference to examine and discuss the necessity for policies and procedures in voluntary organisations. The main speakers were Professor Mari Fitzduff, Director of INCORE, Will Glendinning, Director, CRC and Dr Derek Wilson, Future Ways Project, University of Ulster.

Conference delegates said that this was a neglected area that required more attention. They saw they needed an ethos or culture in their organisations that accepted diversity and differences in cultural identity – but they didn't know how to achieve this. That was the first occasion such a wide spectrum of community-based groups and organisations had been given the opportunity to discuss these issues. It would be repeated.

Counteract Community Unit distributed the *Action Against Intimidation Information & Advice Manual* to all CROs, and held discussions with many community-based groups, encouraging them to adopt the recording system[8] contained in the Advice Manual. They also produced and distributed 5,000 copies of Counteract *Community Newsletter* to community/voluntary groups, youth groups, church groups, trade unions, housing groups and associations, politicians and the press. They set up a research reference library on issues of intimidation and sectarianism. Paul Oakes was establishing the new unit's research database and in discussions with the CABx, District Councils, Churches, Community Groups and so on, promoting the recording system.

In its first working year the Community Unit provided training across the voluntary sector of Northern Ireland.[9] It was involved in a joint initiative with the Housing Rights Service and Law Centre NI providing four two-day seminars throughout Northern Ireland for advice workers in community and voluntary organisations. These aimed to raise awareness of sectarianism and encourage sensitivity when dealing with people looking for advice after incidents of intimidation, and to help workers get the relevant information on housing and funding sources.

Housing has always been – and sadly remains – at the crux of sectarian politics and intimidation in the community, and therefore it was a vital element in the work of the Community Unit. Open Door, Chichester House and Oaklee Housing Association got the unit to provide policy statements and develop procedures with housing managers on neighbourhood and similar disputes. They also asked for training for hostel staff to encourage tenants' awareness in creating a neutral living environment. The Housing Rights Service started developing a training programme then, too.

Counteract Community Unit had an Advisory Panel. This included Maria Graham (ICTU), Janet Hunter (Housing Rights Service), Dr Robbie

McVeigh (Campaign for Research & Development), Will Glenndinning (CRC), Jeff Maxwell (Base 2), Brendan McAllister (Mediation Network), Karen Snoddy (Shankill Women's Centre/ Shankill Women's Network), Derek Alcorn (ASA/NIACAB), Patrick Yu (NICEM), Bob Strong (Association of Independent Advice Centres) and Niall Fitzduff (RCN).

*   *   *   *   *

On another front Counteract was still planning work with young people. CYPHER[10] had been conceived as Counteract Youth Programme on Human & Equality Relations as most young people lived and were educated in a single-identity community and, when they left school, went into youth training programmes that were also likely to be in their own community. As they got no opportunity to address issues of prejudice and sectarianism they went into work with little or no understanding of how to relate to people of a different background. CYPHER was the product of Counteract and NIACTO. It was designed to deliver training to organisations in Belfast, Londonderry and Newry.

Target groups were thirty to forty Management Committee Members, about a dozen Managers, thirty to forty vocational staff and over one hundred and fifty young people. Training by peer educators was to be on site and residential schools were planned to facilitate exchange of experiences of young people from different backgrounds.

Detailed content[11] was researched and included – on achieving awareness of the dynamics of prejudice and how, in specific settings, these take the form of being racist, sectarian or sexist. It would draw on case studies and role-plays that introduced young people to the experiences of those from different and diverse backgrounds. It built up group projects around diversity, practice of good community understanding, gender relations and workplace employee relations. The young trainees would get to experience the concepts of mediation and conflict resolution and develop an understanding of how conflicts emerge and how to distance themselves from rivalries and tensions.

In addressing diversity to help reduce potential conflict at work CYPHER would be valuable[12] to managers, trainers and employers. It would also improve employment opportunities for young people by helping them to consider work across a wider spectrum because of being better equipped to integrate in a mixed workforce. Yet still the negotiations for funding dragged out.

Disappointment was palpable when the T&EA decided against funding CYPHER within 18 months (and hence the entire financing fell through). However, as Billy McCreight recollected, in the end that intention to mainstream anti-sectarian training for young people succeeded. T&EA got its training providers and agencies to give just this kind of training, so that irrespective of who claimed ownership, the change happened and some difference made. Counteract was more concerned to have positive effect than to claim credit, and it was more than sufficient that they could see government approval for anti-sectarian training being enacted.

Further afield, that autumn Billy Robinson attended a two-week training programme at Fordham University, New York, on conflict resolution and mediation. After returning from New York participants met under the auspices of the Study of Conflict to identify where mediation could be developed. This programme was seen by the press as warranting an article on the front page of the New York Times Metro Section.

* * * * *

As the range of Counteract work with employers expanded, so too did the possibility of conflicting interests. If Counteract had been involved with a company that later had to face Tribunal proceedings, it might well be cited as evidence of good management practice – in opposition to the worker's case. This was a considerable conflict of interest for a Trade Union sponsored organisation. One example is that Counteract had been involved with Allied Bakeries about an incident of sectarian harassment on the shop floor. The company sought Counteract help in mediating this matter with an apparently successful outcome. Later, however, the victim lodged a formal complaint. Counteract was asked by Allied Bakeries' solicitors to provide a statement of any discussions that took place. Counteract then had to get legal advice and representation. In the event the case was settled without Counteract having a problem. However, it was a salutary experience.

* * * * *

Following Counteract representation on a visit to Denmark, the Employers' Federation & Trade Unions of Danish Industry came to

Belfast. This was the first of several visits to Counteract. They were welcomed to a dinner with Counteract, committee, staff and guests.

In Committee two paragraphs from the ICTU report were read out,
recorded in minutes and filed for future evaluations.

- *The work of 'Counteract' in Northern Ireland generated a lot of interest
  among the other participants. There was general agreement that access
  by trade unions to such a resource is very valuable and that the approach
  'Counteract' takes to its work is very constructive and could be adapted to
  other civil conflict situations.*
- *The 'Counteract' initiative set up by the ICTU was judged to set an important example in how trade unions can try to resolve conflict.*

On the housekeeping front Billy McCreight had drafted a report on accommodation for Counteract staff, increasing in number and in need
of more space. All agreed that alternative accommodation was required.
Soon they were moving to a larger office (upstairs) in the Unemployed
Centre. This was timely as core funding for an additional worker had
been secured and Paul Burke came on board.

Against the wider political scene, as 1996 ended and the early months
of 1997 unfolded, the key questions for activists and trade Unionists were
'Would there be a victory for New Labour?' and 'Would that bring a New
Politics to Northern Ireland?'

Notes

1. In 1996–97 they delivered talks and had workshops to ATGWU, CWU, MSF,
   SIPTU and AEU. In that period, they provided a stall and spoke at confer-
   ences: CWU (Blackpool and Jersey), ICTU Youth Conference (on Xenophobia
   & Racism in Dublin), ILO (Dublin) Specialarbejderforb undet Trade Union of
   Denmark, Scottish trade Union Council (Glasgow), NI Women's Coalition, and
   Youth Conference on Cross-border Co-operation (Co. Cavan).
2. In February 2001 the SMP involved in advising Dublin resigned within days, such
   was the sensitivity of the issue.

3. RUC Training programmes included input from organisations like NICEM, Women's Aid, Rape Crisis and Disability Action.

4. At that time the RUC's Training Support and Development provided training in equal opportunities, community and race relations for all officers up to NVQ level 3, and was licensed by the Institute of Personnel Development – entailing Quality Assurance.

5. Part one of the promotion examinations was on Law & Procedure. Part two was objective structured exercises which included equality and diversity as core competences.

6. Foreword to 1996–97 Annual Report.

7. The Community Unit was financially supported by European Regional Development Fund – Physical & Social Environment Programme, Central Community Relations Unit.

8. The recording system was a useful idea, but ultimately the information was not in a compatible form for use with other statistics, and so was superseded.

9. They provided training to Oaklee Housing Association, Leonard Cheshire Homes, Youth Link, Kilrea Inter Community Group, Prisoners and Probation Officers at Magaberry Prison, Newry & Mourne, Derry, Lisburn and Omagh Councils, NICEM, National Union of Students/Union of Students in Ireland, Springfield Development Association and the Women's Network.

10. £53,000 was offered to the CYPHER project by donors who wanted no recognition but would give their support privately. Payment was contingent on Counteract raising the remaining 75% of matching funding from the European programme fund Proteus.

11. Partners for the Project were Dr Duncan Morrow, Dr Derek Wilson, Karin Eyben, Future Ways Programme, Centre for the Study of Conflict, University of Ulster, John McVicar, NIACTO, Rosemary Ruddy, Tutor, Belfast Unemployed Resource Centre.

12. CYPHER's value was planned to contribute by helping reduce the negative costs to industry in terms of loss of efficiency, productivity, absenteeism due to flawed relationships. Counteract aimed to develop, accredit and improve anti-prejudice training for young people so that it would become mainstreamed in youth training programmes.

CHAPTER 8

1997: The Poppy and Black Ribbon Disputes

In February 1997 the IRA murdered Stephen Restorick the last British soldier killed in the Northern Ireland conflict. John Hume was reported in the *Irish News* as strongly rejecting a pact with Sinn Féin and demanding an unequivocal IRA cease-fire. That newspaper also reported that a Catholic civil servant, awarded damages for sectarian harassment, had been moved from her post, while the person responsible remained as Baroness Denton's private secretary, against good practice guidelines.

In March Gerry Adams gave an RTE television interview in which he acknowledged the growth of the concerned residents' groups had been the result of three years effort by Republicans and praised those who had done the work. This fuelled the anger and paranoia of many Unionists and muddied the waters for the SDLP.

May 1st was truly a Labour Day as Tony Blair's 'new' Labour swept to power with a huge majority, signalling changes in the working of the peace talks and political economy in Northern Ireland. Mo Mowlam became Secretary of State for Northern Ireland. In June the Irish elections put Bertie Ahern into government with the Progressive Democrats and Belfast got its first Nationalist Lord Mayor, Alban Maginness.

George Mitchell put the deadlocked negotiations on hold until early June. Mo Mowlam declared that a permanent cease-fire from the IRA would ensure a place for Sinn Féin in the talks. The IRA responded a few days later by stopping the Aintree Grand National horse race for the first time in its long history, with a bomb scare. Loyalist paramilitary Billy Wright was transferred to another prison as the UVF would not accept him in their block.

As Garvaghy Road residents and the Orange Order called each other insincere, proposed talks about the forthcoming march in Portadown failed to materialise, and the LVF threatened to kills civilians in the Republic if the march was not let through. After a Twelfth of July fortnight of violence, and small compromises on all sides, the IRA announced the restoration of their cease-fire. Sinn Féin representatives were back in Castle Buildings within days and the DUP and UKUP withdrew permanently from the peace negotiations.

August saw more signs of UVF-LVF conflict with the trashing of a Portadown bar used by LVF supporters. Mo Mowlam told the House of Commons that she accepted the IRA cease-fire as genuine and shortly afterwards Sinn Féin signed up to the Mitchell Principles. Fringe Loyalist parties joined the negotiations in September and all-party talks began despite UUP demands that Sinn Féin be expelled until de-commissioning took place. At the end of the month, Mo Mowlam announced that internment would be taken off the statute books.

Tensions were still rising within Loyalism, as the PUP failed to send representatives to a UDA rally marking the third anniversary of the Loyalist cease-fire. The CLMC was disbanded that month. Protesters from the UUP left Stormont for the day to mark strong opposition to the refusal of the Republic's government to remove articles 2 and 3 from their constitution (i.e. the articles claiming territorial rights over Northern Ireland). In that October Professor Mary McAleese, a Belfast-born lawyer and academic, was elected President of the Republic. In the final weeks of 1997, the Forum for Peace and Reconciliation held its first session for nearly two years, in Dublin. Violent feuding within the Loyalist camp continued. At that time Republicans opposing the peace negotiations formed the 32 County Sovereignty Committee – working as the 'Continuity IRA'. The Leader of the LVF, Billy Wright was shot dead in the Maze prison and hours later a former Republican prisoner was killed.

In 1997 deaths arising from the Troubles were 22. Shootings: 225. Bombs planted: 93. Incendiaries: 9. Firearms found: 105. Explosives found: 1,258 kg (2,775 lb.). Persons charged with terrorist and serious public order offences: 405. Casualties arising from paramilitary attacks: 228.

*   *   *   *   *

By 1997 it was clear that Counteract should review its strategy to make the most effective use of its resources. Responding to immediate demands (fire-fighting) produced only short-lived results, and more lasting solutions were needed as part of longer-term change. Employers and organisations needed to enhance their own induction and training packages. Efforts needed to be concentrated on capacity building, facilitating and increasing knowledge and skills within other organisations so they could deliver and develop their own training programmes – which brought about the beginnings of *Training for Trainers*.

Counteract would identify organisations and groups that wanted training and give them accredited training. This was the *Training for Trainers*[1] project. It would produce self-sustaining support for organisations tackling sectarianism, and a pool of trainer-facilitators and an innovative programme with developed educational resource materials. That proved to be a long-term goal that Counteract continued to work on.

Although the guidelines did not go into print for another two years Counteract used the material in its training. *Trainers Guidelines* listed a series of pointers about its method of training and the relationship between trainer and trainee, at a time when people were sometimes reluctant, if not hostile to training. These included

- Establishing credibility with the participants. Demonstrating that you know what you are talking about and that you are not some sort of idiot;
- Being aware of (and, ideally, informed about) the professional context of participants as you may be providing a professional life line to some of them. Knowing where these people are coming from. You have to be able to 'feel' an audience and whether they are comfortable, hostile or feel trapped;
- Creating a sense of purpose – that this is important work and demands active participation if not commitment;
- Understanding potential conflict of interests – a personnel manager will have a different agenda to the shop floor worker;
- Your role as a trainer requires that you challenge prejudices and engage in hostile arguments when they arise – you are not there to make friends with everybody. People may be wary and resistant and hostile to being 'told' what to do;
- Remembering that people already know a lot of what you'll say. Beware the god complex, you are not the fountain of knowledge;

- Not dominating the debate. Being an active listener. Don't silence people unnecessarily, but be wary of wafflers and saboteurs;
- Confirming the value of participants' input and encourage discussion (but remembering that personal revelations can be difficult to deal with);
- It is vital that everyone understands that the course is in their interests. Providing space for people to express anxiety, resistance and hostility can be the single most effective way of getting people to take training seriously;
- If people are defensive, recognising the need to open up what may initially be a confrontation with some or all the training group. In anti-sectarian work, we avoid such (potentially constructive) confrontations at our peril;
- Remembering that you will be faced with a group of people who feel that your presence is an implicit judgement and they may resent what they feel is outside interference;

And they now had the video package *The Inside Stories*, which was a resource for Counteract trainers but it was also designed for organisations that preferred to deliver their own training. So, they were also training these trainers to use the video package.

It was a break through when the Institute of Personnel Development (IPD) arranged three Counteract sessions using *Trainers Guidelines* in Ballymena that November.

*   *   *   *   *

The *Youth Against Prejudice* campaign began in October 1997 with a Counteract-NICEM conference in Queen's University Belfast. In the first event of its kind, representatives came from youth organisations across Northern Ireland to address the issues of racism and sectarianism. The young people kept proceedings informal and discussions were forthright – this was not the usual subdued and polite ecumenical roundtable. Mo Mowlam spoke at conference and spent a lot of time with the young people before leaving (see Picture 11).

Sectarianism and anti-racist work were the subjects, about which everyone knew. The conference exposed not only the need for anti-racist work but also the less popular fact that the cohesion of Chinese community made them overly protective of their young people, and isolated them further.

Picture 11: Mo Mowlam at Counteract Youth Conference, Queen's University Belfast

Counteract used their experience from a previous session with young people[2] where the topic was approached indirectly by asking people's opinions on what they thought of people from Ballymunn,[3] Kerry, Cork, the McCooeys from Belfast. It revealed prejudice in their perceptions of people who were their neighbours, fellow Irish and so on. From that understanding of what 'perceptions' and 'prejudice' meant, the group went on to discuss how they felt and thought about race issues. Did they have any friends or contact with non-Irish or non-white people?

Approaching racism through their personal experience and perceptions drew out the working of prejudice and let the group analyse prejudice based on their own understanding, and their experience and knowledge of their own community. An indication of how effective the session had been was the fact that it overran, by active consent of the group, by two hours.

Examples of racism had come out as that discussion dug deeper. One young woman talked about how her sister could only go out with her boyfriend at night for fear of repeated racist attacks because he was black. It had started with her own family but even when they accepted him, the local community did not.

Counteract started working with young people but, for lack of time and resources, they could not develop it. It might have been used as pilot work that other agencies could usefully take on board. Indeed, Counteract and Arthur Coldrick, from AC Network did submit a project proposal to IFI for Counteract to deliver awareness training (in dealing with prejudice, racism and conflict) to organisations on both sides of the border. After enlarging and fine-tuning the planned project over two years, they succeeded.[4] Nothing happened quickly in Counteract work – unless it was a serious workplace crisis – and funding was always a fundamental obstacle to the progress that they envisaged.

*   *   *   *   *

Counteract still had close working relations with CRC and Billy Robinson continued on their Council. Support and help from CRC staff remained a mainstay for Counteract, as did its relationship with the FEC – with whom they still developed and delivered joint training seminars to various employers and organisations.

A common feature of sectarian intimidation was the use of 'innocent' emblems to signify the power of an opposing viewpoint. Flags and football shirts were recognised as a way of political and religious bullying and were not allowed in workplaces where management exercised good practice. The more this behaviour was dragged out of the denial zone and recognised, the more subtle the means and versions of coat-trailing became. The wearing of colours was one example, and in the form of ribbons that emerged as a serious area of contention in Desmond's factory in Derry/Londonderry.

Front-page headlines of the *Belfast Telegraph*[5] in March read 'Emblems Crisis Talks. Bid to end sectarian rows in Derry Factory'. The report went on

Business leaders in Londonderry were meeting today in a bid to resolve the controversy over the wearing of emblems in the workplace. The meeting at St Columb's Park House was due to be attended by many of the North West's major employers, along with representatives from economic development groups. The meeting was organised by the Community Relations Council in conjunction with Counteract to address a number of issues including the recent row over the wearing of the Bloody Sunday black ribbons.

A council spokesman voiced the concerns of all involved. The report continued

> Earlier this year the mediation group Counteract was called into Desmond's clothing manufacturers in Newbuildings to help resolve a bitter dispute between Catholic and Protestant workers. The row erupted after Catholic workers wore black ribbons and held a two minutes' silence to commemorate the victims of Bloody Sunday. The move infuriated Protestant workers who claimed to be intimidated by the ribbons. They reacted by staging a series of protests in the factory canteen.
>
> Local DUP Councillor Gregory Campbell today gave a guarded welcome to the meeting. He said 'During the Bloody Sunday Commemorations there were a number of incidents in city centre shops and factories where the sense of isolation was horrendous. If genuine moves are going to be made to prevent the wearing of emblems in the workplace, which causes intimidation, then it has to be totally welcomed.

The black ribbon dispute in Desmond's textile company was presented as a struggle between supporters of Bloody Sunday[6] who were Nationalist and/or Republican and other Protestant and/or Unionist workers. So-called supporters of Bloody Sunday wore black ribbons in work and observed a silence in remembrance of those shot and killed by the British Army in 1971. They were, in fact, hi-jacking an otherwise honourable emblem of remembrance. This was perceived as threatening by others working in the company. Counteract was called into the New Buildings site to mediate.

The wearing of 'simple' black ribbons at the workplace was at the centre of the altercation. As was inevitably the case, when 'simple' emblems of 'respect' were paraded, this indicated that the 'remembrance' had been abused by people wanting to make a statement about an exclusive political allegiance. On this occasion, it was Republicans who wanted to exploit Bloody Sunday as a way of asserting their political strength over Unionist-Protestants in New Buildings – a small predominantly Unionist townland.

Billy Robinson retold the story of how Counteract resolved the crisis, some years later:

> I received an urgent request from Desmond's to visit their factory to discuss a problem by 8.00am the next morning and I cleared my diary to meet at the appointed time. The next morning, I arrived at the factory to find a large mob at the gate with a local political representative and a large group of police officers. I was afforded a police escort through the crowd. Entering the main office, I was met with the director together with all the factory managers and informed that the problem was that a number of workers (Catholics) came to work wearing black ribbons to remember those people shot dead on Bloody Sunday. This caused a reaction from Protestants in the workforce who were demanding that management take action to have the ribbons removed. The Catholics refused to remove them with the result that no one was working until the issue was resolved.
>
> The Protestants occupied the canteen while the Catholics remained at their machines. They were not speaking to each other. Hearing this I thought why did I come up here? What could I do? Where would I start? The managers were standing around the room, and I thought, they are waiting on me waving a magic wand and it would all go away. I asked for a cup of coffee and a copy of the company's policies to create the impression that I knew what I was doing and to give me some thinking time.
>
> My first objective was to get some sort of picture of the culture and strength of political feelings in the factory. So, I arranged a meeting with the trade union reps and from discussions with them I got a clearer understanding of what I was facing. I then asked about the company's policies on displaying emblems in the workplace. Unfortunately, these had not been reviewed in five years and would prove unhelpful in this situation. To compound the problem a few moments later the director received a call from their other factory in another part of the city to inform him that 140 workers in that factory were wearing black ribbons. He responded in frustration and threatened to close the factory if the ribbons were not removed.
>
> I counselled him on the consequences of his actions and the impact that may have on the community – with the potential for escalation, including the destruction of the factory. With the benefit of calm reflection, he rang the factory manager cancelling his previous order. At his request I agreed to go over to that factory to try and negotiate a settlement. Transport was provided and I embarked on a mission into the unknown.
>
> On arrival I discussed the situation with the union representatives. I put it to them that the wearing of the ribbon was causing division amongst the work force. At the conclusion of the meeting I stated that I was going to call a meeting of the workers wearing the ribbon and put a proposal to them. Management agreed to a request to allow those wearing the ribbon to attend a meeting in the canteen.

140 workers attended the meeting and at the outset I illustrated the negative effect the wearing of the ribbon had on their fellow workers. In the course of a very heated debate the rationale for the wearing of the ribbon was that they were simply remembering those people who were shot dead on bloody Sunday. From the outset the trade union reps attempted to direct the debate.

My observations were that there were very strong views in the room – about the shooting by the British army. I decided to take a very direct approach and asked the meeting to recall the reasons why those people who were shot on Bloody Sunday were demonstrating. The response was clear: they were seeking civil rights and equality. I then put it to them 'Would anyone wish to accompany me to the graveyard to witness them turning in their graves, as the action they were engaged on in the factory was contrary to what they had ultimately died for?'

At this, two women passed behind me and whispered that they supported me. I called for a coffee break, during which time I was made aware that there was a young man whose father was shot dead on bloody Sunday. I sought him out and had a conversation with him. He agreed with my analysis and I then asked him if he would just stand a couple of feet to my side when I recalled the meeting – assuring him he'd not have to speak at all. He agreed to my request. I then spoke with the union reps and informed them that I had prepared a proposal for the consideration of the workers. I made it clear that the issue of the wearing the ribbon may escalate into serious conflict in which someone may get hurt or die. However, if the matter was resolved then it had the potential to show the workforce in a very positive light.

I prepared a statement to put to the workers for their approval. 'Although we wish to remember our dead, being aware of what our people were demonstrating for that day, civil rights and equality for all, we do not wish to sully their memory by causing fear and apprehension amongst their fellow workers. Therefore, we will remove the black ribbons.'

When the meeting was recalled the young man stood close by me, and I put the statement to the workers and asked for a show of hands; it was unanimously agreed and the ribbons were removed. Word of this – the discussion and the agreement – was communicated to the other factory and they in turn removed their ribbons.

Addressing 140 people who are involved in conflict in one room is not normally a recommended route to resolving problems. When asked why I took this course of action I outlined that firstly I had to find a quick way to find a resolution. If the conflict had continued beyond the stopping time of the factory the story may have been carried into the community with inevitable distortions and others having an influence for their own political reasons. This would have made it difficult to find a resolution. Positions may have become intractable with the possibility that the factory would come under attack. In calling the workers into the room I was relying on my previous experience as a senior union official within CWU in British Telecom.

> After this the company reviewed its policies and awareness training was provided
> to all their staff. During the training the director approached me to say that three
> women of long-term employment with the company were refusing to attend the
> training as they said they were not sectarian and therefore could see no reason to
> attend. His problem was that they had great credibility with the workforce and
> others may follow their lead and refuse to attend. I suggested to him that as those
> workers had long service with the company, they would have some loyalty to the
> company and that he should go to them and ask for their assistance in delivering
> anti-sectarian training to the workers – which they did.

Having arrived at a point where those with first-hand experience and personal attachment were repudiating this sort of use of the black ribbon in the factory, it was clear it was not doing any 'honour' to their lost relatives. The platform was open for the proposal to be put forward.

As those people who had most credibility in the alleged 'remembrance' felt the dispute was demeaning to the memory of their loved ones, the truth about the reason for wearing black ribbons in Desmond's was revealed. This was gently but clearly exposed as coat-trailing and the inappropriate use of emblems at work to antagonise (if not intimidate) others in the workforce. In getting to the heart of the matter Counteract was able to prepare the company and its workers for reaching consensus. This, simply put, is the story of how Counteract resolved the black ribbon dispute.

*   *   *   *   *

Counteract defined emblems as being 'material or colour worn or displayed from one community' so that it could be identified by one community exclusively, and used for that purpose – and that could be just about anything. Up to that point the definition was restrictive, and confined to things that were identified and listed. Counteract challenged the narrow view going beyond this, demonstrating that manipulating symbolism produced endless possibilities for creating emblems.

The official position was that sectarian emblems came out of thirty years of conflict. Yet very powerful emblems could be created – and not only with the use of the black ribbon, as was instanced when a commemorative Drumcree medal was struck. Anyone wearing a Drumcree Protest medal was making a powerful statement about community and political allegiance, backed by the violence that accompanied these annual sectarian demonstrations. In the twenty-first century, campaigns of all kinds strike ribbons and emblems that become immediately identifiable signifiers of whatever cause is being promoted. Not so in 1996.

Billy Robinson recounted an interview on radio where Bob Cooper of the FEC said that sectarian emblems had come from the thirty years of conflict. He replied 'I'm glad to hear that because now I can feel comfortable wearing my Easter Lily, as it didn't come out of thirty years of the Troubles.'

*   *   *   *   *

More trouble was reported around the display of emblems when the *Fermanagh Herald* led the story 'DOE workers "intimidated" at the presence of Union flags: Catholic staff offended by hand painted emblems'. The report speaks for itself, showing the emblematic power of the flags and the DOE admission that removal of these could endanger the safety of people. Genuinely innocent emblems would not have been a source of fear and danger:

> DOE workers 'intimidated' at the presence of Union flags: Catholic staff offended by hand painted emblems.
>
> Angry Catholic workers based in the Department of the Environment's Silverhill depot in Enniskillen claim they feel intimidated because of the presence of hand painted Union Jack flags on the building in which they work.
>
> Workers at the DOE's premises contacted the 'Herald' this week to highlight the problem but wished to remain anonymous because of fears of reprisals from other members of staff.
>
> The final straw for many of the Catholic staff came on 12th July when the Union Jack flag at the entrance gate was erected and remained up for over a week. One worker said that he himself witnessed the flag being flown on 12th and added that it was widely rumoured that a senior member of staff deliberately displayed the complete band uniform to Catholics at work as he made his way to the parade in Brookeborough.
>
> Apart from the flag pole at the entrance to the depot, there are also two hand painted Union Jack flags on the outside of the building which are believed to have been there for 10 years, one of which is clearly visible from the main entrance.

Speaking to the Herald one worker said

> The Union Jack is flown up to three or four times a year but they normally leave them up for a couple of days which they are not supposed to. There also used to be four or five flags painted in the garage but they were painted over a number of years ago. All the Catholics workers are outraged by the flags, the Union Jack on the flag pole

is bad enough but the hand painted ones are permanent and really offensive. The workforce is split 50/50 (Catholic and Protestant) and I have to ask why Catholics have to endure the Union flag stuck in their face every day.

However, a spokesman for the DOE said there had never been any complaints about the flags before but they would now be looking into the matter. There are certain designated days when the flag is flown and I believe it was actually up there before the 12th July for the Queen's birthday which I think is on 9th July. There was an instruction for it to be taken down shortly after but for some reason it wasn't.

Regarding the subject of the painted flags, he said that they had been there for a number of years and as nobody really objected before their position is to wait until someone objects.

'Since they were put up staff and management have changed but now that it has been brought to our attention we will see if it should be removed. DOE policy is to talk to people in an area and staff to find out their feelings about the matter. We also have to ensure the safety of people, if the flags were removed.'

While there no longer exists legislation to prevent the flying of flags after the Flags and Emblems Act of 1954 was repealed some time ago, a Press Officer at Stormont said any flag or emblem can be flown so long as it does not breach public order or cause a breach of the peace. Although he did say that staff could complain through the avenue of Fair Employment or Public Order acts, where there are rules which relate to workers having the right to a neutral workplace. However, he did point out that as regards the flying of the Union Jack for the Queen's official birthday the actual date is 15th June. (Fermanagh Herald, July 1997)

This dispute caused enough difficulty that Counteract was brought in. It is interesting, too, that the *Church of Ireland Journal* (20th August) carried a feature 'Sectarianism and intimidation' and gave Counteract a window – and thereby some cognisance.

Disingenuous claims of 'innocent' displays of flags and emblems were a constant catchphrase in prejudiced resistance and hypocrisy in every organisation that called in Counteract to mediate such disputes. As one form of coat-trailing was outed as sectarian or intimidatory to one section of the workforce, another sign or form of symbolism would be created. Ultimately, as Counteract understood, it was the intention of such actions that mattered, and management's challenge or condoning of this that made for disputes or a neutral working place.

*   *   *   *   *

Both the statutory view and Counteract line tallied as regards displaying or wearing emblems in the workplace – it was unacceptable. Where Counteract and the FEC differed radically was in their position as regards the wearing of the Poppy in work.

The official line, and that of all statutory bodies, including the FEC, was that the Poppy was not an emblem. In sharp contrast Counteract, with characteristic forthrightness, disagreed, arguing that the Poppy was an emblem and was used – besides its legitimate purpose of remembrance of war dead – for sectarian purposes. This disagreement had gone on for some years, coming to a head in 1996 and 1997.

The Poppy disputes of 1996–97 thrust the issue of emblems in the workplace into the mainstream and in 1997 Counteract into the arena of government and a temporarily high profile in the national media.

So, what was all the fuss about something no greater than a little flower that was to commemorate the honour of those who died in war?

The Poppy has been at the heart of many disputes as the symbol of respect and remembrance in British traditions and the epitome of exclusion in Irish traditions. The facts and historical realities of who fought in both World Wars were misrepresented on both sides, and made the Poppy open to political and sectarian abuse – providing space for strong denial that the Poppy was used in aggressively sectarian ways throughout its history in Ireland North and South.

The UVF fought in the Battle of the Somme. Their followers and the Unionist tradition honoured only the Protestant/Unionist dead.[8] Since Nationalists were excluded from this tradition and the Catholic Church was anti-Poppy, conflicting allegiances and narratives evolved and were woven into the fabric of Irish society. Until the early years of this century wearing a Poppy in the Republic of Ireland was controversial, whereas not wearing it was regarded as a political issue in Northern Ireland.

In practice the sectarian wearing of the poppy was understood widely but, until the 1990s, simply denied. Why else would Catholic workers in places like the Shipyards have been forced into buying them? From a traditional British perspective, it seemed inconceivable that the little flower that marked respect for those who died fighting fascism could be a tool of discrimination and used to identify targets for intimidation – on both 'sides'. To this day that view prevails in Britain – as does the naïve notion that the Union flag is always displayed as a neutral symbol.

Flags and emblems have been at the centre of innumerable disputes in the workplace and throughout the streets of Northern Ireland for all its history. Rules on displaying flags and emblems became an effective way of dealing with this form of intimidation.[9] Flaunting flags, emblems and regalia at work had been the cause of cases lost by employers in Tribunals. So, what was once established practice was brought into serious question and seen as intimidatory. Even the wearing of clothes, like the most blatant examples of football shirts, to send sectarian messages was 'outed' and employers had to acknowledge what had long been denied – that they tacitly permitted sectarian and political disputes to be silently played out in work.

*   *   *   *   *

Was the Poppy an emblem? What counted as appropriate display of the Poppy? What was deemed to be an emblem? These questions were more clearly defined for Counteract than for the FEC. Counteract had always regarded the poppy as an emblem. The FEC differed.

In response to enquiries from the Belfast and District trades Council in April 1997 the Chairman of the FEC wrote[10]

> Although the wearing of 'emblems' and sectarian harassment are not in themselves defined in the legislation as offences, in line with sexual or racial harassment, sectarian harassment has been identified by the Fair Employment Agency and subsequently the Fair Employment Tribunal as direct discrimination, contrary to the Fair Employment (NI) Act 1976. ...... [I]t would be for a Tribunal to decide whether unlawful discrimination had occurred, on the basis of the specific circumstances of the case.

The different working assumptions did not prevent the FEC and Counteract working together and Counteract was grateful for the support of the FEC in many areas. However, the culture of the FEC was one that promoted the provision of advice and information. Counteract's strengths lay in its understanding the dynamics of prejudice and intimidation. They used language from grass roots that management and employers sometimes did not understand until it was explained. Just as managers might not see graffiti in the workers' toilets, they did not always know (or admit to knowing) their workers' language (whether be that of their own political persuasion or otherwise).

This was sometimes a genuine ignorance but it was often a rather thinly veiled denial – as was demonstrated by the case of a manager who told the Fair Employment Tribunal that he did not recognise the tune of the Orange Order anthem *The Sash* when whistled by someone allegedly harassing a Catholic colleague at work.

The FEC was tasked to provide statistics on the religious and political breakdown of employment, and give advice and information on legal obligations and good practice in Fair Employment. Counteract was tasked to tackle sectarianism and intimidation in the workplace, and so had to confront the practicalities of how prejudice and harassment operated. Counteract had to provide an understanding of intimidation rather than information about rules about allegations and complaints. The two had distinct roles and remits.

That November the issue of wearing the Poppy in work would reach fever pitch with intense scrutiny from press and the media, and questions asked in the House of Commons about the dispute in the Coates Viyella fashion manufacturing plant.

*　*　*　*　*

This case demonstrates the complexities of doing business and succeeding in good management practice in Northern Ireland. The dispute arose in Coates Viyella in Derry/ Londonderry in the autumn of 1997. The company had a policy on flags and emblems and on the wearing of poppies at work. Wearing a Poppy was permitted within stated times and dates. Employees and managers were aware of these agreements, but problems surfaced when some employees insisted on wearing poppies outside agreed times.

The dispute came up because the company had appropriate policy and procedures, and took disciplinary action – suspending a number of staff for breaching agreed rules. Coates Viyella accepted that the Poppy had been used to create division and conflict in the factory, and therefore it had to be seen and managed within that area of policy. Unlike other companies that had no such policies, or ignored sectarian disputes at work, they were looking like a victim of their own good practice. Recognising and acting to manage workplace conflict had apparently generated problems and potentially bad press. There was a bigger agenda in Derry that autumn, increasing pressure on Coates Viyella to settle things because contested marches coincided with the Poppy dispute.

Tensions heightened in the City when politicians became embroiled, notably the local DUP MP Gregory Campbell who alleged the Poppy was banned and 'ordinary decent people' were being victimised for simply remembering the war dead. David Trimble, UUP leader raised the matter in Westminster at Prime Minister's Question time. The debate was heated because, officially, the Poppy was not an emblem. Counteract argued that anything that could be used to intimidate or create conflict and division at work (or in the community) was *de facto* an emblem. The Poppy dispute became the focus of intense media scrutiny once questions were asked in Parliament. This dispute was created by people making political capital out of the Poppy and Remembrance Sunday, pretending that this was about demonstrating respect for the war dead.

*   *   *   *   *

Indeed, the Poppy was not an issue confined to the factory or shop floor. It was, and remained, an issue for corporate business, the public sector and all sections of the economy. A year before the dispute in Coates Viyella, the BBC had faced a storm of criticism and controversy over wearing the Poppy. BBC TV newscaster Donna Traynor refused to wear a Poppy and, after a flood of complaints, was taken to task both internally and by the local press. It was BBC policy that all newscasters should wear the Poppy for the week running up to Remembrance Sunday. She held the view that the Poppy was an emblem as was the shamrock and were seen as symbols of division:

> In a bid to avert further criticism, the presenter and the corporation agreed a compromise, changing her shift pattern for the week. Last year the BBC offered its presenters a similar arrangement – giving them the choice of wearing poppies onscreen or taking off-screen jobs.[11]

So, for the BBC all those appearing on screen were to wear the Poppy, with individuals choosing to opt in or out. A similarly ambivalent corporate response was indicated in the relocation of the sales of poppies – from the main reception area to the restaurant. 'Since the refurbishment of the reception area in Broadcasting House, as part of an overall corporate re-design, flag days are now represented in the restaurant rather than recep-tion.'[12] This was akin to a 'whatever you say, say nothing' strategy.

All such disputes were taken up by those with a sectarian-political agenda and were inevitably distorted. On Armistice Day in 1997 Mary McAleese was inaugurated as President of the Republic against a back-ground of mounting pressure on her to 'make a symbolic stand against those who dared to politicise the poppy'. Press opinion was that she should make a gesture showing that the poppy belonged to both traditions. In the event she took a line on emblems and adhered to it – she would wear no symbols or emblems other than the shamrock which was the national emblem. A year later her spokeswoman reported 'Throughout her first year in office, President McAleese has often been asked to wear symbols representing a variety of causes but her position has not changed.' The President did, however, mark Remembrance Day at a religious service in St Patrick's cathedral in Dublin and joined the Queen at a special cere-mony in Belgium three days later to honour Ireland's war dead and jointly unveil a new memorial.

* * * * *

How did the company and Counteract resolve the Poppy dispute? Counteract was assured that company policy and the disciplinary suspen-sions and appeal procedure were sound practice in fair employment. The issues were those in any sectarian dispute: fear, feelings and lack of trust. There was fear that Protestant/Unionists were losing the right to wear the poppy in a traditional and 'Unionist' way (i.e. for as many days or weeks as they wanted). There were feelings of bitter resentment that 'their' poppy and symbol was being controlled (and put out of commission as a powerful pro-British, and therefore anti-Catholic symbol). And there was a lack of trust between workers and management, and Unionists and Nationalists.

Having established that correct company procedures were in place Counteract set about educating the entire organisation on the issues of sectarianism and harassment at work. The 'untouchable' subject of the Poppy had already featured in Counteract training and was included in the sessions at Coates Viyella. The company arranged an 'away-day' for managers, workers and unions. Karen Eyben from UU Future Ways, Billy Robinson from Counteract and the FEC facilitated a very difficult day, facing intense hostility in a threatening atmosphere.

The issue was not about disrespect for the Poppy. There had always been ostentatious sectarianism on both 'sides'. Billy Robinson recounted his experience of witnessing a priest castigate a man wearing a poppy, from the pulpit, to such a degree that the worshipper was intimidated into leaving chapel immediately. The message was 'We remember our dead exclusively.' Appropriating the Poppy as belonging to one tradition only suited sectarian interests in both Unionist and Nationalist camps.

This was not a time of great conversions, or a sea change in attitudes. Confronting a hitherto 'untouchable' subject challenged the denial – that 'the poppy is just a little flower' – and brought about a more honest recognition that the use of the poppy was open to being questioned.

The effect of bringing all interest groups together was to diffuse tensions to some extent and lay the basis for an inclusive agreement. Communication had to be open and transparent so that the disputed situation could not be manipulated by people both inside and outside the company who had a political-sectarian agenda.

Meanwhile the issue of disciplinary action had to be resolved. At that time, company suspensions and appeals were handled by a Human Resources manager in England. Decisions on appeals were due to be announced two days before a controversial march in the city – leaving room for yet more altercation about what was company business and what was sectarian-political. As it turned out the manager in England suffered a very bad bout of flu and was not able to come to the factory until the following week. By that stage the steam had gone out of the situation. Suddenly there was no burning issue. Timing, on this occasion, had been a vital factor.

Some years later Billy Robinson recalled how he experienced events:

> Counteract arrived at site to find a large crowd and a local Politician picketing the premises in support of wearing the poppy in the work place. The police were present in large numbers.

> After discussion with management to gauge the extent of the problem we decided to spend some time walking round the factory, looking at how people worked, physical

contact, what if any groups existed, spoke to workers in the canteen, to get a feeling of the culture on the site.

There was a committee of workers – union representatives, managers, and some dissenters. You keep your friends close and your enemies even closer! The committee was organized to oversee a change program – they were engaged in a training program to raise awareness of the issues and to process a solution. Discussions around the company's equality policy and policy on flags and emblems in the workplace facilitated debate. The framework policy included that the poppy could be worn on the premises for three consecutive days during the remembrance period and that a minute's silence would be observed in the canteen for those who wished to attend on Remembrance Day.

The entire work force attended training on prejudice awareness and harassment, together with presentations on the changes to the company policies. Sessions were attended by twenty participants at a time. There was some hostility in the sessions and at times very heated debates, but we managed to get a general consensus on the way forward.

Later, during remembrance week, four workers were suspended for wearing the poppy in work after the allocated time period. The HR manager was to come to the factory to deliver the verdict on the discipline to the individuals on a Friday. I rang her about this and suggested that a bad flu may prevent her attendance until the following Tuesday. Without hesitation she informed me that she was going to the doctor that evening.

The disciplinary meeting was held that Tuesday. The HR person rang me to ask why she had taken the flu. I informed her that on the Saturday there was a very large contentious parade in the town and if she had delivered her judgment on the Friday the factory would have possibly have been caught up in any violence that may have occurred.

Shortly after this Mr. David Trimble asked the question of the Prime Minister Mr. Tony Blair what was his position on people being penalized for wearing the wearing the poppy in work.

The BBC then interviewed me in relation to the Prime Minister's statement. I agreed with the PM view that the poppy could be worn at work. I was then asked by the interviewer how this sat with the Coates Viyella discipline of four workers wearing the poppy in work. I responded that those individuals were not disciplined for wearing the poppy in work but for wearing it outside the company's policy which was an allocated time-frame of three days. They were therefore challenging the company's policy – which was a disciplinary matter.

Issues like this at times can be escalated to a political level very quickly, and then can create bigger conflicts in society.

Counteract had two main tasks in the Coates Viyella situation. They had to establish that company procedures and policies were appropriate, in place, and properly put into practice. They also had to work with others to open up heated discussion as safely as possible, while encouraging the company to keep communications open with all interested parties – inside the factory and outside. The process included all interested parties and fear of any 'hidden agenda' was reduced if not eliminated – so the real issues and underlying problems emerged. The sectarianism causing disruption and intimidation was challenged successfully.

Gregory Campbell (DUP) welcomed the policy changes and Counteract training at Coates Viyella adding, somewhat disingenuously, and getting some facts wrong:

> It was unfortunate that it took such a protracted dispute involving people losing their wages for the principle of being allowed to remember the war dead to be established. The new agreement between management and workers simply established the poppy as an emblem which can and should be worn by everybody.[13]

More than two years down the line Andrew Lowden from the company recalled the dispute and those controversial times saying it was the worst time of his working life.

The Poppy issue was still evident a year later but the Coates Viyella dispute did not arise again. The *Belfast Telegraph* reported Alban Maginness (SDLP), first Nationalist mayor of Belfast, on his views on Remembrance Day, saying, 'The most important thing is being at the Cenotaph to remember the dead and respecting the traditions of the Unionist community.' Clearly, Nationalists felt that the poppy was not an emblem belonging to their tradition. Equally clearly the Unionist perception was that respect for this emblem was compulsory, not a cross-cultural gesture.

*   *   *   *   *

Counteract staff worked right across Northern Ireland throughout the year[14] and this training was integrated into seminars for the (EU) Independent Funding Bodies (IFBs) and funding recipients.

The profile of their work and Counteract credibility had risen to the point where others were taking a lead from them – and attitudes, actions and industrial relations were changing, in the workplace and in the realms of community and politics.

Plans were being laid as Future Ways (UU) partnered Counteract to start developing a model for embedding best practice in community relations in organisations.

This model was to be called Relationships in Equity, Diversity and Interdependence (REDI). It would pilot an initiative to take community relations from the periphery of organisations and embed it within the mainstream, over the coming two years, 1998–2000. The objective was to assist in creating a model of change for employees in local government (as well as business and the community) and for local politicians. As 1998 approached some lessons were to be learned.

The Management Committee[15] remained trade union dominated, with two nominees from voluntary organisations working in the area of housing and the unemployed. The links with the trade union movement were still central to its work and networking. In its Annual report Counteract applauded the outcome of the multi-party negotiations:

> We particularly welcome the commitments to equality and justice and specifically – 'the right to freedom from sectarian harassment'. We trust all those seeking election to the assembly and participation in the civic forum will operate in a way conducive to promoting good community relations and equality of treatment. While rights may be enshrined in legislation, North and South, we look forward to those rights becoming reality.

Notes

1. This project was funded jointly by The Community Bridges Programme, International Fund for Ireland and EU Sub-Committee, Community Relations Council.
2. This was at a 1996 ICTU conference, in Bray, County Dublin.
3. Ballymunn housing estate had a reputation as a 'sink' estate with huge social, economic and drug problems.
4. Counteract and AC Network (Dublin) were later to co-ordinate a development programme for community leaders and activists concentrating on project-based

consensus-building activities. The programme, supported by IFI, ran May–December 1998. No fees were involved.

5. *Belfast Telegraph*, North West Edition Thursday 20 March 1997.

6. Sunday 30 January 1972 was 'Bloody Sunday' in Londonderry/Derry when the British Army opened fire killing thirteen people.

7. *Fermanagh Herald*, July 1997.

8. Time and history have redressed the balance somewhat as the sectarian exclusion of Northern Ireland's only Victoria Cross holder, Mr Magennis, is now remembered alongside others who fell in the many battles in World War One, and afterwards.

9. It is an interesting point that when DuPont set up shop in Maydown Co Londonderry in 1960 the wearing of emblems was forbidden in the workplace.

10. Quoted from FEC letter of 17 April 1997, *'Although the wearing of "emblems" and sectarian harassment are not in themselves defined in the legislation as offences, in line with sexual or racial harassment, sectarian harassment has been identified by the Fair Employment Agency and subsequently the Fair Employment Tribunal as direct discrimination, contrary to the Fair Employment (NI) Act 1976. … [The] Tribunal has given guidance on issues such as the relevance of the Code of Practice, the need for employers to take a proactive approach to the promotion of good and harmonious working environment and on the acceptability of the display of materials which may have a sectarian significance, the wearing of football shirts etc.*

    With regard to the wearing of 'emblems' consideration needs to be given, not only to the nature of the emblem itself, but also to the context, manner etc. in which it was being displayed. Ultimately … [it] would depend on all the circumstances of the case. … There is no exact formula which can be applied to ensure harmony in all workplaces. …. I have outlined our general view on the specific issues raised.

    Some football shirts/sportswear can have the effect, whether intended or not, of giving clear sectarian messages connected with community strife in Northern Ireland and other apparel, for example, Union Jack/red, white and blue/green, white and orange T-shirts can be worn with the intention of giving a sectarian message. This case is clearly recognised in Brennan – v – Short Bros. Plc. In our view, given the difficulties associated with 'drawing the line' on clothing/apparel, it may be appropriate to ban the wearing of all sportswear, ties, scarves and other regalia, including that linked to any football clubs (this would include Gaelic football clubs). However, if agreement can be reached with the workforce on a more limited restriction, then this may be an acceptable option.

    In addition to the disadvantages of 'manifestations of the community' the Fair Employment Tribunal has outlined the dangers of regalia, apparel, or indeed conversations, which reflect the community divisions in Northern Ireland which exist outside the workplace. For this reason, we have taken the view that emblems or displays in the workplace, which are linked to the community strife over the past 30 years and/or local politics, clearly have the potential to cause disruption to a good and harmonious working environment as such are unacceptable.

On the other hand the Commission is of the view that the respectful wearing of emblems which do tend to distinguish one community from the other but which are not directly connected with the community strife over the last years, such as crosses/crucifixes, ashes, pioneer pins, Christian Union badges, and fiannes, as well as Poppies and Shamrock when worn at appropriate times, are unlikely to be regarded as creating an atmosphere in which an individual would feel under threat or intimidated, as outlined in the Code of Practice (5.2.2).

That said, employers and trade unions would need to guard against any attempt being made to use the wearing of these emblems as some form of statement. It would be unacceptable if someone was made to feel uncomfortable for not wearing these emblems or if they were being flaunted or forced on someone not wearing them:

> … In our view, ultimately it is for employers to decide on the appropriate policy to deliver a good and harmonious working environment in the workplace. This may mean that in some situations that no emblems will be considered appropriate, whilst in others a wider range may be considered acceptable. … [I]t would be for a Tribunal to decide whether unlawful discrimination had occurred, on the basis of the specific circumstances of the case.'

11. Dan McGinn, writing in the *Belfast Telegraph* October 31, 1998.
12. Ibid.
13. *Belfast Telegraph*, North West Edition.
14. This was in Newry & Mourne Council, Border Project, Lisburn, Limavady, Strabane, and Enniskillen District Councils, PJ Halls, Coates Vyella, Unipork, Phoenix Gas, Co. Monaghan Training Project, Training Consortium and the Ireland Fund.
15. Terry Carlin ICTU, Maria Graham ICTU, Billy McCreight (CWU), John Cassells (SIPTU), Jonathon Smyth (NATFE), Brenda Callaghan (BTC), Brendan Mackin (Director, Belfast Unemployed Resource Centre), Janet Hunter (Director, Housing Rights Service UU).

CHAPTER 9

1998–99: New Dispensation – New Mainstream Vocabulary

1998 saw the continued sectarian targeting of Catholic taxi drivers, and several were murdered in the opening weeks of that year. As parties were excluded from and/or left discussions, peace negotiations made slow but steady progress. This provoked leading DUP members to team up with the LVF at a Loyalist protest rally in Portadown, after which Dr Ian Paisley denied any paramilitary connection with the rally.

A UN investigator's report in April concluded that there should be an inquiry into the RUC's involvement in the 1989 murder of Belfast solicitor Pat Finucane. The world's media was expecting another event, however, and the grounds of Stormont heaved under the weight of the world's press and media who camped out waiting for news of the Belfast Peace Agreement. Although it was due to be hammered out by Thursday, it was not until the early hours of Good Friday that the Agreement was finally signed by all parties in the negotiations.

From this came a referendum[1] resulting in a yes vote of over 71% with the highest voter turnout since 1921 at 81% and forthcoming elections for the local Assembly. Near hysteria was reported in the media with the 'No' camp overstating and the 'Yes' camp understating the implications of the agreement. Policing and de-commissioning of paramilitary arms formed the primary thorns in the side of the Unionist electorate. Trust was essential for the process but in predictably short supply.

So-called 'punishment' beatings, bombings, shootings and sectarian intimidation would continue in a cessation of violence, demonstrating the precarious nature of the 'peace'.

In mid-May the Chancellor of the Exchequer underscored the economic importance of the peace process by announcing an investment package of £315 million for Northern Ireland. The business community was almost completely won over, at a public level at least. At the same time, with only 55% Protestant-Unionist backing and 96% Catholic-Nationalist endorsement, the Belfast Agreement would not be easy to implement. Unionist fears and the perception that Nationalists had 'won' would dog the process and threaten to bring it down – on a regular basis.

Mo Mowlam announced eight members of what would become the Patten Commission on the reform of the RUC that June. The Police Authority said it would press for legislation forcing RUC members to declare membership of groups such as the Orange Order. In the same month, UUP leader David Trimble criticised re-routing decisions made by the already beleaguered Parades Commission, and declared the Commission was not viable. By the end of the month Assembly elections had produced the makings of the new administration, including all the minority parties except the UDP.[2] The electoral failure of the Loyalist UDP, largely the consequence of the split Unionist vote in West Belfast was to have serious repercussions because it left the UDA and LVF political representatives with no stake in the 'new dispensation' of a Stormont Assembly and created a power vacuum.

July was a blood-curdling month when LVF and Loyalist extremists filled that political vacuum with violence. Possibly the most shocking murders of the whole of the Troubles was the murder by fire of three Catholic boys Richard (11), Mark (10), and Jason Quinn (9) as they slept in their beds. Despite Dr Ian Paisley's very public assertion that this was a drugs-related offence, it was a sectarian attack. The murders rent the heart of Orange-ism with bitter attacks on those who now called for an end to the Drumcree stand-off. A fortnight later estimates were that the cost of damage associated with the Drumcree protest that year was £3 million as compared with £10 million in 1997 and £20 million in 1996.

Late July saw the start of legislation on the early release of prisoners, and later the revelation that to rehabilitate paramilitary prisoners into society cost £3,500 each – a total of £1.4 million for 400 ex-prisoners.

No-one then believed such an outrage as the Omagh bombing could happen, but that August it did. Twenty-eight people and two unborn children were killed and three hundred and sixty people injured after a Republican bomb exploded. One of the injured later died, bring the death toll to thirty-one. Sinn Féin condemned the bombing but this horrific event soured the peace process and broke the fragile trust.

Sectarian and economically motivated attacks continued in the community throughout the autumn as the Stormont Assembly met and wrangled about procedural matters. As rows raged over de-commissioning and the NIO threatened to halt early releases if paramilitary beatings did not stop, David Trimble and John Hume received the Nobel Peace Prize. The withdrawal of troops and closure of some security points continued, while controversy arose over suggestions that the RUC was to be disbanded. Unionist John Taylor made a speech paralleling the peace agreement with the failed Sunningdale power-sharing agreement of 1974. Rather more aptly Seamus Mallon (SDLP) described it as 'Sunningdale for slow learners'.

Sectarian violence continued spreading (predictably enough) onto the football pitch. RUC figures showed that Loyalists were outdoing Republicans in the number of 'punishment' beatings. Housing figures leaked to the DUP showed that the level of intimidation was such that more families had been put out of their homes than for twenty-five years; and that 60% of these were from members of the security forces. The '*I know where you live*' approach was being employed as never before. This message was intended for members of the security forces, who already tended to live in 'mixed' and middle-class areas for fear of intimidation – and was perpetrated by Loyalists as well as Republicans.

The year ended with the token de-commissioning of Loyalist arms and Christmas paroles for paramilitary prisoners.

Fifty-five deaths were 'arising from the Troubles' in 1998. Shootings: 211. Bombs planted: 243. Firearms found: 88. Explosives found: 883 kg (1,945 lb.). Persons charged with terrorist and serious public order offences: 459. Casualties arising from paramilitary attacks: 216.

*   *   *   *   *

1998 began with hope and trepidation about the slow progress of peace negotiations. Beyond the reaches of bilateral, multilateral and other convoluted negotiating structures, it would end with the people of Northern Ireland going about their business in various states of expectation, fear, frustration and confidence.

For Counteract 1998 had a positive start as a new Trainer/Development Officer Stephen Nolan took up post in February. Counteract had met with Gerry O'Sullivan, Head of Public Relations, Telecom Eireann in Dublin to discuss the possible provision of a rent-free office for Counteract over a three-year period. Although this was not to materialise as a viable development at that point, it was indicative of the credibility of their work, and its perceived value by one of Ireland's biggest corporations.

Other ongoing tasks for the staff and Committee continued. Publication of the bulletin *Counteraction*, with Noreen Moore patiently waiting for articles, went ahead. And there was a Training Sub-Committee, Staff Training, ongoing research and a Personnel Sub-Group work on Draft Contracts of Employment.

In April Counteract launched *Doing Business in a Divided Society* under the slogan *Diversity enhances business*. As the Business Newsletter reported

> The project has been co-sponsored by the Province's leading morning newspapers, the Newsletter and the Irish News and endorsed by Counteract, the trade union anti-intimidation unit which has seen enquiries from companies increase triple-fold over the last year. Speaking at the launch in Belfast Will Glendinning Chief Executive of the CRC added that while the law requires employers to ensure the workplace is free from discrimination and harassment, 'Doing Business in a Divided Society' goes beyond that.
>
> Ten thousand copies of the guidelines which cover four main areas – good practice in doing business with suppliers, working with the community, managing the workplace and business with customers – will be distributed to members of the CBI, Institute of Directors, the Chief Executives' Forum, the Institute of Personnel and Development, the NI Chamber of Commerce, the Federation of Small Businesses, the Institute of Management, the NI Quality Centre and Business in the Community.

NIE was a prominent player in this initiative and gave Counteract credibility in the business community. As more small and medium sized companies came forward for help on policies and procedures, the business case for tackling sectarianism and harassment was at least a small part of the changing commercial environment.

Easter brought the Belfast Agreement, also known as the Good Friday Agreement. Such was the desire for peace that many believed it presaged an end to all violence and intimidation. This posed the question Was Counteract to become redundant? After reaching agreement, some said openly that there was a limited need for its services. However, the work of creating sustainable peace was only then beginning.

Counteract argued that peace could not be understood in negative terms as 'an absence of war' but had to be regarded as positive development towards 'a state of harmony between people and groups'.

Another immediate question was whether or not the proposed merger[3] of the existing statutory equality agencies would be a positive part of that process. Counteract highlighted a concern. How could a merger of the existing Commissions best address the equality issues in Northern Ireland? Might it not result in losing the effective single focus approach that was then the focus of each of the constituencies? Also, the recently created Commission for Racial Equality, and the hoped-for Commission on Disability, would not have time to develop their own approaches, and so that their development might be curtailed within a unified commission. In the event the Equality Commission was set up and oversaw the introduction of the duty to promote equality of opportunity and Equality Schemes required by law for every designated public authority in Northern Ireland.

On a more pragmatic note Counteract was under-financed. The video was still a centre-piece of Counteract work,[4] although it was not earning much income. Despite a second round of funding requests made to Trade Unions, response had been very poor. There had been a shortfall in income for that year. On Brendan Mackin's suggestion Counteract successfully re-negotiated funding levels with CRC.

*   *   *   *   *

Changes were happening within Counteract. The representation in its Management Committee had altered from being trade union only to a more mixed make-up. Six of eleven committee members represented trade unions,[5] two from the community sector, one was from education, one represented employers and one came from government. Representing voluntary organisations working in the area of housing and the unemployed were Brendan Mackin (BURC) and Janet Hunter (Housing Rights Service); for education Sara Hunter (Equality Department, UU), employers John Ellison (BT representing the CBI) and government Margaret McGurk (DFP). This much increased the range.

It was a time of enormous change in the political economy of Northern Ireland. The implications of political, social and economic events of these were yet to unfold. Counteract knew that it had work to do in making its contribution to the peace process:

> Counteract, as part of the trade union movement, seeks to promote economic and social policies and stresses the need for social partnership and an inclusive approach on the basis of an integrated approach to achieving effective economic growth, tackling inequality and creating social cohesion. Peace, stability and progress will not result exclusively from an end to violence. We have to address the question of building trust to create a lasting peace, and in tandem with those is the question of economic development which is an essential ingredient in creating a just and progressive society. We remain concerned at the lack of emphasis given by the statutory job creation agencies to inward investors on the employment legislation in Northern Ireland, particularly Fair Employment. There needs to be a strengthening in the area; sectarianism cannot be tackled exclusively at grass roots level.

Counteract regarded local area partnerships as increasingly important as they could harness energy, skills, local strategies and resources to tackle unemployment, poverty and social exclusion. Their geographical organisation and community divisions also made them aware that they too had to confront sectarianism.

*   *   *   *   *

By this time the public and private sectors understood they could not function efficiently if they ignored the prejudice and intimidation that spilled into or came from within the workplace. These were such obvious barriers to success. Irrespective of any ethical debate, sectarianism would affect both business profit and efficiency, and therefore the long-term survival of companies – which in turn would affect jobs and investment in the local community. There was also a more widespread recognition of the danger of legal costs, bad publicity, loss of contracts and boycotts.

In the public sector, providing vital services to the community, there had also been an ethos of 'ignore it and it'll go away'. It had not gone away. Any issue that prevented an equal delivery of services to the community needed to be dealt with. Sectarianism and intimidation were huge issues that had to be confronted if the public sector was going to fulfil its social contract with the community and the new positive duty – to promote equality of opportunity and good relations. This was now mandatory.

So far Counteract training[6] forced people to confront personal prejudices as well as structural discrimination in organisations. It was not a style designed to make friends but to challenge certain behaviour and working practices. Within the criteria that Counteract had set itself these objectives were being met.

There was less denial of the realities of discrimination, intimidation and harassment but it was apparent that a different approach was required. It took more than a series of workshops for an organisation to change, and for its employees to work free of intimidation. A well-meaning mission statement and paper policies were not enough to mend flawed relationships. Nor could they begin to create an ethos that overruled any form of discriminatory or intimidatory practice.

Changing the working culture of an organisation needed full commitment (at all levels) to eradicating sectarian behaviour and developing a neutral if not harmonious working environment. Counteract had already established a series of building blocks with which to create such an ethos. In the terminology of the new administration, they were trying to get an ethos of equity embedded in the mainstream of both public and private sector organisations, as well as in the community and voluntary sector.

In this respect Counteract had stumbled on a methodology for implementing part of the legal enshrining of the Belfast Agreement – Sections 75 and 76 of the 1998 Northern Ireland Act which mandated an end to discrimination and (for public authorities) the positive duties to promote equality and good relations. Of course, that was not fully recognised in Counteract, but they knew that good community relations had to be tied to equality – and they understood that changing the culture and ethos of an organisation was a mammoth task.

In Counteract there was no critical questioning of the terminology of 'equity' or the accepted community relations model. Strategically committed to broadening the effect of its work Counteract was intent on helping organisations develop an ethos of equity (believing that to be equal opportunity) and spreading that as widely as possible. 'We look forward to employers putting customer service, product quality and equality on an equivalent footing.'

That strategy was rooted in practical experience. Some businesses and organisations knew they needed Counteract help but they were selective in how they used advice. For example, one firm launched their new policies and procedures without sharing them with Counteract and with no reference to the joint declaration of ICTU-CBI. Later they had to come back for help when this failed, and the old sectarian problems arose. Tackling prejudice and inequality at work was not possible with a 'quick fix' or taking an 'add-on' approach. It required permanent new relationships and ways of working.

*   *   *   *   *

A key part of the Counteract strategy was to increase the pool of trainers operating in all the sectors of employment. So, the Equity & Diversity Trainers Certificate (formerly referred to as Training for Trainers) was launched on 8 May 1998 in the Wellington Park Hotel, Belfast. Coates Viyella not only sponsored the launch but also offered bursaries to the community/voluntary sector to participate in the programme. Personnel Director for Clothing Divisions for Coates Viyella UK, Max Playfer was the main guest speaker. He spoke about the difficulties his company had experienced with the Poppy dispute, and emphasised how important the support of Counteract had been at that time. He said the situation could have been significantly improved if there had been access to this type of training when they developed their in-house programme – before the dispute. Coates Viyella nominated members of their management team for the programme and actively recommended that other public, private and community/voluntary organisations do the same, as the way forward into the new millennium.

As the first accredited course of this kind in Northern Ireland the Equity & Diversity Trainers Certificate was a significant landmark in the improvement of anti-sectarian community relations training. Paul Burke had re-written Training for Trainers for this programme, presented it for accreditation, developed materials, recruited students and delivered the course.

The Certificate course gave a unique opportunity to re-evaluate personal bias and prejudice, and re-appraise and update existing organisational policies and procedures in light of new information and thinking. It would also provide access to relevant statutory and voluntary anti-discriminatory bodies on the one platform, and develop up-to-date adequate and appropriate training resources:[7]

> What if an organisational policy relating to sexual harassment is too narrow in the light of current thinking? What if it does not make adequate and appropriate reference to harassment or discrimination on the basis of sexual orientation? How should it be adjusted? What are the ramifications of not making adequate and appropriate adjustment?

Training was to equip participants to answer this kind question.

Throughout this programme participants were challenged to examine and evaluate both the personal and professional effects of prejudice, discrimination, harassment and intimidation. They were asked to look at how their own bias and prejudice could adversely affect promoting equality and the acceptance of diversity where they worked. Underlying the course was a recognition that sectarianism, sexism, racism and disability discrimination permeate society, at every level. This was timely in the year of the Peace Agreement.

The Certificate was piloted with weekly training days and two residentials that autumn; and a wide range of training professionals from public, private and voluntary organisations completed the course.[8] Input for training was comprehensive – coming from Counteract staff and FEC, EOC, CRE, Disability Action, FCWE, Lisburn Women's Centre/Rainbow, Belfast Travellers' Education & Development Group, NICEM, CAJ and PMG Planning.

*   *   *   *   *

On the wider European platform Counteract met the *European Foundation on Living & Working Conditions* to discuss the programme's relevance within Europe. The Training Consortium established by the European Programme was still receiving a very positive response. However, there was still a wide gap between Counteract and ICTU thinking and that of other European trade unions.

Further work was completed with Newry & Mourne, Border Project, Lisburn, Limavady, Strabane, and Enniskillen District Councils, PJ Halls, Coates Viyella, Unipork, Phoenix Gas, Co. Monaghan Training Project, the Training Consortium and the Ireland Fund. Counteract training was integrated into seminars for the (EU) Independent Funding Bodies (IFBs) and funding recipients. As ever, organisations in trouble came to Counteract, which still handled crises and gave training sessions.

The use of the video training package by certain non-Counteract consultants and trainers still caused concern but they were not in a position to challenge companies who had bought the package and were using it, albeit in an imperfect way, for training purposes. Counteract lost out as others made a tidy profit from its ground-breaking work.

Following up its work in *Youth Against Prejudice* they established a joint working party of young people to develop an anti-sectarianism/ anti-racism training manual, to be used in training for young people. Counteract Community Unit's successful May 1997 conference[9] had prompted community groups throughout Northern Ireland to ask Counteract for advice and/ or support. They gave a number of seminars in areas such as Down, Newry & Mourne, Newtownabbey, Cookstown, Fermanagh, Armagh. They took part in a two-day residential conference for a range of community organisations in the Newtownabbey Community Relations Group which identified how community groups could address conflict within their community more effectively. They also put out a roadshow throughout Northern Ireland in Omagh followed by Derry, Ballymena, Newry and Bangor.

As the Community Unit was one of the projects being supported by a European programme CCRU asked Joe Law to do a presentation on Counteract in Ballymena. The Unit also gave in-house training to the Ulster Peoples College and Paul Oakes was invited to give a presentation about their Database[10] and Research Library.

Counteract and AC Network (Dublin) began co-ordinating a cross-border programme for community leaders and activists concentrating on project-based consensus-building activities.[11] The key elements in this programme were relevant participant ownership,[12] networking and reciprocating exchange of ideas and information, mentoring and development support, and a small series of informal workshops with other participants.

A typical participant profile would be someone currently active in a leadership or co-ordinating capacity within her/his own community who had the support of other community activists and could involve them in their selection and implementation of a chosen project selected for the programme. They would be interested in meeting other community-based colleagues and sharing ideas and information and welcome a challenging role for agreed mentor(s) who would make available back-up knowledge and information. The course required a commitment of around four hours a week to develop projects and go to informal workshops. They also had to be prepared at the end to write up the project as a case study with support from mentor(s).

They would publish case studies giving transferable learning on a range of approaches to conflict resolution.[13] The network that came from this was a valuable catalyst for future Counteract initiatives in the community.

It also attracted the attention of Dermot Ahern, Irish Minister for Social, Community and Family Affairs, who visited Counteract and went on walkabout in Belfast (see Picture 12).

Picture 12: Joe Doherty, Dermot Ahern, Joe Hinds and Billy Robinson

Meanwhile, publicity about Counteract involvement with Coates Viyella and the poppy dispute had been positive and gave them profile and prestige. Counteract was ambitious to develop methods to embed the ethos, policies, and practice of Equity Diversity and Interdependence (EDI) in public institutions.

To accomplish this Counteract forged a partnership with Future Ways (UU) to develop a model for embedding best practice in community relations. The model was called REDI (Relationships in Equity, Diversity and Interdependence). This took equality and community relations work from an organisation's periphery and put it into the mainstream. REDI's practical design allowed the integration of current good practice with new ways, while helping the organisation to address issues of equity and diversity.

REDI identified both internal and external relationships in an organisation, and where capacity building was necessary – that is, scope to make strides towards more fair, stable and accommodating working practices. The method was finding the most sustainable ways to promote and embed core concepts of Equity, Diversity and Interdependence. How this happened depended on the context; there was no 'one-size-fits-all' method.

REDI had to engage people at all levels. In District Councils for instance, it would involve people at the level of councillors, senior management, council departments, non-management staff and the wider community. And, as the programme developed, new relationships would consolidate along three axes: vertical, horizontal and between the council and the community.

Developing these strategic models with Future Ways partners was a new challenge, but Counteract had never been envisaged as an organisational development agency. Its task was to tackle sectarianism – subtle or otherwise. That was how they helped organisations address if not mend flawed relationships. The aim of REDI was to create a positive and dynamic ethos in organisations and into the wider community to foster the evolution of a new working culture. Billy Robinson was not an academic, but a hands-on practitioner – as later became clear.

*   *   *   *   *

In October Counteract was among a contingent of trade union delegates visiting the Los Angeles Simon Wiesenthal Centre's Museum of

Tolerance[14] to investigate the possibility of a similar project for a Belfast Museum. The experience was a two-way learning process as delegates listened and talked, and shared views and expertise. Counteract gave a seminar dedicated entirely to its work in Northern Ireland for the benefit of those at the week-long Los Angeles School.

*   *   *   *   *

During 1998 Counteract was also helping at the Cantrell & Cochrane bottling plant in East Belfast giving training sessions to a hostile workforce on the night shift. The spirit of peace and reconciliation had not got that far, as Billy Robinson's candid account of the session makes clear:

> Counteract was engaged by Cantrell & Cochrane to deliver awareness training to all its staff. One problem was that they could not take the night shift off to take part in the training during the day so Counteract agreed to deliver the training at night. The factory was situated in a part of east Belfast which was a very Loyalist – delivering training I was a bit frightened.
>
> The training session started at about 10.30pm with approximately 20 people, all male with one manager present. He was the only manager on the site. The session was the most difficult I ever delivered. The persons present did not want to be there, so they were going to have a go at me, by challenging me at every moment – and in a very intimidating manner, with statements like 'Who did I think I was?' 'A fenian (that's a Catholic) coming into their work to tell them they were sectarian, as there was no sectarianism in this factory!'
>
> At times some of them were getting out of their seats. My way of defusing the situation was to be as challenging as them. So, instead of standing up in front of them and being a target, I walked in between them and to be close to those who were most hostile to me. For if I was standing up front in the room, they could challenge from the comfort of feeling the support of their colleagues, and to some degree feel safe in the crowd. To say that I was frightened is an understatement, as I smoked ten cigarettes in one hour!
>
> At a certain point I would show the counteract training video, and because I knew the video backwards, and knew it was very challenging and touched on some very sensitive issues, I decided it was better that I wasn't the room when they were watching it. So, I left the room and went outside.
>
> Outside I walked to the security gate as there was flood lighting – just in case anyone intended to come after me. At the gate I observed a number of police land rovers sitting, and wondered what they were doing sitting there. I went back in and by the end of the training session those present were more relaxed and even offered me

cigarettes. When I asked how they felt after the training, they stated that it was 'not that bad once you got into it'.

At the end of the training the one manager present informed me that he never seen anything like it. At one point he was frightened that I would be physically attacked and as he was the only manager on the site, he was fearful that he would not be able to do anything. So, he had rung the police and informed them of his fears and requested that they be present near the site. That's why the police land rovers were at the gate.

This dramatically illustrates the demands of what was called 'challenging' work at a time when sectarian murder remained a 'normal' part of life in Northern Ireland – and shows why so many feared and avoided anti-sectarian work.

*   *   *   *   *

A variety of requests came in that year. Gary Fettis asked for a presentation to British Telecom managers and awareness training, initially in Portadown and Enniskillen. Counteract also made a presentation to teachers in the Integrated School Hazlewood College, Belfast. Sara Hunter met Billy Robinson and decided to have Counteract deliver awareness training to all staff in the four Ulster University sites beginning in December.

Trade Unions continued to use Counteract. They delivered sessions as part of the internal shop stewards training programmes for Unison and ATGWU and contributed to NIC ICTU Equality Committee. They facilitated a two-day school for shop stewards on harassment in the workplace for Unison. They trained on the T&G advanced shop stewards' course and designed a training programme for use in future years. An FEC, NIC ICTU and Counteract anti-sectarian seminar in 1997 revealed the need for greater understanding of Fair Employment Law and practice – after which they designed up a unique course. *Developing Fair Employment Practices in the Workplace*[15] was tailor made for people with experience as trade union representatives who would commit to completing the course.

The course was based on comments made at that seminar:

Basically, any information on courses relevant to shop stewards or members would help us to become more pro-active rather than re-active;

Need for information on a regular basis;

Now we hopefully have a better appreciation of the subject – a course on the application of the procedures, particularly representational skills and the art of allaying fears and encouraging members to challenge bad practices;

How to deal with these issues within my organisation without damaging the reputation of my organisation; and

My union needs a more structured approach to harassment. Training is required for representatives and members.

Participants spent a day a month for 15 months learning about the unions' role and policies on fair employment, case law, legislation, best practice and comprehensive skills development. This course was delivered in BIFHE and later offered to all shop stewards and officials in the trade union movement.

* * * * *

Counteract continued to receive core funding from CRC supplemented by donations from ICTU-affiliated unions, and maintained its excellent working relationships with the CRC and FEC. The FEC's winter 1998 *Fair Comment* devoted an entire edition to the subject of Sectarian Harassment. Their Annual Report recorded employers' changing demands over the past three years, showing a clear pattern of the increasing importance of sectarianism at work and the FEC response. The percentage of FEC training time spent on sectarianism increased dramatically as the table shows.

Training Area	% in 1995–96	% in 1997–98	% in 1998–99
Recruitment & Selection	52	38	34
Sectarian Harassment	19	38	41
Equality Awareness	17	10	10
Legislation & Work of FEC	12	10	9
Section 31 Review	–	4	4
Total	100	100	100

In its 1998–99 report the FEC paid tribute to the work of trade unions and specifically NIC ICTU and Counteract as partners in tackling harassment and discrimination, throughout the 1990s:

During 1998–99 Commission staff assisted with the design of a modular training programme for trade Unionists being developed by NIC ICTU and Counteract and accredited through the Open College. Staff also participated in the Equity and Diversity training programme delivered by Counteract.

The powers the FEC had in the 1990s were unique within the UK. No other statutory body had the legal power to encroach into all businesses and make its findings public. After years of a culture of employers' rights, FEC concentration on employers' duties, and equal opportunity and fair employment, made stark contrast. As the FEC reached its 21st anniversary its powers were no longer controversial.

*   *   *   *   *

As the year closed the matter of an ongoing evaluation of Counteract had yet to be addressed. The organisation had grown and developed beyond anything that NIC ICTU, Jim Quinn, Billy Robinson and Noreen Moore had ever imagined possible. Their work and their core relationships had developed, as the CENI evaluation had noted:

> They are considered to be effective because of their relevance and their realism. They use real life situations and scenarios and … have had practical experience of dealing with intimidation and harassment both personally and professionally.

It also notes that where sectarianism was not already recognised by employers '… *the impact of awards [made by tribunals] was much more likely to force employers to put this issue on the agenda than any pressure from Counteract or indeed the trade union movement.*'[16]

Project evaluation is a standard audit tool – used most often by funders. As neither CCRU (or its policy administrators since) nor CRC have a history of robust auditing for effective community relations practice it seems likely that the impetus for the CENI evaluation was the internal politics of Counteract and the Trade Union movement. If that was the case, its findings would not have made for comfortable reading:

> Those who established Counteract hoped it would have a central role in combating sectarianism through the trade union movement. It has certainly become a facility and a resource for the trade union movement on sectarianism and intimidation and it very quickly developed an authoritative voice on these issues. However, key informants point out that the existence of Counteract may have allowed the movement to

'appear' to be doing something about sectarianism while not having to face the issue directly; that in fact, rather than being central Counteract was 'semi-detached'. One example of this is the fact that despite having two nominees from NIC ICTU on its management committee Counteract's Co-ordinator was only recently invited to join NIC ICTU's Equality Committee. There was no exclusion of him, it simply did not occur to people that they had this resource in their midst.

It is telling that the approach to Counteract from NIE came from management and not unions and indeed when Counteract did a training session with the joint negotiating committee in NIE, a minority of the trade union representatives turned up whereas all the management side did! (CENI 1997).

As regards the relationship with the Trade Union movement CENI said

The origins of Counteract lie in the vision and commitment of trade union activists. However, the trade union movement in Northern Ireland found it difficult to deal with the issue in the past because of fear of splitting the membership. Trade Unionists would say that unions have tended to take the point of view that as trade Unionists its members needed to unite around issues of pay and conditions and that sectarianism was 'politics'. However, there were activists and education officers who sought to persuade people that 'conditions' included safety from feeling fear in the workplace and that it was necessary to recognise that members of trade unions in Northern Ireland reflected all the attitudes and bigotry of the society from which they came.[17]

Counteract had transcended those attitudes and had now convinced others in industry, politics, economy and community that sectarianism should and could be effectively challenged. The committed trade union women and men who had given unstinting support to Counteract over eight years were exceptional – that is beyond doubt. However, Billy Robinson had taken Counteract beyond the movement and outside their comfort zone.

* * * * *

At a more personal level the strains of the work had become apparent as both Billy Robinson and Paul Burke suffered heart attacks that year but Counteract continued to deliver its services.

* * * * *

The year ended with press reports on the 'Price of prejudice warning' as the FEC revealed figures on FET cases and damages. The message was

Picture 13: Counteract and Making a difference in Keeping the Peace

getting through. Counteract was making an impact in the media and political circles – if only privately.

Notes

1. Referenda were held in both the Republic and Northern Ireland. Overwhelming
    support for the Belfast Agreement was registered in both.
2. The UDP was the political party of the UDA and LVF. Their absence from the NI
    Assembly would presage alienation amongst the UDA and its supporters given the
    failure to provide realistic political options. It also signalled future UDA/UVF feuds.
3. This was proposed in the white paper 'Partnership for Equality'.

4. It was bought by trade unions (CWU (London), CWU (Postal), UNISON, MSF (Belfast), MSF (London), NIPSA, NUS/USA, ATGWU, SIPTU, Danish Trade Union), local councils (Lisburn Borough Council, Derry City Council, Newry & Mourne District Council, Belfast City Council), Employers and community groups, (Women Together, Sports Council, Youth Action, YMCA Ireland, Chief Executive's Forum, Moypark, Bowring Marsh McLellan, Golden Vale, Allied Bakeries, Colin Glen, South & East H&SST, Oaklee Housing Association, Northern Ireland Housing Executive, Croft Inns, Royal Mail, Engineering Employers Federation) and the NI Civil Service (Department of Finance, NI Police Authority, NI Civil Service, MOD, RUC, and Industrial Tribunals [for hire]).

5. The ICTU remained as Terry Carlin and Maria Graham. Affiliated Union nominees were Billy McCreight (CWU), John Cassells (SIPTU) and Bill Hastings (NATFHE) and the Belfast & District Trades Council nominee was Brenda Callaghan (Counteract Chair, withdrew in June; her contribution was formally commended).

6. The majority of this work came under the heading of 'Anti-sectarian Awareness Training'. This involved the development of anti-discriminatory policies and procedures, training for harassment advisors and investigation officers, creating a greater understanding of what constitutes sectarian harassment/intimidation, information on equality legislation etc., addressing issues of diversity and the reality of living in a divided, sectarian society.

7. The programme was accredited by the Northern Ireland Open College Network at level 3.

8. Trainers came from CRC, EMBARC (Ortus), BT, CWU, RUC, Telecom Eirann and PHAB Northern Ireland.

9. This was held for community groups to look at the question of a need for policies and/or procedures to address sectarianism.

10. The Community Unit database had agreed input from Housing Rights Service, Base 2, CABs, Peace & Reconciliation Group, Derry and being considered by Churches. They would try to get NIHE involved also.

11. The programme was supported by IFI, so no fees were involved. It ran over the period May–December 1998.

12. Identification/ownership by the participant and by his/her community of the subject area chosen. Subject areas for a project were selected from topics like, ageism, business generation, disability, sectarianism, discrimination, communication, employment, equity, gender, race etc. However, the central concern would be the direct relevance to the community involved.

13. 'Consensus building for community leaders/activists' was produced in 1999.

14. Los Angeles Times, Metro Section page 1, 22 October 1998. This was reported widely in the Jewish press The Jewish Chronicle and Jewish Journal featured these plans in their papers.

15. This was accredited by OCN (Level 2) and would be provided in the ICTU education programme.
16. Community Evaluation Northern Ireland's 1997 report recorded that feedback on Counteract's effectiveness in training was very positive.
17. Community Evaluation Northern Ireland 1997 report.

1998–99: Consolidating Alliances – Building on Networks

1998 had been a roller coaster year for formal politics. Finally, Mo Mowlam triggered the d'Hondt mechanism and the Assembly started, stopped, and restarted, with the Ministerial appointments finally coming in December. New arrangements established the Equality Commission for Northern Ireland (comprising and extending the remit of CRE, EOC, FEC, and Disability legislation) and the Human Rights Commission. Brutal sectarianism and internal feuding among paramilitaries continued. Assertions of links between drug trafficking and paramilitary factions increased. Early release of prisoners, Loyalist picketing of Catholic churches and dissident Republican violence continued. Northern Ireland battled to maintain its funding levels if not its Objective One status in the European Union.

The murder of Lurgan solicitor Rosemary Nelson in March brought allegations of RUC intimidation and collusion with the Loyalists who bombed her car. The Chief Constable of Kent and the FBI were invited to investigate these matters by RUC Chief Constable Ronnie Flanagan. Weeks later he announced that John Stevens would head the inquiry into the murder of Pat Finucane. Later the Law Society of Northern Ireland would overturn its own Council's decision and call for an independent inquiry into the Finucane and Nelson murders – matters not resolved in the next two decades.

The political year was one of halting, fitful progress as the peace process staggered from one clarification and redefinition of the Belfast Agreement to another and the level of sectarianism and intimidation rose, predictably, with the summer Loyal Order marches. Polling popular support for the agreement kept a lot of people in work.

Headline news in April was that David Trimble met the Pope when in Italy for a two-day seminar. There was outcry and Unionist dismay when Bairbre de Brun and Martin McGuinness took up their Ministerial positions with some Unionist school children protesting when the Education Minister visited secondary (state) schools. UUP dislike of Mo Mowlam reached fever pitch and the party leader asked Tony Blair to replace her. Mowlam's cult status with the British and some of the Northern Irish electorate gave her short-term leverage, and she refused to go. However, she did not see out the year in Hillsborough and was replaced as Secretary of State for Northern Ireland by the rehabilitated Peter Mandelson.

As Minister for Economic Development, Reg Empey headed up a new department and made a series of very optimistic announcements about jobs and investments, although this was under the shadow of the marching season, and the threat of another Drumcree protest to match the massive disruption that had occurred in 1996. For him, like his fellow UUP members, Peter Mandelson was someone they were prepared to tolerate if not gladly do business with. Disillusion with the Belfast Agreement was steadily growing, while the business community had now come to realise that peace was their only hope of sustainable survival and growth. It was a time of oddly conflicting loyalties and interests, but the economic interest argument won out.

In Dublin the Equality Authority (replacing the Employment Equality Agency) and the Office of the Director of Equality Investigations were established in March 1999[1] in parallel to ECNI in Northern Ireland. A quarter of a century, after a start with the FEA, the outgoing FEC could review the sea change it had created. Bob Cooper and his staff began first with policing, and then gaining acceptance of the strongest employment legislation in the UK. The development of an equality agenda in Northern Ireland was substantially the product of work by the FEC and enlightened forces in the London government, civil society, academics and the trade union movement, including Counteract.

*   *   *   *   *

Movement and change were indicative of the year. At the end of May Counteract moved to larger premises in Philip House, York Street. BT transferred the telephone system free of charge as a donation to

Counteract. Arrangements for administration of staff wages now fell to Noreen Moore. A Finance & General Purposes Committee was also set up to cover a wide range of administration matters. Contact was made with the Joint Council for Local Government Services to establish key benchmarks to help them in any review for current and future employees. More changes were due after the Management Committee considered and adopted the recommendations in the Initial Development Plan for 1999–2004.

Counteract and its partners wanted EDI embedded in the policies, practice and ethos of public institutions and private companies. To consolidate progress every Counteract programme operating in local authorities and the commercial sector was brought under the umbrella of what they called the 'Institutional Programme Area'.

The purpose of the Institutional Programme was to build capacity of individuals and groups in organisations so they could act as advocates for change. Training now went beyond awareness raising, seeking to create organisational 'equality proofing'. Counteract and Future Ways were to be external partners so that public/private bodies would have complete ownership in a process of changing to a more equitable ethos. The challenge was for Counteract and partners to gradually disengage over two years so organisations and their development groups took ownership of these new ways of working. It was later suggested that the term 'institutional' needed rethinking and a better description might be 'organisational'. However, whatever the wording, Counteract was working to facilitate change within the scope of the equality agenda.

There was also positive movement in the continuing work of the Counteract staff. The Community Unit had been set up so that community groups and voluntary organisations could deal with sectarianism at both an individual level and as a whole. The unit was providing advice and training to get anti-sectarian policies, procedures and practices adopted by the voluntary sector.

Joe Law and Paul Oakes of the Community Unit were working with both the Newry & Mourne[2] and the Cross-Border Projects. Fermanagh District, Belfast City, Coleraine Borough, Derry City, Castlereagh Borough, Ards Borough and Limavady Borough Councils were all interested in bringing Counteract on board. Paul Oakes' post had developed into Trainer/Development Officer, and CRC were to fund a Researcher for the Unit. By December they were involved with twelve of the twenty-six local Councils and expected more to approach Counteract in the near future.

They were also associated with Youthnet and its subsidiary groupings, delivering training to the IFI-funded Wider Horizons Programme.[3] The Community Unit helped eight youth organisations develop community relations policy and practice, as the 1998–99 Annual report states

> Having accepted the reality of the New Deal, we have recently been working in part-nership with the Armagh New Deal Project. We are designing a week-long training package examining the historical nature of the current conflict and how our different interpretations of history and politics prevent us from engaging in a more rational debate about the past.

The Community Unit also teamed up with Claire Killen, CRO in Castlereagh to produce an introductory course in Ballyoran Community Centre, *History, Politics and People – Part 1*. Using the early history, archae-ology and mythology of the British Isles and specifically Ireland a new per-spective was reached. This form of awareness raising was new to Counteract and proved effective in the short term as the Centre continued to develop training resources. However, teaching history and linguistics was not an area Counteract would develop. Others such as the Ulster Peoples College and the WEA had already broken new ground in this form of developmental political and identity education and Counteract was not in the business of duplicating existing work. Nevertheless, the Community Unit was in high demand and their work took them across Northern Ireland.[4]

*   *   *   *   *

Consensus building for Community Leaders & Activists was the product of work carried out in 1996–97 in an IFI-funded project run by Counteract, AC Network in Dublin, and the Labour Relations Agency exploring a range of strategies and techniques for consensus building and conflict resolution at local level. That programme ran through 1998–99 with pre-liminary awareness raising, and workshops to develop techniques for conflict resolution and consensus building.

Arthur Coldrick of AC Network reported

Fourteen community activists formed the core group of the project and a further twenty-six persons participated in one or more of the workshops or discussion groups. It is estimated that, in addition, nearly 200 people were involved in project related activities. Nine projects were undertaken by the activists and their groups, five based in Northern Ireland and four in the Republic of Ireland. … Project support came from informal monitoring from a panel set up by AC Network and Counteract. Each project had a named mentor who maintained links with the designated project co-ordinator and thus a constant connection was maintained with the groups, with informal advice and assistance rendered as necessary.

There were nine core participating groups.[5] The trends identified in the case studies were documented in *Consensus building for community leaders/activists* and demonstrated eight key elements.

- The importance of perceptions in all consensus building and how false perceptions connected to assumptions undermine well-intended activity. Unfounded or incorrect assumptions added to perceptions can also underpin prejudice;
- Direct dialogue is a powerful tool in promoting understanding;
- Identifying and interacting with 'key players and institutions' is vital to creating consensus and better understanding between community groups and the wider society. Projects in Belfast and Cork were seen to use these elements as core in their work;
- Central to consensus building is the re-appraisal of positions, policies and strategy with the passage of time;
- Groups can underestimate their potential and capacity. The energy, commitment and unrecognised expertise in local groups is a powerfully enabling factor in gaining insights and achieving results not possible through more established means;
- Innovative decision-making (and an appropriate, facilitative leadership style) are often needed plus a degree of risk-taking (which is not characteristic of many formal institutions);
- It is practicable to build bridges and/or make alliances with other groups or institutions to achieve common aims, even where conventional viewpoints suggest this is not possible;
- State and Voluntary bodies, Employer and Trade Union interests, Protestant and Catholic groups etc. can and do identify issues of common concern where joint action is appropriate in their

respective interests. Such joint actions can stimulate further mutual understanding.[6]

Documenting this knowledge and experience gave a wider audience access to understanding how consensus building and prejudice reduction was achievable, empowering and could be replicated at community level and in partnerships. The project provided concrete evidence for policy makers as well as funding bodies, and grass-roots practitioners, as Arthur Goldrick said in the Counteract Annual report:

> Consensus building has been shown to be a core element, directly or indirectly, of community group activity, and the building blocks of consensus building activity such as positive listening, refining perceptions and the understanding of diversity, have been shown to be relevant to a variety of contexts, for example political disadvantage [and] social exclusion.

*　　*　　*　　*　　*

Trade Unions continued to take Counteract training and services. A previous FEC, NIC ICTU & Counteract anti-sectarian seminar in 1997 showed a lack of knowledge on Fair Employment Law and practice, after which Counteract and the FEC drew up a unique and accredited course *Fair Employment Practice in the Workplace*. This course developed with the FEC and ICTU on fair employment was delivered in BIFHE to shop stewards and officials in the trade union movement.

Progress was made publicly with the launch of *Doing Business in a Divided Society*. This was a new set of codes to promote good practice. The News Letter headlined with *the battle to combat prejudice*:[7]

> Central to the guidelines, which have been co-sponsored by the News Letter and the Irish News, and endorsed by Counteract, the trade union anti-intimidation unit, is the understanding that 'managing diversity is good management practice' but that 'individual difference is to be valued, not feared.' ... The CBI, Institute of Directors, Chief Executives' Forum, Institute of Personnel and Development, NI Chamber of Commerce, Federation of Small Businesses, Institute of Management, NI Quality Centre and Business in the Community will distribute 10,000 copies of the guidelines to all members to promote discussion within the business community on the issues raised.

*　　*　　*　　*　　*

The Newry & Mourne Council project, Relationships in Equity, Diversity and Interdependence (REDI) had started well and was bringing increased interest from a number of District Councils. This benefitted Counteract, both financially and with prestige. Similar projects were being considered or developed with Coleraine, Antrim, Dungannon, Lisburn and Ards Councils. Furthermore, Counteract had noted that the new Equality Commission's forthcoming Equality Review would increase local Councils' motivation to use the Counteract services.

Forthcoming Chief Executive of Newry and Mourne District Council, Tom McCall and Chairperson Councillor Josephine O'Hare reported

> REDI has raised more questions than it has provided answers but it is a tribute to the professionalism of Counteract and Future Ways staff that we have made so much progress during the last year. The commitment, dedication, patience and enthusiasm that Counteract personnel brought with them to the Council has been so infectious and contagious that we have a real commitment throughout all levels of our Council to make the REDI project truly work. We at Newry & Mourne are deeply appreciative of the important work Billy Robinson and his staff has enabled us to embark upon. We have a long way to go but we are looking forward to the journey.

So, what was REDI about? The idea for an initiative that would 'fire-proof' rather than 'fire fight' was the result of many discussions between Joe Hinds and Billy Robinson in the later 1990s.

Counteract saw the need to embed an ethos of equality into the structure, strategy, planning and operation of organisations and – to use Billy Robinson's words – that meant addressing flawed relationships. An anti-sectarian culture had to be created and sustained if organisations were going to 'fire-proof' rather than just 'fire fight' – and the community relations agenda of 'equity, diversity and interdependence' seemed to cover all contingencies. Nothing less would effectively address prejudice, harassment and intimidation at work. Making such fundamental changes to an organisation required a new set of methods, and would need much more than a series of training sessions.

Thus, REDI came about as a first attempt at organisational change 'to embed the principles of fairness and respect for difference at the core of Newry and Mourne's policy and practice'.[8] The Council recognised the

need to address the serious under-representation of Protestants in their
workforce and build better relations at work – as the FEC had identified
significant employment inequality. As there was no pre-existing work or
knowledge in this area the task for those involved in REDI was to develop
a model. The IFI backed Counteract in this intricate experiment.

REDI was the outcome of the persuasive relationship between Joe
Hinds and Billy Robinson, and Newry and Mourne Council. Future Ways
and Counteract made a partnership and reported back to IFI after two
years work with Newry and Mourne Council. REDI was one of the most
significant processes that had evolved in the Council in recent years. Many
lessons would be learned from this pilot venture so that Newry and Mourne
Council were in a position to make changes and act as a catalyst for change
in other Councils. It was an ambitious attempt at embedding good community relations at the core of Council work – as a means to achieve fair
employment and copper fasten equality. Where community relations had
previously been undertaken by a temporary-contract CRO, it was periph-
eral work with community projects, 'out there'.

REDI was to bring about structural changes so that the CRO became
permanent, promoted in status, working under the Chief Executive Officer
in a new Equality Unit that had power and influence across all departments,
in a proofing role. The Council employed a second CRO, out of its own ex-
penditure, as distinct from CRC or government funding. In this way both
'good relations' and equality work were being embedded in the structure
and core function of the Council. By 2000 REDI would be at the stage
where EDI thinking was integral to senior management, so it became part
of strategic and operational planning in all Council departments. All the
key managers needed to understand and appreciate the implications of
EDI to their work, and implement the changes needed. They would also
have to monitor those changes.

REDI surpassed what was required by ECNI as regards compliance
with the positive equality duty and equality schemes required under Section
75 and Schedule 9 of the 1998 Northern Ireland Act. As ECNI recognised,
equality schemes could not change the culture of organisations. They could
begin at the stage of having policy proofing over a three-year period – but
beyond this, they could not make demands.

Counteract and Future Ways worked with management and staff in awareness training, and formed a Development Group. This work lasted for four years, complementing the political discussions in the Elected Members' Forum and created a genuine understanding that the 'complacent Nationalist culture'[9] was excluding Protestant-Unionists – in the Council and the district.

This value of this project is described in greater depth elsewhere[10] for those interested in reading the detail. Suffice to say that REDI made significant changes in the Council – though whether these would stand the test of time is another question. What is beyond doubt is the fact that this was ground-breaking work that dove-tailed with other initiatives to bring Council management and staff, Councillors and civic groups into discussions that were far ahead of any other local government Council. As the evaluation points out, this was a process and a method – neither a quick fix nor a project to be copied wholescale:

> The learning in Newry and Mourne was particular to them and the same lessons may not apply in other Councils to the same extent. One therefore has to be careful to view the REDI project as a process, through which learning was obtained and not a rigid programme which is 'applied to' an organisation.

Press reports – one of which included Mo Mowlam's imprimatur boosted Counteract's credibility.

In 1999 Counteract continued to run the Equity & Diversity Trainers (E&DT) Certificate course. This offered tutorial sessions as well one-to-one support. As training was competence-based it required variety and breadth of trainers, and experiential rather than purely knowledge-based learning. From the first two pilot courses lessons were learned and adaptations made.

The value of the certificate course was to be seen in its practical transferable use for people training in their own organisations.[11] Kate Fleck from PHAB developed a new model on equity and diversity as part of the RSA part-time Youth Workers Certificate. Others, like the participants from Ortus, took their training back to spread throughout their organisation.

The second E&DT Certificate course began in February 1999. People from the RUC, CROs from Coleraine and Lisburn, Derry Peace & Reconciliation Group, IVS (NI), NICEM, Edward Street Hostel, The

Group aims to stamp out sectarianism

19.11.98

By **Nevin Farrell**

COUNCILLORS are being urged to avoid using sectarian language in town halls and council chambers under new anti-discrimination initiatives.

Representatives in Newry and Mourne district council are the first in Northern Ireland being warned to be careful with their comments.

And the group behind a scheme to eradicate alleged sectarianism throughout local councils and all workplaces across the Northern Ireland — Counteract — have been praised for their work by Secretary of State Mo Mowlam.

Belfast-based Counteract — which was born out of the trade union movement — yesterday met with Dr Mowlam to explain their work.

The group's director, Billy Robinson, told how Counteract used to be called in to workplaces to "fire-fight" specific problems but now they were striving to help businesses and councils adopt strategies to eradicate sectarianism.

He said they were now more proactive in their approach to combating sectarianism.

For instance, Newry and Mourne district council brought the group in to make community relations a key part of the council's work.

Mr Robinson said the project, which had been running for three years, even looked at the language councillors used, encouraging them to make political points without falling into a "sectarian pit".

He added they had also been approached by a number of other councils to look at ways of improving their whole ethos.

The smothering of offensive conduct in the workplace, Mr Robinson said, was the "adhesive of the peace process".

Dr Mowlam told *the Irish News*: "I think Counteract is a very good step forward. Their work is increasing all the time and I think people are becoming aware that this is important.

● **PRAISE... Mo Mowlam**

"It's a partnership issue and there is no doubt that people are doing everything they can and Counteract is a good example of that happening," she added.

Dr Mowlam heard about Counteract's equity and diversity training certificate scheme which she said "delivered a powerful message against the pernicious effect of sectarianism in the workplace".

She added: "I have no doubt their work in the Newry and Mourne area will set a new benchmark for improving relationships based on mutual respect across political and religious divisions."

Picture 14: Mo Mowlam's approval. *Irish News* 19 November 1998

Boys and Girls Clubs (NI), Springwell Centre Lurgan and the Out and About Project Armagh took part. The course was then made to be available outside Belfast in the North West and South West:

> A year down the line we can actually see how the programme does underline and facilitate the practical application of current government thinking in relation to equity as put forward in the new Equality Scheme Guidelines. It has provided a platform for debate and strategic training, which addresses the pertinent issues in a practical manner. We hope that the course will continue to offer in house capacity building, the sharing of skills and experiences and most importantly the multiplication of good practice and new learning. (Paul Burke, Counteract)

Mo Mowlam visited the course and was impressed with both the training and the proposed Standard. She described the standard as 'the practical implementation of PAFT' (Policy Appraisal and Fair Treatment) (see Picture 14). A note of this visit was prepared by her secretariat and forwarded internally to senior civil servants. She wrote formally to Counteract and meetings were set up (see Picture 15).

Picture 15: Mo Mowlam, Joe Hinds and Billy Robinson with the ubiquitous Counteract cuppa

Demand for the E&DT Certificate course was high with over 30 enquiries, plus interest from the Gardai and talks were ongoing with FAS (The statutory Irish Youth Training body). Counteract Management Committee agreed to the employment of a second trainer provided this could be self-sustaining through fees. That became an issue in its own right. Counteract was having to adjust to market thinking, however reluctantly. As core funding decreased the course needed to generate enough fees to keep that part of the service running.

*   *   *   *   *

A key part of Counteract work that year was creating a quality instrument to establish the principles and practice of equity and diversity at the core of mainstream organisations. This was being explored by Counteract and Future Ways (UU) in their EDI Standard. This Standard (or Award depending on how the records described it) would be similar to the Total Quality Management Award under the BSI standards. Billy Robinson had met John Hunter, Under-Secretary DFP hoping to take this initiative forward and received a very positive response. Counteract secured funding from CRC, CRU[12] and a contribution in kind from the IPD to fund an eighteen-month action research and training programme to launch the Standard. By the end of the year Billy Robinson had negotiated the secondment of a principal officer from DFP to assist in the action research, and Pascal McCulla was about to join the team. This initiative was to become the Equity, Diversity and Interdependence Framework (EDIF) in 2000. As Pascal McCulla remembered

> The project ran between January 2000 and September 2001. I had the title of Project Director. It was known as EDIF (Equity Diversity and Interdependence Framework).
>
> It was a joint venture between the University of Ulster/Counteract. The project focused on planning the design, delivery and application of a management methodology to apply Diversity in organisations. It essentially was to demonstrate that what was generally called Diversity could be mainstreamed in Northern Ireland across all sectors.
>
> This project included designing a new way of thinking of diversity, as a mainstream management competence, and applying the framework in a range of organisations across the public, private, and community and voluntary sectors.
>
> We worked with a range of senior managers in DCAL, HMCR, Eircom and the Rural Community Network to develop them as managers in the EDIF skills. For

each organisation I produced a manual with module descriptors and quality assurance documentation including tutor manuals. The framework produced was infused with the work on learning by Peter Senge and Chris Arygris. (Pascal McCulla, 2020)

This is discussed in more detail later in the book.

The IFI[13] funded the publication of materials Counteract had developed over the past two years – so they could then demonstrate and share crucial information, from their experience using practical anti-sectarian techniques. Early in 1999 *Community Relations – A Counteract Perspective, Trainers' Guidelines, Understanding Affirmative Action, Sectarian Harassment at Work, Anti-Sectarianism Means Business, Total Quality Management and the Anti-Sectarian Ethos*, and *Understanding the Law on Fair Employment* were in the public arena.

Counteract was getting their message out, although it had taken some years to put this into print – and their manuals made the anti-sectarian case in a measured but no less passionate manner than in their training.

What is sectarian harassment?

- Actions, behaviour, comments or physical contact which causes offence or is objectionable;
- Behaviour which makes a person feel threatened, humiliated or patronised or which creates an intimidating working environment;
- It is defined by *the impact on the recipient* and *not* by *the intention of the harasser*.

Written harassment includes the circulation of sectarian notes, letters and other written material containing offensive language.

Visual displays of offensive material refers to the presence of sectarian posters, graffiti, flags, bunting and emblems in the workplace.

Offensive behaviour includes sectarian name-calling, 'banter', physical threat, assault, and insulting behaviour or gestures, isolation, non-co-operation at work, exclusion from social activities,

interference with job performance, unfair allocation of work, pressure to join or make contributions to religious or political groups.
Source Counteract, 'Sectarian harassment at Work'

The FEC could take on complaints, with an inquisitorial style, and a
Tribunal could fine those found wanting – up to £30,000 until that ceiling
was broken in 1998 and the potential damages became unlimited. Counteract
had to rely on the powers of the FEC and Tribunal judgements to substantiate – at least in part – the business case for tackling intimidation and harassment. Indeed, the very existence of the FEC opened doors to management
and employers who might not otherwise have engaged with Counteract:

What must be done about sectarian harassment?

The employer's responsibility – in law, ignorance is no defence – made management
keen to use the services of Counteract. A company could train managers, supervisors and staff. Also, they could engage Counteract to help them create or review
policies, procedures and good practice in dealing with allegations of intimidation
or prejudice at work.

Unfortunately, some managers wrote up policies and put procedure into print but not
into practice. Many of them ended up losing FET cases and returning to Counteract.
Sectarianism was to be handled like health and safety issues – and not an add-on
in crisis situations.

Every employer has a responsibility to:

• Uphold Fair employment legislation;
• Follow recommendations in the Fair Employment Code of Practice;
• Identify and implement appropriate policies and procedures to prevent and deal
  with sectarian harassment in the workplace;
• Ensure appropriate action is taken to deal with any incident of harassment;
• Provide appropriate training for individuals with designated roles under the policy
  and procedure;
• Take regular steps to actively promote the policy and procedure, e.g. awareness
  training;
• Ensure there is no further problem or harassment, or victimisation after a com-
  plaint has been resolved;
• Monitor the incidence of harassment;
• Regularly review the effectiveness of policy and procedure;

- Where appropriate, work with trade unions or employees' representatives to ensure the creation and maintenance of a good and harmonious working environment.

(Source Counteract, Sectarian harassment at Work)

However, the FEC had neither the remit nor resources to provide general equality and anti-sectarian training and education. And their style was different to Counteract. Facing an audience which was cautious, if not hostile to fair employment, they aimed to establish a grudging acceptance – leaving other more hard-hitting presentations to Counteract hoping this would not 'disrupt' the atmosphere. The FEC was known, by its more outspoken detractors, as the 'Fenian Employment Commission'. All equality work in Northern Ireland began with serious opposition from those who believed that if some won rights and fairness others would automatically lose out.

The FEC was clear about its role, the law and the role of shop stewards. By contrast Counteract prided itself that it '… did not talk about coreligionists without mummies and daddies – it's fenian bastards and orange bastards isn't it?' (Billy Robinson) Statutory professionals were not tasked to rake up and then deal with that intensity of hostility, and were not experienced enough to 'let them let off steam'. However effective they proved to be, the methods Counteract used remained contentious:

Why do people stay silent about sectarian harassment?

Fear that they will not be believed, that they will be ostracised or victimised for complaining or that they will lose their job or promotion. People also fear for their personal safety, because of lack of confidentiality.

Others remain silent for fear that they too will become victims. This reflects on the management since it shows employees lack either awareness about or faith in the organisation's ability to eliminate intimidation in the workplace.

(Source Counteract, 'Sectarian harassment at Work')

* * * * *

The imminent arrival of a seconded civil servant came after a Counteract session with 500 civil servants, as part of a move to prepare them for working in the new 'peaceful' Northern Ireland. Billy Robinson brought Jane Elliott, whom he had met in the USA at Fordham in 1996, to give a presentation of 'A class divided: Brown Eye Blue Eye' (used in a Channel 4 TV documentary in 2020). Her personal appearance was the star attraction and made a dramatic impact on the audience (see Picture 16). The connection between racism in the US and sectarianism in Northern Ireland was made – and the importance resonates in 2020 with the Black Lives Matter movement.

Picture 16: Jane Elliott, PA, Pascal and Olaf

Of its numerous partnerships and collaborations, a central one for Counteract was with Future Ways (UU). Karen Eyben summed up the constructive partnership between them:

> As a result of its history and knowledge base Counteract seeks to quickly crystallise the problem in order that a solution and 'way out' be rapidly effected. Future Ways works from a different context and seeks 'ways out' by giving people the space to discover greater complexities about themselves. However, both groups share a common belief that the freedom to engage in new relationships can only exist in secure, inclusive and fair structures.

Their partnership required that agreed structures and working practices were put in place. These lessons are especially useful to forming and sustaining any partnership, and so are included below:

Agreement between partners has to be reached on

- *Who's the boss?* Who makes the decisions and how are these processed?
- *Who holds the purse-strings?* Agreeing on financial structures and accountability is often the base of a successful partnership.
- *How are the rules and responsibilities allocated and are these complementary?*
- *Is there a common value base?*
- *Is there a commitment to non-disclosure and confidentiality of information?*
- *Is there freedom to challenge each other's language, models and assumptions?* Is there enough trust in the relationship to question and criticise often dearly held assumptions?
- *How is administration structured?* Who chairs meetings, takes minutes etc.?
- *Is reflection a legitimate strand of the partnership?* Partnerships can generate a lot of new learnings and issues, and these need to be articulated and captured.

Clearly, there was a need to establish boundaries, and written agreement on these, which may indicate that there were some difficulties in the partnership.

* * * * *

Counteract went through development on a number of fronts in 1999. Central government agreed to fund a three-year Researcher post. As it was important to employ an experienced researcher with a commitment to the ethos of Counteract, both the Management Committee and an academic were involved in the selection procedure. In autumn 1999 Stephen Bloomer took up post.

The Community Unit took on extensive new work with companies: Prudential Insurance Company (500 staff), North West Housing Association (200 staff), Moypark (Management training), Milk Marketing Board (650 staff) and P. J. Halls (200 Management/staff). They were also being engaged by Dungannon and Coleraine Councils, embarking on a similar project to Newry & Mourne.

A Counteract article written by Stephen Nolan and Billy Robinson was published in a special edition of the prestigious Fordham International Law Journal. *Counteract: Working for Change*[14] put the anti-sectarian unit in an international forum, and recording the work for interested scholars of law and conflict resolution.

*   *   *   *   *

The Counteract team was engaged in discussion strategic developments and Joe Hinds facilitated an unusual in-house workshop (see Picture 17).

Pat McGinn formally presented of his draft Development Plan (1999–2004) to the Management Committee, based on an ongoing evaluation. Although this gave a focus to building better organisational skills, it emphasised the fact that adequate funding was clearly also necessary[15] if Counteract was to be more effective and efficient.

Picture 17: Joe Hinds, Stephen Nolan, Joe Law, Sara Hunter, Joe Burke, Billy Robinson, Billy McCreight, Paul Oakes and Stephen Bloomer

The Committee agreed to act on key issues in the Plan. Pat McGinn recommended strongly that they ensure that Counteract was seen as a separate entity from the BURC and NIC ICTU (new premises achieved this in part), develop staff training, update training materials and set up a small ad-hoc group to carry forward such matters.[16] The Committee would have to play a full and active role, be given more advance briefings from the Director and staff, form a General Purposes Sub-committee and take a more strategic role. It was also said that the Committee would benefit by including representatives from other bodies and increasing their number to develop the future sub-committee system.

Pat McGinn believed Counteract could become the leading provider of Equality, Diversity and Interdependence training and advice – but only if it undertook more refined organisational and developmental measures. His report emphasised the importance of 'synergies between programmes' keeping excellence in each, and pointed to the importance of clear guidelines for staff. It was politely pointing out that both the organisation and line management needed immediate attention.

The Plan suggested that reference to Counteract as a Trade Union sponsored Anti-intimidation Unit was outdated at this juncture and was perhaps off-putting to potential users. This was an issue for detailed future discussion and consultation. It remained a hotly debated subject for the rest of the organisation's time

Benda Callaghan and others from the Trade Union movement who had been involved in Counteract since its formative years remained strongly opposed to this change. She was passionately against the proposal to drop the strap line 'trade union sponsored anti-sectarian unit', believing that the links with the movement were essential:

> Why deny Counteract's background? Why remove its roots, suppress knowledge of its roots? It risks losing the original drive and ethos. Counteract was sold on its trade union base and had its independence. I would need deep convincing why you'd remove the strap. It places it in its sector of society. Counteract was not and should not be seen as other than 'Fairness, Work and Progress'. It is like the WEA denying its trade union background.

The recommendations and proposed development plan were still at a draft stage – but suggestions for change were not well received by Trade Unionists.

Notes

1. This was under the provisions of the Employment Equality Act (1998).
2. Work with Newry & Mourne District Council was continuing, a scoping study had just been completed and a sub-committee has been established within the Council. This project expected to have a three-year duration. Steven Nolan and Joe Law went to Birmingham with the Newry & Mourne Development Group on a study trip looking specifically at how local authorities deal with and manage an extremely diverse workforce, deliver services to a diverse community and manage a close working relationship with the West Midlands Police Force.
3. This work and the direction of the Unit would have consequences for the Equity & Diversity Trainers Certificate course, bringing the Youth sector into its training.
4. There was other educational and practical input from Counteract when the Community Unit went to Lurgan Community Trust, Community Network Portadown, Ulster Peoples College (CR certificate), the Armagh Unemployed Centre and E-Force Training. (A week-long course for E-Force trainee journalists was designed to consider how personal prejudice and ideological representations influence how reporting is carried out.) On top of this, the unit worked with Armagh Inter-Church Group, The Quakers, Craigavon Partnership Board, The Princes Trust, Springboard, The Cornerstone Community and the Community Development Health Network 'Policy to Practice training for H&SS professionals on CR and Community Development methods of working'.
5. Five groups came from the North (Shankill Women's Group, North Belfast Community Development Centre, St Colm's Park House, Link resource Centre and IVS NI) and four from the South (Cork City Network – Irish Council of People with Disabilities, Dundalk Resource Centre, Irish National Organisation for the Unemployed and Irish Trade Union Trust). Others taking part included Springfield Inter-Community Group and Confederation of Small Businesses (North) and Community Response and Energy Action Ltd. (South).
6. Page 6 of 'Consensus building for community leaders/activists'.
7. News Letter 20 April 1998.
8. Quoted from a draft report for the Community Relations Unit Evaluation of REDI Project, by Research and Evaluation Services.
9. These are the words of the REDI team, describing District Council in 1998 quoted in 'The Smaller Peace Process' PhD Thesis, Roz Goldie, Queen's University Belfast, 2008.
10. *'Problem, Process and Product: Implementing Key Reforms in Local Government in Northern Ireland Since the Belfast Agreement'*, Roz Goldie, Local Government Studies 1–13, 2012.

11. During the course of the training programme, the RUC trainers had indicated that a number of other police services in the UK and elsewhere had discussed the possibility of joint training. It was agreed to investigate the possibility of a summer school.

12. CCRU had become CRU in OFMDFM.

13. IFI Community Bridges Programme gave Counteract support and advice and eventually funded the publication of important documents on the learning of several years' work.

14. The article by Billy Robinson and Stevie Nolan in *Fordham International Law Journal*, Volume 22, Number 4, April 1999.

15. Minutes of the Management Committee record that 'salary levels were still somewhat behind comparable organisations.'

16. The ad-hoc group included Billy McCreight (as Chair of the Committee and trade union nominee), Margaret McGurk (statutory nominee), Janet Hunter (community/voluntary nominee) and Billy Robinson (Director).

CHAPTER 11

2000: If You Do What You've Always Done, You Get What You've Always Got

The millennium year was one in which the equality agenda finally reached throughout Britain and Ireland. In the Republic, equality schemes (albeit voluntary) were introduced. In Britain the debate was heated about the inherent racism in the terms British and English. The Runnymede Trust reported on a study in *The Future of Multi-Ethnic Britain*[1] causing massive media attention and widespread denial that 'there ain't no black in the Union Jack.' Lessons could and should have been learned by those who looked down on the pariah state that was Northern Ireland.

Law and policy moves had put prejudice much further forward in the public consciousness in Northern Ireland than had happened elsewhere. It was telling that there should even have been media comment on the fact that the new Speaker in the House of Commons, Michael Martin, was a Roman Catholic; allegedly the first to hold the position. It was indicative of institutional prejudice that for the first time all the leaders of Britain's religions were invited to be present at the Cenotaph in London on Remembrance Sunday:

> Non-Christian organisations will participate in the Remembrance service at the Cenotaph, the Home Office said yesterday. Sikh, Muslim, Buddhist and Hindu groups will be allowed to take part in the ceremony as a tribute to their sacrifice for Britain during the two world wars. Lord Weatherill, who served in the Indian Army in the Second World War, said: 'I am thrilled. I had the privilege to serve with the Indian soldiers who proved to be extremely loyal in fighting in two wars that really had nothing to do with them.'

This shocked many people who had never even known that they had been excluded for over half a century.[2]

The politics of the Northern Ireland Assembly became increasingly convoluted in 2000. The smaller parties were eclipsed and the two dominant parties, the UUP and SDLP, vied to hold centre stage – in danger of being obscured by the third and fourth largest parties, Sinn Féin and the DUP. The two DUP Ministers and other party members played a cynical game of pretending to abstain from Stormont while, in fact, taking their seats and doing only the politically expedient parts of their work.

The state of the over-stretched NHS was as much a focus in health matters as the Sinn Féin minister herself. In the event, all pro-agreement parties did work together, though with little noticeable short-term effect, as budgetary limits had been set in London before d'Hondt was triggered. Still, as Northern Ireland got its first locally agreed budget for thirty years, there was a palpable sense of achievement.

Issues that exercised the public consciousness in 2000 included the bitterly disputed requirement that all barristers swear allegiance to the crown – in order that they might become, eventually, Queen's Counsel. After much wrangling and wringing of Unionist-biased hands, the profession accepted that such a requirement would be offensive to certain traditions. So, another bastion had been stormed, according to the perceptions of many at the bar in Northern Ireland.

The politics of the UUP were in a state of continuous crisis as the anti-Agreement camp gained ground and the Orange Order put maximum pressure on the leadership of the party in February. David Trimble's political majority was reduced to a perilous 3%. The loss of the UUP seat in South Antrim to the DUP's Rev. Willie McCrea in September threatened another crisis. The UUP had to decide whether to stand its ground or field a 'No' candidate in the hope of appearing nearer to the DUP. In the event, the latter strategy did not work. At the same time, progress on IRA weapons de-commissioning was very slow, some said non-existent, which did not help the UUP maintain its stance of governing with Sinn Féin in the Assembly, in the teeth of DUP electoral gains.

Education was in the hands of Martin McGuiness (Sinn Féin) whose opposition to the 11-plus selection exam was well known. The Grammar Schools' lobby, which had rushed into action in 1999, feared the worst when independent research proposed five options, only one of which was to keep the current set up of academic selection. The debate carried on into 2001 and through the next two decades.

The degree to which the UUP was losing ground with its electorate was possibly overstated to gain leverage in the debate on the Policing Bill. However, tensions ran high as the moderate pro-Agreement Unionists strove desperately to show the Protestants of Ulster that all was not lost in staying with the peace process.

Tony Blair's besieged administration was preoccupied that summer with the Labour party conference overshadowed by the summer's woes, the fuel crisis and the revolt of the grey lobby on old age pensions. Northern Ireland was not his top priority – until the October meeting of the Unionist Party Executive exposing the threat to David Trimble's small majority. Inherent instability in the peace process – and the potential for the ending of the local assembly – came from the 'rock and the hard place' of Patten's police reform and the de-commissioning of paramilitary arms. Arms still in the hands of the IRA and proposed reforms to policing made this a last-ditch-stand for Unionists – and became more central after the UUP lost to the DUP in the autumn election in South Antrim. In the event, the Trimble compromise won an 8% victory, but at the expense of including Sinn Féin in the North-South Inter-governmental process.

The year came towards an end with the First Minister refusing to sign up to Sinn Féin ministers attending these cross-border bodies in the teeth of opposition from the SDLP and the Republic's government. Sinn Féin poised itself for a legal challenge to the First Minister's embargo.

The Belfast Ship Yard Harland & Wolff had always been a touchstone of the feelings on one side of the sectarian divide and symbolic of the economic and political supremacy of Unionism-Protestantism. During the boom times of the 1920s, the yard had 40,000 employees and sustained that number for approximately 30 years. The fortunes and fate of the yard were regarded as being indicative of the condition of Unionist Northern Ireland – and had traditionally been most acutely felt in East Belfast. By October 2000, it was on the verge of closure again after years of uncertainty, low or no orders and the general decline of the industry. Press reports stated that the 140-year-old yard had been reduced to a staff of 600 and that closure was imminent. As if to mirror the precarious progress of the peace process, only last-minute orders saved the yard from closure late that month.[3]

On 2 October 2000, European law, in the form of the long-awaited Human Rights Act (1988), came into force in Northern Ireland – which underwrote the equality agenda in the Northern Ireland Act. This copper-fastened the legislative basis for the equality agenda already in place and heightened interest in how equality could be made to work, and particularly across the public sector.

In mid-October, the press reported reaction to the Port Inquiry[4] into the murder of Lurgan solicitor Rosemary Nelson. East Londonderry UUP MP Willie Ross demanded details of spending and expenses entailed in the inquiry – thinly veiling the inherent sectarianism by adding a request for costs relating to the investigations into the murders of Pat Finucane (another lawyer killed for upholding the rule of law in cases brought against Republicans) and the Loyalist prisoner Billy Wright (killed inside the Maze Prison). Paralleling objections to the cost of the Bloody Sunday Inquiry, this move towards justice and human rights was resented by many as being too costly.

*   *   *   *   *

As a strategic part of its development Counteract embraced the EDI principles. This begged the question of whether the broad scope of the new single Equality Commission would lead to weakening the focus on anti-sectarian work. Was there still a specialist niche for Counteract if ECNI pursued the path of holistic anti-prejudice work? And would sectarianism cease to be the biggest issue on the equal treatment agenda in Northern Ireland? Interviews conducted at this stage highlighted the dilemma. Would a Counteract policy of taking all major forms of prejudice into account affect its unique position of providing anti-sectarian solutions and training and education?

Racism had long been part of the Counteract agenda and was increasingly a core issue as spurious immigration scares emerged and governments and press used derogatory language including terms like 'bogus asylum-seekers'. Whereas both Ireland and the UK needed immigrant labour to keep their economies growing, the public panicked about 'floods of economic migrants'. What was laughingly called a debate was in fact a virtual publicity campaign that pandered to the racist populations of both states.

Northern Ireland managed to achieve the dubious status of being 'twice as racist as sectarian', according to the London Commission for Racial Equality journal *Connections* in a 'Call for Change in Northern Ireland', Summer 2000. Researchers from UU interviewed 1,267 people with the startling results that twice as many people

> were unwilling to accept or mix with members of ethnic minority communities as they were with members of an 'opposing' religion. And attitudes towards specific groups appeared to be getting worse. The survey found that 54% of people were unwilling to accept a south Asian person as a relative, compared with 37% in 1995/96; while 53% did not want a Chinese person as a relative, compared to 32% in 1995/96. The report called for the Equality Commission for Northern Ireland to produce a broad strategy to reduce racial prejudice. It also recommended specific training for all staff and users of public authorities; for the NI Housing Executive to co-ordinate initiatives between Travellers and settled people; and for the Department of Education to introduce a multicultural and anti-racist element to the National Curriculum in Northern Ireland and the Youth Service Curriculum.

The peace process in Northern Ireland had not improved race or community relations.

*   *   *   *   *

The Counteract strategy in the late 1990s was to develop their Equity, Diversity and Interdependence Framework (EDIF) into a Programme and a practical tool to embed the EDI ethos and implement the equity agenda in organisations – and to do that Counteract had to expand existing partnerships, hoping an enlarged network would build on that with pragmatic, achievable benchmarks.

Counteract and Future Ways produced a tool for organisational self-assessment and a standard indicator for Equality. This emerged as the EDIF Programme with a Director, Pascal McCulla,[5] on secondment from DFP. His experience brought in-depth knowledge of applying the concept of diversity in the Northern Ireland Civil Service mainstream management and quality management standards. He also brought extensive experience in management standards (such as Investor in People and EFQM's Business Excellence Model).

Craig Cameron, former Director of Personnel, Du Pont UK also gave specialist advice as Programme Consultant on a pro-bono basis. The Project was managed by a Board[6] and funded by CRC with assistance from the EU Special Support Programme and the central government's CRU.

The EDI Framework was designed to support organisations trying to operate on the three principles of fairness, valuing difference and mutuality. EDIF moved beyond the customary silence and avoidance. It stated

> by recognising that to be different is to be human. It affirms that exploring diversity can enhance how people develop individually, within organisations and ultimately as to how society benefits.

> Equity is about ensuring that people from all sections of society have equal opportunities to participate in economic, political and social life through redressing inequalities arising independently from people's choices.

> Diversity is about being free to shape and articulate our identities as individual human beings and as members of different groups.

> Interdependence is about acknowledging that we are shaped by our relationships, and that our potential as human beings and as a society is dependent on the quality of our relationships and networks.

> The Framework is:

> - A process to support the leadership and people within an organisation, deepening their understanding, confidence and skills in managing relationships based on difference and equity;
> - An internal self-assessment framework, which allows an organisation to plan, implement and measure against previous internal benchmarks and, if the information is available, in comparison with other similar organisations;
> - A foundation process and a set of values underpinning and enhancing existing standards and quality management initiatives.

EDIF was to complement and reinforce existing (good) practice – not to be an add-on or stand-alone measure. EDIF was promoted as a measure of whether organisations reproduced the wider social inequalities and prejudices in their work practices, values and relationships. It concerned the costs of avoidance to business and claimed to help organisations develop core business strategies to make them more openly diverse, fair and effective.

Moving beyond sectarianism, it covered all exclusion and prejudice – focusing on how tensions, conflicts and fears generated by the political/ religious divisions were reflected in and reinforced by poor organisational practices. It placed sectarianism within the wider setting of exclusion and prejudice.

Counteract and its partners knew the importance of equipping organisations to change their working culture. Compliance with the requirements of fair treatment legislation, and the significant clout of Tribunals, had been the leverage that Counteract had used within organisations it had wanted to help develop. However, legal compliance was not sufficient to embed an ethos of EDI and, consequently, the EDIF pilot project was a necessary new departure.

EDIF was about going beyond fixing single disputes and problem-specific situations. The difficulties of flawed working relationships might be solved in the short term, but the culture of the organisation did not change and therefore similar problems would simply recur. EDIF was about reaching the intricacies of those attitudes, beliefs and feelings that shaped the way individuals and groups behaved and organisations operated. It was a tool to identify the tacit culture of organisations; whether it meant finding an understanding of how the 'glass ceiling' operated or unravelling the dynamics of exclusion. Disputes arose repeatedly, albeit in different or subtler forms, because the underlying reasons for them were not addressed. Counteract training exposed both the obvious and the more subtle forms of prejudice, discrimination and intimidation, reminding organisations that compliance with the law was necessary.

This approach was based on Peter Senge's ideas in the 'Learning Organisation', where the working culture is open to learning, accepts that people make mistakes and can learn from them. In learning organisations, improvement comes because people are able to admit openly to making mistakes – which decreases rather than increases the rate of error. Getting past the fear of being wrong was a basic component of achieving EDI or not – and it was the job of leadership to direct and help individuals begin to see and understand their own behaviour and how they contributed to negative aspects of 'how things are done around here' – that is, the tacit culture.

* * * * *

By examining the tacit culture organisations identified the roots of many problems created by bullying, intimidation and discrimination and prejudice at work, they find solutions to and change these. For profit-making organisations, the pay-off was clearly financial and derived from the business case for EDI. For non-profit making organisations, the incentive was to meet objectives and targets set by funders, government etc. In all cases a key issue was absentee rates.

Yet, in whichever sector it operated, tentatively as it was still at a pilot stage, EDIF appeared to yield most when it involved people who were eager to make changes. It worked best for organisations where failing to change led to some loss (through lack of competitiveness, poor levels of productivity, high levels of sickness leave, or bad press and public image).

Twenty years later the management fashions of the Learning Organisations, IIP and TQM seem quaintly outdated, and EDIF is not mainstream management vocabulary. However, the everyday language of 'the tacit culture' was crucial and remains useful for those interested in seeing improvements in how things are done.

* * * * *

Tacit culture is a catch-all phrase that Billy Robinson used and understood to mean the unspoken rules of an organisation's staff. In popular speech the phrase is 'canteen culture' which maybe gives more of a hint that it may conflict with official policy.

Generally, people whose 'faces fit' tend to succeed more often than those whose don't. The unsaid rules are to 'play the game' and that means being just like others who succeed. The woman who does not go for a drink after work or the man who does not laugh at the boss's jokes is unlikely to get promotion as quickly as 'one of the crowd'. Exploring what the unspoken rules dictate and critically appraising both the attitudes and what is acceptable behaviour is the way to uncover what the tacit culture is and how it works. It is only at that level that enhancing the working culture can take place.

In the new methodology there was a new vocabulary – full commitment to change in senior management was a critical factor because these 'drivers' or 'champions' of change had to agree the EDI principles from the start and support this by creating developmental and working groups, in co-operation with outsiders such as Counteract and its partners.

The new approach was not confrontational – and that was something of a culture change for Counteract which negotiated and trained in a largely combative style. It marked a significant move away from tackling or fighting prejudice towards engaging with organisations. Counteract was no longer waging a battle against employers and factions permitted by employers to perpetrate intimidation and discrimination. It was a partner in a co-operative venture and saw a role for management as well as unions in making a sustainable difference.

At the end of 2000, EDIF was still in the pilot stage with a number of partner organisations across the public, private and voluntary sectors testing the relevance and applicability of its ideas. The pilot phase lasted until March 2001 – when publication of findings, provision of training programmes, learning networks, advice/support for organisations and a policy platform was planned.

The ultimate success or failure of EDIF has always depended on the will of the statutory and private sectors and whether there was a genuine desire to shake the foundations of a culture of prejudice.

*   *   *   *   *

Returning to the 'coal face' of its work Counteract facilitated International Voluntary Service (NI) and began a ground-breaking programme with Loyalist ex-prisoners in 2000. Positive Action in Community Training (PACT) was a pilot project, funded by the IFI Bridges Programme, that started with three groups of key activists within brigade structures, with a total of 45 participants from outside Belfast. It provided ten training sessions on themes of single-identity work, political education and community development. These sessions were consolidated with two residentials and three one-day seminars.

A core aim was to identify and build on appropriate relationships and educative processes to encourage core members of particular paramilitary organisations to get the skills to move away from a militaristic violent culture to one of non-violence and engagement with the perceived enemy. This was done with the official endorsement and participation of each organisation. The project also aimed to move these people into more constructive relationships within their own communities.

A number of key lessons came from the pilot project. These were

- Much of the programme was learnt by doing in lieu of a previous approach or model for this work;
- Initially the facilitating organisations had difficulty gaining the trust and participation of people in the programme;
- Programme participants were not adept or comfortable with critical engagement or analysis;
- The internal structure of the organisations of the groups were extremely hierarchical with designated leaders who approved or disapproved of particular sessions, discussions or events;
- Perhaps not surprisingly there was a significant amount of ignorance, not only about Protestant/Loyalist/Unionist culture and history but others' cultures;
- There was in some cases a complete lack of basic social skills;
- At the time, in Loyalist paramilitaries, there was a constant undercurrent of factionalism and fragmentation that disrupted the cohesiveness and consensus of the groups;
- A progressive programme could have impact only where an 'enlightened' leader gave authority, space and permission to explore previously 'taboo' subjects;

On a more positive note it was also found that

- There was a significant number of people from the first phase who wanted to continue and develop their own leadership potential;
- A significant number of participants built up relationships of trust with the facilitators, sometimes to a disturbing degree in the context of their past activities;
- This work could only have its fullest impact if/when it was continued over a much longer time and was seen to be of benefit to participants.

Initially, attendance was good, but in one of the three groups, half dropped out within weeks. The pilot programme lasted a couple of months, and was evaluated. One of the lessons learned was that former 'combatants' were not ready to meet the 'other side' within a few weeks of training sessions. Asking Mid-Ulster Loyalists to talk with Republicans from the Bogside after so short a time had been a mistake. Counteract and IVS went back to the drawing board to re-appraise the work, its impact on the facilitators and the potential for developing this radical programme.

In hindsight, the lack of support and counselling for the facilitators had been a key lesson. It demonstrated the 'macho' culture in some of the working methods that Counteract had developed. Working under stress in extremely confrontational environments and pressure, they neglected the emotional side of its development. Not all Counteract staff had the 'emotional intelligence' or resilience of Billy Robinson – and both these were needed to withstand the corrosive effects of working with potentially violent situations on a regular, if not daily basis.

It may seem obvious that building the necessary relationships of trust would bring about disturbing as well as positive results. If people were to change how they behaved – even using a facilitative learning environment – they would bring their past into the process, if only to dump 'that past' before moving on. That is what happened in PACT. It is not a traditional British/Irish male characteristic to admit to fear and ask for help and support. Counteract faced up to the need to incorporate new support systems for some of its staff who encountered very threatening situations in their work.

It was also evident that short-term schemes would not do more than raise some basic questions. Certainly, work like the PACT project needed to done, but would take months (or years) rather than weeks to make a difference. Counteract never had the resources – financial or otherwise – to maintain that. And, there is anecdotal evidence that elements of the Loyalist paramilitary hierarchy were determined to 'spike their guns'.

To compound the difficulties for PACT, in 2000 the Loyalist feud in West Belfast that summer and autumn demonstrated the extent of internal factional problems. This played into the hands of those Loyalists who did not want to see PACT or anything else that eroded violent paramilitary activity on the ground.[7]

*   *   *   *   *

Through the 1990s Counteract became inured to the hostility it encountered. By 2000, they were being positively welcomed in some quarters as a provider of methods for promoting EDI. The language had changed from anti-sectarian to Equality, Diversity and Interdependence – although there was little emphasis on the Interdependence in EDI work. It remained a challenge to copper fasten the need for interdependence, as examples were few on the ground. This threw up the question of whether there had been changes in the core values of Counteract over the previous decade.

Counteract started as a trade union–based unit challenging sectarian intimidation and acting as a champion of oppressed and intimidated workers. Initially, recruitment for jobs in the unit required experience of trade union work. At that time, Counteract reflected best practice and a minority view within trade unionism. By 2000, it had moved beyond working exclusively for the victims of sectarianism, realising that fire-fighting and one-off training had been 'like putting lipstick on a bulldog' and didn't change the animal. However, adapting to the new times, methods and terminology it was to face a series of internal challenges.

The Management Committee now sought nominations from organisations reflecting the breadth of their service users – which meant going even further outside the ambit of the trade union movement. It needed to widen its contacts, and represent itself as other than a 'cloth cap' organisation that was anti-management. That generated internal debate and was also an issue, though a smaller one, for many of the larger companies and senior public service figures with whom it worked.

The place of trade unions was an emotive question for many associates, especially those who had been involved since the early days. The business community had been part of the problem faced by the anti-intimidation workers and the trade unions in the early 1990s – not part of the solution. The business community, which had not endorsed their early work, was regarded by trade Unionists as an opponent of a campaign for the rights of intimidated, endangered and murdered workers.

The argument put forward that, just as the larger political arena depicted changing views and allegiances throughout the decade, the smaller scene of Counteract work was visibly changed. The peace process and addressing EDI required the business community to be fully involved. If there was to be change in workplace behaviour and a new ethos, employers and management had to be part of the inclusive approach – meaning that they also had to have a stake in Counteract. Those who had been 'part of the problem' became 'part of the solution'. However, this was too big a change of heart and mind for some to accept.

At the same time, interviews conducted at this time showed that large employers – in both the public and private sectors – were still a touch reluctant to be seen to be using Counteract for dealing with prejudice and intimidation. While they appeared happy to be seen as proactive in adopting EDI and were willing to address difficult issues in private, they were concerned that being involved with Counteract would attract negative publicity for their organisations.

In light of its experience over a decade Counteract saw the EDI Framework as an opportunity for people to 'move up a gear' – by identifying the cultural issues in their organisation and dealing them effectively, closing the gap between the stated or official values and actual practice.

Billy Robinson saw the Framework and Programme as somewhat academic, but trusted that it would be an advance. Having operated as crisis management in search of instant solutions to sectarian intimidation Counteract was not a management consultancy. Its roots were in the Trade Union movement and this was a new departure. What neither Trade Unionists nor Counteract partners noticed was that the business case was not underpinned by a rights agenda.

While there were obvious benefits to Counteract in having the support, publicity and funding to develop EDI, this was the strap line for the Community Relations Council and not the Trade Union movement. Diverging from the Trade Union emphasis on workers' rights and the new legislation on equality and human rights Counteract did not see the difference between equality to equity as a problem but it was taking them down a new and as yet uncharted path.

*   *   *   *   *

The CENI evaluation of Counteract concluded that spending public money to support its work and development was justified, particularly as private consultancies were copying Counteract, purely for profit:

> There is evidence that the private sector consultancy firms are moving into this market. However, organisations that are motivated by profit may not want to challenge

management practices – given that it is management that is paying. Counteract's influence and credibility among the workforce lies in its alliance with the trade union movement, whereas management consultants would be seen as just management's consultants and thus are less likely to be effective.

There are serious drawbacks to providing this kind of service entirely on a consultancy or fee-paying basis. Firstly, as one manager stated [of Counteract], 'They were seen to be there to solve the problem, not earn money.' He also stated that organisations might stint on the amount of time for which they used the service. Especially before they fully understood its value.

Its effectiveness had never been measured before – quantitatively or qualitatively. Nor could it be, in hindsight, other than by the crude indicator of whether or not a certain crisis or problem had recurred within a particular organisation. However, this evaluation was an evidence-based endorsement of its work. And if measuring the efficacy of equality and anti-sectarian work was less than an exact science, gauging the success of EDIF was even more elusive.

* * * * *

More often than not, the outcome of Counteract work was not apparent until a lot later, when the progress or lack of it was documented. The Youthquest 2000 Survey Community findings were published in October 2000[8] demonstrating the need for more and better-quality community relations teaching and training in schools and the Youth Service. This survey showed that young people had strong views about the Belfast Agreement and powerful experiences of the conflict which had not been met with an adequate response. Among the young people who conducted this fieldwork, there was a clear recognition that politically expedient talk of young people being 'our most important resources' and 'our future' were not being matched by provision of anything like the appropriate education and training.

Five years previously Counteract experienced the characteristic fear of educationalists and youth trainers. The findings of the Youthquest 2000 survey vindicated the early Counteract ambition tackle these problems. Denial that there was a problem and the outright rejection of offers of Counteract education and training had served nobody well.

This was a point where government policy seemingly supported education and training for teachers and trainers as well as young people, and it remained a vital aspect of moving towards a *Cohesive, Inclusive and Just Society*. The Programme for Government (draft form for consultation) stated

> In working together to create a new future, we have to deal with the very deep and painful divisions in our society. After decades of division and 30 years of conflict there is a high level of distrust between the two main traditions within our community.[9]

Counteract looked to the devolved, if shaky Northern Ireland government to take the lead in this. If there was a real political will to tackle inequality and to develop better and more trusting relationships throughout society, education and training would necessarily reflect this in changed and improved curricula and provision, echoing the values of human rights, equality and inclusiveness.

*   *   *   *   *

Seconded to Counteract from DFP, Pascal McCulla considered that possible future scenarios for Counteract would depend on the outcome of the political process. If that process worked well, and policy achieved what it claimed on paper, Counteract could develop its contribution. Astutely, he also saw the future role of Counteract as being tied into the broad context of future progress in politics and society in Northern Ireland:

> There are doors opening now that have been closed and never would have opened. They're only peeking out and saying 'well maybe'. And that's where the EDI framework is coming in – to institutions in our society that turned a blind eye and has learned to cope with the whole thing. In learning to cope with sectarianism, I think what they learned to do was to sweep everything else under the carpet. As long as you can bury it and keep it in the bowels of the organisation somewhere, you cope. It is a cultural thing, happening in society, where you just baton down the hatches to get through.
>
> Now the 'all clear' has gone and somebody's saying 'it's all right you can open up the hatches' and everyone's saying 'Ah, but we've heard this all before. We'll keep a wee eye on some of these pioneers and see how they do. If they survive, we'll come out behind them.' The global context, with international trade is another aspect – that brings in issues like racism and prejudice that are beyond the Northern Ireland arena. There will be a greater recognition that maybe some of our problems are not unique or eccentric aspects of Northern Ireland. Diversity is an issue in the bigger picture. (Pascal McCulla, 2000)

From business, commerce, public and private sector service providers to the Draft Programme for Government, the language of EDI was being used in the mainstream. Depending on political progress, of course, Counteract work would be taken on by the broader economic community. There was a widespread acceptance, if not the fullest understanding and commitment to these ideas and strategies. From the days when its vision and development came from the back of an envelope, Counteract had grown into something that was part of the general move towards a more OFMDFM policy for a 'cohesive, inclusive and just society':

> Northern Ireland can have a prosperous future. To achieve this, we need to concentrate on some key themes ... and take action – everyone in Northern Ireland must have a stake in economic success. The benefits must be shared fairly and we need real partnership in our drive for common goals and social cohesion.[10]

This posed two major questions about the future of Counteract as the wider scene pushed EDI to the top of the agenda. Could Counteract maintain the substance of its pioneering work? Would putting its vision, values and work into the mainstream dilute its calibre? And what structure was the organisation of Counteract to take as the increasing demands on the small workforce grew?

Would this weaken the core values and practice of Counteract?

> There are pockets of substance in CRC, Future Ways and so on. And how do you get that drawn together. A lot of thinking has to be done. And how do you protect it for the future, because if it gets diluted now, it will get lost again as things progress. There are models, where organisations have people whose job it is to protect the values and uphold the underlying thinking. So, one idea we had is to create what probably will have to be a consortium because it's diversity in action that would protect these. So that's one possible scenario we're looking at. Business in the Community, the Institute of Management and the Equality Centre seem interested. Those are the sort of players with Counteract and Future Ways that you could create as a consortium. This could be a core to protect it and it could be developed. And that is one route through this. I think a big chunk of it has to be the real engagement of the business sector. (Pascal McCulla, 2000).

Acknowledging that 'there can be no quick fix solutions', the primacy of *Equality and Social Cohesion* included a commitment to equality in its broadest context – in accord with the legislation of the time. The Strategy 2010 report was one of the most significant of the times, signposting that the thinking and vision of pioneers like Counteract, and their partners had become accepted – and appeared to be leading towards something more tangible than 'ticking boxes' and paying lip service.

For Counteract it was progress when equality, inclusion and social cohesion were stated as key parts of both local and the international political economic agenda. The challenge was to engage with the wider business community and government without losing Counteract core values.

A major problem for Counteract – and many others – was that every policy on promoting good relations was risible and justifiable criticised – and although it changed it did not progress over the following decades.

*   *   *   *   *

In 2000 conflict and violence had not gone, nor had the bitterness felt by some in every class and creed, but there was a widespread desire to move on and to grasp the opportunities for making changes that could bring a future in a society where conflict and unresolved disputes were manageable – as they were unlikely to be eradicated.

Was moving from its identity as trade union–based seen as softening the Counteract approach? By no means! – as was clear in Chris Ryder's feature on Counteract.[11] It declared

> 'Violence is in your face. Prejudice is in your face. Conflict is in your face. You can't confront them if you're nice.' … 'everybody is racist and sectarian, but Counteract worked every day to overcome it. That sometimes made the difference'.

Counteract success came from this direct approach – as Chris Ryder was told:

> We assist people to have difficult conversations. There must be no denial or avoidance of fundamental issues. There are no easy answers and sometimes we have to let people blow off a lot of steam before we can make any progress. However, we have found from experience that where the process is a collective one, with management and all sides of the argument involved, and solutions are not imposed, but agreed by a combination of consensus and accommodation, that even the most intractable difficulties can be overcome. Indeed, that way of working creates a sense of ownership and allegiance to the policy we devise.

*   *   *   *   *

By 2000, the organisation had reached Whitehall, Stormont, USA, Europe and beyond. Then, it planned to work with the Imperial and Northern Irish Civil Service, Police (North and South of the border), as well as local government and large companies. Its services had been especially in demand that year as the first of the equality schemes were being drafted by all public bodies in Northern Ireland. The question was whether this small outfit could muster the capacity needed to meet the enormous demands being made of them and their partners. There were various options between remaining as a small employing body and remodelling to become a clearing-house or agency for consultant and specialist free-lance staff.

One thing was for sure. Counteract might change with the political and economic climate in Northern Ireland, and its work would almost certainly develop further, but there was no sign that its services would be redundant in the foreseeable future.

*   *   *   *   *

Looking back to the 1990s, long-time associate Brendan Mackin believed that its work on the poppy and black ribbon disputes, and with the police at a time when it was an extremely dangerous enterprise showed how crucial Counteract was in the years before the peace agreement. It also demonstrated the limits of the trade Union movement from which Counteract sprang:

> These epitomised Counteract where the trade union movement would have been damaged by sectarian and political splits in both the workforce and unions. Counteract engaged with the security forces when others were being shot for that. CAJ held a conference on police brutality one day, and the next Counteract had thirty new recruits training on the image and perceptions of the RUC.

The scope and direction of Counteract had changed since it began in 1990, as the CENI Evaluation reported. 'The change in emphasis from offering designed training packages to providing organisational consultancy and capacity building has led to a drop in numbers of individual participants and a small reduction in numbers of organisations.'[12]

This evaluation was meant to inform the final version of the 1999 draft Development Plan – which the Management Committee had agreed to act upon.

A proposal to drop the Counteract strap line and trade union reference was part of that strategic evaluation and planning. It had brought the anti-sectarian unit to a critical point as the organisation had grown and needed change in its management structure, staffing, education and services. There were no records in 2001 showing any action of this sort was planned or agreed.

Counteract did not last long enough to drop the strap line. It continued its work but the records available when the original fieldwork for this history was done end in 2000.

What was not recorded was the fact that Billy Robinson was on the Honours list for 2000. The following spring, he was awarded the MBE by the Queen for services to good relations – and took it as a mark of much-deserved recognition for Counteract.

It is clear from what he later had to say about Counteract work and the 'Lessons Learned' that flags and emblems were and would continue to be the litmus test of sectarianism at work – with all its ugly manifestations – intimidation, violence and the threat of death. The civil unrest of a decade later that accompanied the 2012–13 flags dispute[13] in Belfast was a political problem that required both mediation and a law-and-order response – some years after the demise of Counteract.

Notes

1. *The Times*, Thursday 12 October 2008, p. 1 and 'The argument for becoming a nation without a name', p. 6.
2. 'Many faiths to march at Cenotaph', *The Times*, Monday 30 October 2000.
3. *Sunday Life*, 1 October 2000, pp. 12–13.
4. Colin Port, Chief Constable of Norfolk was brought in four weeks after the March 1999 murder of Rosemary Nelson, to investigate allegations that there was RUC collusion in the Loyalist murder of the solicitor.
5. Pascal McCulla (MBA) had a background in management development and training is assisting organisations implement major change initiatives. He worked for three years on a project in the civil service (NICS) 'Value Diversity and Maximise Potential' initiative – exploring the application of diversity in its widest

sense into the mainstream management of NICS, including the importance of making the business case for applying these issues to any organisation.

6. The Board was Billy Robinson (Director Counteract), Sara Hunter (Chairperson Counteract), Karin Eyben (Research Officer, Future Ways) Duncan Morrow (Co-Director Future Way – Lecturer in Politics) and Derek Wilson (Co-Director Future Way – Senior Lecturer in Community Relations).

7. Another of the conclusions reached was that single-identity community relations work is good (at best), but not enough to create equality and inclusiveness. One example from Counteracts experience was the pilot project with Loyalist ex-prisoners that was carried out in 2000. Single-identity work is a method of establishing a safe space to talk around safe topics. It allows people to take pride in who they are and where they are from and can offset feelings of insecurity and loss that a group may have. However, when groups and people hate each other, single identity work and pride can feed hatred and prejudice and can provide a hiding place for collaborating with old and counterproductive mind-sets. While there is little effective value in 'starving' hatred, it must be understood that hatred can be nourished when pride (or insecurity) go unchallenged. So, the value of single identity work is that it is a means to an end. It cannot be left at that, without addressing multiple identity issues.

8. Conflict Impact on Children and Joint Society for a Common Cause *The Youthquest 2000 Survey: A Report on Young People's Views and Experiences in Northern Ireland*, Marie Smyth and Mark Scott with Leigh Whittley, Paul Reid, Davy Millar, Judy Cameron, Carl Graham, Tracey Robinson, Sean Hughes, Paul Turley and Ronan Graham(Pluto Press, 2000).

9. 'Draft Programme for Government', OFMDFM, October 2000, 1.3, p. 10.

10. Report by the Economic Development Strategy Review Steering Group, March 1999.

11. 'Bridging the Gap': European Union Peace Programme, CRC, Belfast, 2000.

12. CENI 'Counteract: An Evaluation Commissioned by CRC' February 2000. Belfast.

13. Goldie, R. and Murphy, J., Belfast beyond Violence: Flagging Up a Challenge to Local Government? *Local Government Studies*, 41/3 (2015), 470–88.

CHAPTER 12

The Limits, the Lessons and the Legacy

Counteract was set up as an advice and support campaign with the limited objectives of highlighting the brutal effects of sectarian intimidation at work, provide advice for workers who had been victims and to research the facts – never recorded in official statistics. It set out to build on the foundations of Trade Union education and awareness training. Its aim was to change people's actions not their attitudes. This set positive limits.

Tackling sectarianism in the workplace never a 'hearts and minds' exercise to change attitudes or mindsets. Counteract challenged behaviour, not attitudes. 'It's what you do that counts. Whatever you may believe or think, it is only your actions that we are challenging.' Reasons, motives or deeply held convictions were not up for discussion. The focus was on violence, bullying and intimidation – by displays of flags and emblems and/or actions causing fear and distrust.

*   *   *   *   *

Later, as a source of mediation in workplace disputes, it entered the terrain of threat, risk and hostility, confronting sectarianism head-on.

Counteract resolved workplace crises like the Poppy and Black Ribbon disputes and provided training in a practical partnership with the FEC. As Tribunals made determinations against employers the cost of falling short of fair employment was clear and, over time, intimidation at work became less blatant. This required Counteract to develop nuanced skills to identify the dynamics underlying the immediate crisis and find solutions – eventually leading to partnerships outside the Trade Union movement with employers. As Billy Robinson recorded, their progress led to changing the style of training and the realisation that training on its own was not enough:

> Examples of training varied. There were sessions with a hostile night shift in a Belfast bottling plant, with a predominantly Protestant workforce, in the early 1990s. Then

Counteract took a confrontational line, despite the very real potential of physical threat. By contrast, in the later 1990s the predominantly Catholic employees of Newry & Mourne Council were given what was by then a standard Counteract training package with information about what constituted intimidation, the experience of harassment and the legal responsibilities of employers, managers and supervisors, as well as employees. Although this awareness raising was an integral part of the process of making changes and was necessary, it was not enough in itself to make a difference to the way in which people worked and related to each other.

To make enduring changes there had to be organisational change – something that was outside the limited expertise and skills of the movement and Counteract. At this point the limits to their knowledge and appropriate experience necessitated working with academics – who used rather different methods.

A straightforward verdict is that the unit's Trade Union origins and ethos limited the scope of this practice – and would eventually produce problems that would never be resolved.

*   *   *   *   *

Awareness raising was a step towards getting companies to understand the importance of these issues – and the economics of prejudice, discrimination, bullying and intimidation. Initially, the role of Counteract was restricted to crisis management, until employers came back to them, sometimes very reluctantly, to ask for more help. So, it became clear that 'fire-fighting' was not enough. 'Fire–proofing', by creating a different environment in the workplace (and ultimately changing the tacit culture), was necessary if organisations were to make lasting changes.

However, it had to go further than, as Billy Robinson called it, 'Putting lipstick on a bulldog'. This meant tackling the tacit culture – that is, the reality of life in the workplace rather than official policy (if such existed) on sectarianism. Opening up genuine discussion of sectarianism and other prejudices was and remains the key to making changes. Counteract was always clear. Everyone knew exactly how intimidation, harassment and unfair treatment happened. Everyone had a firm grasp of how it operated, despite it being systematically hidden in a pervasive culture of silence and denial.

For Billy Robinson, the tacit culture was what needed to change. Mediating disputes, awareness training and anti-sectarian policies had to be backed up with changes to the organisation itself. To do less was, as the image suggests, only cosmetic.

*   *   *   *   *

As Trade Union funding was limited, the unit needed to generate more income than core funding from community relations grants. So, Counteract Services had to be set up. That development would eventually create ideological differences because Counteract would then have to work with management, business and mainstream government. Even though the movement had been happy to comply with government requests for mass public demonstrations for peace in the 1980s and early 1990s, this development would be taken by some as 'selling out' on Trade Union values and principles.

Billy Robinson did not see, or chose not to see, potential conflict in forging business partnerships, since this was essential for Counteract to reach its aim of embedding organisational and cultural change across the private and public sector. It appears that the move from fire-fighting to fire-proofing was deemed to be taking Counteract too far from the coalface and crisis management – although hands-on trade union support in that work was rarely to be seen.

*   *   *   *   *

Over the mid-1990s Counteract looked for the tools to identify and measure the culture sustaining sectarianism at work – the organisational ethos and practices that left intimidation unchecked. The Ulster University Future Ways team and Counteract began developing a set of principles and a framework, using the EDI principles – Equity, Diversity and Interdependence. It was an attempt to map the critical path from sectarianism to delivering the 'product' of organisations free from this culture and behaviour.

This advance produced organisational and operational dilemmas in Counteract. Firstly, it was now fire-proofing with the EDI work but still fire-fighting, and the staff were not adept at combining or understanding these two distinct approaches. After Pascal McCulla came on board the EDI Framework was more fully developed. This was a new organisational approach and required an entirely different set of skills – to complement the in-your-face training, crisis management and problem solving. It was a difficult balance to maintain and perhaps more than was fair to ask of people from a Trade Union background who had been hired to face physical and verbal hostility on a regular basis.

*   *   *   *   *

EDI work was based on a community relations model of conflict resolution and did not fit precisely with the Trade Union traditions of putting workers first. The two ideologies were not well-matched.

More fundamentally the EDI work and the framework for organisational change was limited – as Pascal McCulla recalled in 2020:

> In the end EDIF could not get scaled up. I am not sure we had political sponsorship from each side. … With Sectarianism institutionalised in the Executive structure – the two main sides had four ministers and eight Spads and still couldn't reach agreement (on promoting equality and good relations). … As Billy said, 'deal with it or it'll come back – and it's still there'.
>
> That begs the question 'Is politics capable of making change or does it just react to events on the ground?' I realise that the counter argument is that to mainstream anything there can be a bottom up build-up. However, that groundswell never materialised.

The distinct lack of political sponsorship was a crucially limiting factor for anti-sectarian work. The politics of sectarianism were open for all to see. This was exemplified in the Poppy dispute, when the local MP very publicly backed the employees who had defied company policy on wearing the Poppy – and went as far as the UUP leader raising the matter at Question Time in Westminster. However, there was never that degree of public support and political sponsorship for Counteract – from the parties at Stormont during the 1990s. It remains questionable whether there is sufficient political will and understanding of policy since the 1998 Belfast Agreement to create viable political support for combatting sectarianism from the major parties.

*   *   *   *   *

There is a certain irony in that the high media and political profile created by the Poppy dispute paved the way for a change in the official position on the Poppy. After questions in Westminster the story hit national headlines and the ensuing debate changed the authorised perspective. The

Poppy was recognised as an emblem – albeit only in a Northern Ireland context. That is a forgotten legacy of Counteract.

*   *   *   *   *

Counteract provided lessons for employers and even regulators like the FEC but it also learned lessons – and some the hard way.

The 1995 weekend school for GPMU/CWU women's committee members was the first women-only seminar organised by Counteract. It revealed some uncomfortable truths including the fact that Counteract looked at sectarianism from a male perspective. Women experienced problems when their harasser was male, giving them the dual problem of sectarian/sexual harassment. The event exposed other issues, so it was decided future women-only seminars could develop a feminist perspective. This was quite a challenge as Counteract had, like the Unions, a predominantly male culture. However, this was never fully explored – and could be considered a lesson not learned.

*   *   *   *   *

Working with former combatants was not a success in the Positive Action and Community Training (PACT) initiative. Aside from paramilitary opposition to the project, it was short-term stand-alone training. In hindsight Counteract realised that it needed time to build relationships of trust, and that the open discussions would bring out disturbing as well as positive results. PACT was an attempt to transform young men in the wake of the Belfast Agreement and the peace process. However, if these young men were to change how they behaved – even in a facilitative learning environment – they would bring their past into the process – if only to dump 'that past' before moving on. That is what happened in PACT. It is not a traditional British/Irish male characteristic to admit to fear and ask for help and support. Counteract faced up to the need to review the scope of this form of transformational work – if indeed they had the resources for such a long-term project. They also needed to revisit support for some of its own staff who had found the work extremely threatening:

> We reached the conclusion that single-identity community relations work was good (at best), but not enough to create equality and inclusiveness. One example from

Counteract experience was the pilot project with Loyalist ex-prisoners carried out in 2000. Single-identity work is a method of establishing a safe space to talk around safe topics. It allows people to take pride in who they are and where they are from and can offset feelings of insecurity and loss that a group may have. However, when groups and individuals hate each other, single identity work and pride can feed hatred and prejudice and can provide a hiding place for collaborating with old and counterproductive mind-sets. While there is little effective value in 'starving' hatred, it must be understood that hatred can be nourished when pride (or insecurity) go unchallenged. So, the value of single identity work is that it is a means to an end but not an end in itself. It cannot be left at that, without addressing multiple identity issues. (Draft report on PACT)

*   *   *   *   *

Where work with former combatants was 'in your face' and physically threatening, sectarianism in the workplace had changed by the end of the 1990s. Intimidation was becoming more subtle and complex. The use of emblems became increasingly shrewd – as when poppies were displayed in cars in work car parks, rather than pinned to clothing, or when coloured T-shirts and ribbons were worn to signify sectarian allegiances. The dynamics of sectarianism exhibited new methods of expressing old and unchanging prejudice. There was often considerable and heated debate about what counted as being an emblem, but the job of Counteract was to critically investigate the actual and intended meaning of actions and allegations – not the surface appearance. This required more than the traditional confrontational Counteract approach.

*   *   *   *   *

A lesson that Counteract learned to its financial cost was that it did not have much business sense. Having found the funding for *The Inside Stories*, a unique training video package, it did not have it copyrighted and sold it at a price that lost out on income stream, as others exploited a rather unsuspecting Counteract who lacked entrepreneurial nous. These and other naïve financial judgements almost certainly came from their Trade Union origins and ideological opposition to profit-making. A more developed sense of finance might have left Counteract less dependent on community relations money from government and CRC – and its inevitable leverage in Counteract thinking.

*   *   *   *   *

After much time and effort Counteract learned they had overestimated the value of accredited learning. What had been *Guidelines for Trainers* went through the lengthy and convoluted process of accreditation with the Open College Network (OCN). This gave individuals on the course an official recognition. However, over time it emerged that this was not a great motivator for people who already possessed professional qualifications. On its own, certification was of no value to the organisations that sponsored them. The acid test was whether the E&DT certificate course delivered the skills that people needed. Piloting and attempts at refining the course provided a series of lessons. The demands of OCN for certification required a huge amount of portfolio work that was off-putting for participants. Also, the course was not flexible enough to keep all the participants enthralled. By winter 2000, Counteract learned the painful way that a learning organisation needs to reconsider even its most precious elements.

*   *   *   *   *

And there was another lesson – one that was not learned when Counteract was in operation. Perhaps it was due to his lack of educational qualifications and his dyslexia but, whatever the reason, Billy Robinson was somewhat overawed by the academic dimensions of the progression into EDI – and did not see the gap between this community relations model and his own principles. On an ideological level the politics of Counteract was based on the simple traditional Trade Union values of equality and the protection of workers' rights. The EDI principles were a community relations model – and potentially in opposition to the equality agenda.

This is a lesson that was not learned at the time, and a debate that is yet to be settled. It stems from the legal and political complexities of the Belfast Agreement and relevant sections of the law that enshrined the peace settlement. So, what did this legislation provide to strengthen anti-sectarian work? The 1998 Northern Ireland Act had two relevant sections – Section 76 on anti-discrimination and Section 75 on promoting equality and good relations. On the surface these seemed to add to existing protections against sectarian intimidation in the workplace – but like many aspects of the negotiations, peace process and implementation of law, it was more complicated than that.

Firstly, the Section 75 duties applied only to designated public sector organisations. Secondly, there was no legal definition of what 'good relations' meant. Thirdly, and most importantly, the legislation did not match the expectations or aspirations of Nationalists and Republicans on parity of esteem for those claiming Irish citizenship.

Behind the scenes the parties negotiating the Belfast Agreement and their advisors wrangled over both the substance and detail of 'equality' and 'parity of esteem' (Hayward and Mitchell, 2003) Then legislation was drafted so that ambiguities covered any obvious divergence from the settlement. In general, the 1998 Northern Ireland Act passed without significant argument – with the exceptions of the positive duties in Section 75. These obliged all designated public bodies to promote equality of opportunity and good relations.

Some in the community relations lobby then argued that promoting equality would create community tensions. The opposing faction argued that 'equality' should be stronger than equality of opportunity. Although the first objection was based on absurd logic, and the second too much to ask of New Labour, each argument had some purchase – as debates in Hansard demonstrate.[1] Equality in the form of anti-discrimination and the duty to promote equality of opportunity was as much as the more radical lobbyists would get, and the Section 75 equality duty was stronger than the good relations obligation – so 'good relations' could never trump 'equality of opportunity'. However, even with that safeguard, the fact that 'promoting good relations' replaced 'parity of esteem' was viewed as 'blunting the harder edges of the human rights and equality agendas so as to soften the blow for unionists.'[2]

This is not just an academic point – because it formed the basis of a political-ideological stand-off where the community relations model of EDI fundamentally differed from the human rights and equality agenda. Those who had most strongly supported human rights and equality, like the CAJ, had been partners with Counteract in times before it adopted the EDI principles and framework.

In failing to see that the equity of EDI was not necessarily equality Counteract left itself outside the virtuous circle of the CAJ and Human Rights activists. Counteract records did not reveal whether this informed the thinking of the Trade Union movement – but it is worth noting that the issue was not addressed in any written Counteract records or mentioned by any person interviewed for this book.

*   *   *   *   *

There are many examples of Counteract successfully challenging 'acceptable levels of prejudice'. Part of its legacy is the anticipation of now popular and common causes. In bringing Jane Elliott to Belfast Billy Robinson saw the value of putting racism on the agenda for 500 senior managers from the private and public sector – two decades before the Black Lives Matter movement.

*   *   *   *   *

The most poignant aspect of the legacy of Counteract is that, despite the risks in the 'Dangerous Pursuit', sectarianism is still a defining factor in Northern Ireland – albeit in more subtle forms in the workplace, if not always as understated in politics and on the street. Achieving the radical change needed to eradicate it remains unfinished business. Flags and emblems remain contentious (Bryan and Gillespie, 2005)

Both before and after his time in Counteract, Billy Robinson worked with courage and good faith to achieve anti-sectarian behaviour and principles. In 1969 he was tackling sectarianism at work, as his brother Gerry recounted:

> He worked for Beltex clothing factory in Ardoyne, where it all started. I'd say one of his first experiences of negotiation. It was a mixed workforce, predominantly Protestant. Bill got along well with the management.
>
> This day they put flags up – bunting. One side wasn't going to come in – they'd take it down and put theirs up – the others said they'd take it down – the place was up in arms. The Manager came to Bill 'Right what do we do?'
>
> He had no idea because nobody had faced a situation like that before and said, 'No matter what I do the place is going to get burned down – if I take one side down that'll [annoy] the others – what'll I do?'
>
> Bill says, 'I'll tell you what to do – take all of it down, put it in a big box, set it on a table and when everybody comes in, in the morning, bring them into the canteen. And you tell them all – "This is a place of work – you leave your politics at the door. Anybody who does not agree with that take your bunting and flags and leave."'
>
> The manager did that the next morning and says, 'Bill, will you stand with us?'

And Bill says, 'Yes'.

Nobody walked out.

He didn't have the ticket [qualifications] but, as the manager said, he had the skills.

He knew ordinary people weren't all they were painted to be – they just wanted somebody to help. … It's like kids at school who want to be told not to mitch off – and that's what it's like in the workplace – the bullies put it up and all they wanted was somebody please come in and cut across this and knock the bully down – that's what Bill did and the trade unions [saying] 'No that's not what's going to happen. This is a place of work.'

So, long before 1990, and Counteract, Billy Robinson was 'telling it like it is' – and after Counteract he spent his time still doing that. Driven by an intense desire to create a society that could sustain peace rather than simply manage division and sectarian hatreds. His views and those who began Counteract are reflected in the writing of George Mitchell, who chaired the peace negotiations after June 1996.

Senator Mitchell understood the complexities of peace-making and the fact that agreement does not bring certain or sustainable peace:

Finally, in the late afternoon of Good Friday, an agreement was reached. It is important to recognize that the agreement does not, by itself, provide or guarantee a durable peace, political stability, or reconciliation. It makes them possible. But there will have to be a lot of effort, in good faith, for a long time, to achieve those goals.[3]

Counteract had indeed put in 'a lot of effort, in good faith, for a long time' and its successes were part of the peace-making process.

In 1998 Senator George Mitchell summed up what the peace process was about, what lessons Northern Ireland holds for other conflicts:

First, I believe there is no such thing as a conflict that cannot be ended. They are created and sustained by human beings. They can be ended by human beings. No matter how ancient the conflict, no matter how hateful, no matter how hurtful, peace can prevail. …

A second need is for a clear and determined policy not to yield to the men of violence. Over and over, they tried to destroy the peace process in Northern Ireland; at times they nearly succeeded. … A third need is a willingness to compromise. Peace and political stability cannot be achieved in sharply divided societies unless there is a genuine willingness to understand the other point of view and to enter into principled compromise. That is easy to say, but very hard to do because it requires of political leaders that they take the risks for peace. ...

A fourth principle is to recognize that the implementation of agreements is as difficult, and as important, as reaching them. That should be self-evident. But often just getting an agreement is so difficult that the natural tendency is to celebrate, and then turn to other issues. But as we are now seeing in Northern Ireland, in the Middle East, and in the Balkans, getting it done is often harder than agreeing to do it.

Once again, patience and perseverance are necessary. It is especially important that Americans, busy at home and all across the world, not be distracted or become complacent by the good feeling created by a highly-publicized agreement. If a conflict is important enough to get involved, we must see it through all the way to a fair and successful conclusion.[4]

Nearly two decades after the demise of Counteract the brute facts of sectarianism remain with walls that divide and signal the implicit threat of a less intense form of conflict in Northern Ireland – at sectarian interfaces – and sadly the number of these increased after 1998. George Mitchell considered them of enormous consequence:

There is a final point that to me is so important that it extends beyond open conflict. I recall clearly my first day in Northern Ireland, nearly four years ago. I saw for the first time the huge wall that physically separates the communities in Belfast. Thirty feet high, topped in places with barbed wire, it is an ugly reminder of the intensity and duration of the conflict. Ironically, it is called the Peace Line.

On that first morning, I met with the Catholics on their side of the wall, in the afternoon with the Protestants on their side. Their messages had not been coordinated, but they were the same. In Belfast, they told me, there is a high correlation between unemployment and violence. They said that there, where men and women have no opportunity, or hope, they are more likely to take the path to violence.

As I sat and listened to them, I thought that I could just as easily be in Chicago, or Calcutta, or Johannesburg, or the Middle East. Despair is the fuel for instability and conflict everywhere. Hope is essential to peace and stability. Men and women everywhere need income to support their families, and they need the satisfaction of doing something worthwhile and meaningful with their lives.

The Universal Declaration' also recognizes this basic right. Article 23 states: 'Everyone has the right to work, to free choice of employment, to just and favorable conditions of work and to protection against unemployment.[5]

Had not the Trade Union movement set up Counteract, the fundamental US constitutional right to work, and the internationally recognised Human Right to life, would have been reason enough for the anti-
intimidation unit. It was vital that someone had the courage to 'tell it like
it is' as Billy Robinson always said Counteract did.

Notes

1. 'The Smaller Peace Process' PhD Thesis, Roz Goldie, Queen's University Belfast,
   2008 – Sections 3.8 and 3.9, pp. 73–79.
2. Quotation from McVeigh, Robbie and Rolston, Bill, From Good Friday to Good
   Relations: Sectarianism, Racism and the Northern Ireland State. *Race and Class*, 48/
   4 (2007), 1–23, London, p. 8.
3. Quotation from 'Toward Peace in Northern Ireland' *Fordham International Journal
   International Law Journal*, 22/4 (April 1999), 1139.
4. Quotation from 'Toward Peace in Northern Ireland' *Fordham International Journal
   International Law Journal*, 22/4 (April 1999), 1140–41.
5. Quotation from 'Toward Peace in Northern Ireland' *Fordham International Journal
   International Law Journal*, 22/4 (April 1999), 1141.

Bibliography

Andersonstown News, 4 November 1995.

Bew, Paul and Gillespie, Gordon *Northern Ireland: A Chronology of the Troubles 1968–1999*, (Dublin, Gill & Macmillan, 1999).

157,457 say Stop the Killing, The Belfast Newsletter, Belfast, (19 Nov 1993, P1).

Belfast Telegraph, Belfast, 11 March 1991.

    2 July 1991;
    3 July 1991;
    10 February 1993;
    4 August 1993;
    28 September 1993;
    11 November 1998.

Counteract poses the question, should TQM address Sectarianism? Belfast Telegraph, Business Telegraph (30 January 1996, p. 24).

Emblems Crisis Talks. Bid to end sectarian rows in Derry Factory, Belfast Telegraph, North West Edition (20 March 1997).

Birmingham Evening News, 15/16 November 1990.

Bryan, Dominic and Gillespie, Gordon, *Transforming Conflict: Flags and Emblems* (Belfast, Institute of Irish Studies, Queen's University Belfast, March 2005).

Commission for Racial Equality, *Call for Change in Northern Ireland* (London, Connections, Summer 2000).

Community Evaluation Northern Ireland, *Counteract: An Evaluation Commissioned by CRC* (Belfast, CENI, February 2000).

Community Relations Council for Northern Ireland, *Accommodating Change Conference Report* (Belfast, Community Relations Council for Northern Ireland, February 1996).

Daily Mail 15/16 November 1990.

Dan McGinn, *Belfast Telegraph*, Belfast, 31 October 1998.

Eyben, Karin; Morrow, Duncan; Wilson, Derick; Robinson, Billy, *The Equity, Diversity and Interdependence Framework, A Framework for Organisational Learning and Change* (Belfast, University of Ulster Future Ways, 2002).

Fair Employment Commission, *Fair Comment*, Sectarian Harassment edition (Belfast, FEC, winter 1998).

Fermanagh Herald, DOE workers 'intimidated' at the presence of Union flags: Catholic staff offended by hand painted emblems, July 1997.

Goldie, Roz, 'Problem, Process and Product: Implementing Key Reforms in Local Government in Northern Ireland Since the Belfast Agreement', *Local Government Studies*, 38/1 (2012), 1–13.

Goldie, Roz, *The Smaller Peace Process* (Belfast, PhD Thesis, Queen's University Belfast, 2008).

Goldie, Roz, and Murphy, Joanne, 'Belfast beyond Violence: Flagging Up a Challenge to Local Government?', *Local Government Studies*, 41(3) (2015), 470–88.

Goleman, Daniel, *Working with Emotional Intelligence* (London, Daniel Bloomsbury Paperbacks, 1998).

Hayward, K. and Mitchell, C., 'Discourses of Equality in Post-Agreement Northern Ireland', *Contemporary Politics*, 9/3 (2003), 293–312.

"The Inside Stories" Counteract video available on Youtube.com (https://www.youtube.com).

Irish News, Belfast,

> 15/16 November 1990
> 30 January 1991
> 2 February 1991 "Row over Union Jack Policy"
> 11 March 1991;
> 13 March 1991;
> 3 July 1991;
> 4 July 1991;
> 20 October 1991;
> 28 September 1992;
> 17 October 1992;
> 22 October 1992;
> 21 September 1993;
> 19 November 1998.

Irish Times 3 July 1991;

> 22 October 1992;
> Monday/Tuesday 25/26 October 1993.

McVeigh, R. and Rolston, B., 'From Good Friday to Good Relations: Sectarianism, Racism and the Northern Ireland State', *Race and Class*, 48/4 (2007), 1–23.

Mitchell, George, 'Toward Peace in Northern Ireland', *Fordham International Journal International Law Journal*, 22/4 (1999), 1136–44.

Morning Star, 24 October 1991.

Northern Ireland Committee, Irish Congress of Trade Unions, Congress Report, Belfast, 1990.

Newsletter 3 July 1991;

> 22 October 1992;
> 31 October 1991;
> 20 April 1998.

Office of First Minister and Deputy First Minister 'Draft Programme for Government' (Belfast, OFMDFM, October 2000).

Quinn, Jim, 'Stop Watching – Get Active' in *Fair Comment* (Belfast, Fair Employment Commission, Summer 1993).

Robinson, Billy and Nolan, Stevie, 'Counteract: Working for Change', *Fordham International Law Journal* 22/4 (1999), 4–23.

'Sectarianism and Intimidation', *Church of Ireland Journal* (20 August 1997).

Smyth, Marie and Scott, Mark with Whittley, Leigh; Reid, Paul; Millar, Davy; Cameron, Judy; Graham, Carl; Robinson, Tracey; Hughes, Sean; Turley, Paul and Graham, Ronan. Conflict Impact on Children and Joint Society for a Common Cause *The Youthquest 2000 Survey: A Report on Young People's Views and Experiences in Northern Ireland* (London, Pluto Press, 2000).

Sunday Life, 14 August 1994.

Sunday Times, 18 October;
       15 October;
       1 November 1992.

Sunday World, 8 November.

Sunday News, 6 January 1991.

The Times, 'Many faiths to march at Cenotaph', Monday 30 October 2000.

The Times, 12 October 2008, p. 1 and *The argument for becoming a nation without a name*, p. 6

Transport and General Workers Union, T&G News December 1990.

UK Press Gazette (front page), 26 October 1992.

Index

Reimagining Ireland

Series Editor: Dr Eamon Maher, Technological
University Dublin

The concepts of Ireland and 'Irishness' are in constant flux in the wake of an ever-increasing reappraisal of the notion of cultural and national specificity in a world assailed from all angles by the forces of globalisation and uniformity. Reimagining Ireland interrogates Ireland's past and present and suggests possibilities for the future by looking at Ireland's literature, culture and history and subjecting them to the most up-to-date critical appraisals associated with sociology, literary theory, historiography, political science and theology.

Some of the pertinent issues include, but are not confined to, Irish writing in English and Irish, Nationalism, Unionism, the Northern 'Troubles', the Peace Process, economic development in Ireland, the impact and decline of the Celtic Tiger, Irish spirituality, the rise and fall of organised religion, the visual arts, popular cultures, sport, Irish music and dance, emigration and the Irish diaspora, immigration and multiculturalism, marginalisation, globalisation, modernity/postmodernity and postcolonialism. The series publishes monographs, comparative studies, interdisciplinary projects, conference proceedings and edited books. Proposals should be sent either to Dr Eamon Maher at eamon.maher@ittdublin.ie or to ireland@peterlang.com.

Printed by
CPI books GmbH, Leck